1|2   3⁰⁰

POWER
TOOLS

POWER TOOLS

AN ELECTRIFYING CELEBRATION

TOOLS

AND GROUNDED GUIDE

Written and Photographed by

● SANDOR NAGYSZALANCZY ●

The Taunton Press

TO GERALD BOWDEN, my good friend, tireless supporter and scourge of the local flea market. Thanks to his eagerness and savvy bargaining abilities, this book is resplendent with many interesting (as well as some odd) vintage power tools.

Text © 2001 by Sandor Nagyszalanczy
Photographs © 2001 by Sandor Nagyszalanczy (except where noted)
Illustrations © 2001 by The Taunton Press, Inc. (except where noted)

 The Taunton Press
Inspiration for hands-on living™

The Taunton Press, Inc., 63 South Main Street, PO Box 5506, Newtown, CT 06470-5506
e-mail: tp@taunton.com

Distributed by Publishers Group West

COVER AND INTERIOR DESIGNER: Carol Singer
LAYOUT: Mary McKeon
ILLUSTRATOR: Mark Sant'Angelo

LIBRARY OF CONGRESS CATALOGING-IN-PUBLICATION DATA:
Nagyszalanczy, Sandor.
    Power tools : an electrifying celebration and grounded guide / Sandor Nagyszalanczy.
        p. cm.
    Includes index.
    ISBN 1-56158-427-4
        1. Power tools. I. Title.

TJ1195 .N34 2001
621.9--dc21   2001033097

Printed in Great Britain
10 9 8 7 6 5 4 3 2 1

About Your Safety: Working with power tools is inherently dangerous. Using hand or power tools improperly or ignoring safety practices can lead to permanent injury or even death. Don't try to perform operations you learn about here (or elsewhere) unless you're certain they are safe for you. If something about an operation does not feel right, don't do it. Look for another way. Please keep safety foremost in your mind whenever you're working with tools.

The following manufacturers/names appearing in *Power Tools* are registered trademarks: Bakelite, Biesemeyer T-Square, Bondo, Bosch Clic System, Coke, Cool Blocks, Festo Systainer, Firestorm, Freud Performance System RP2000, Jet Xacta, Kleenex, Leigh Jigs, Makita, Metabo, Milwaukee (Enduro, Magnum, Sawzall, Super Sawzall, Tilt-Lok), Oster, Portalign, Porter-Cable (Porta-Band, Riptide, SawBoss, Speed-Bloc, Speedmatic, Tiger Saw), Ridgid (Indi-I-Cut, Sure-Cut), Rockwell Speedmatic, Ryobi (Power Pen, VersaTable), Sears Craftsman Redi Drill, ShopMate, Skil (Skilsaw), Teflon, Thermos, The Ugly, Torx, Timesavers.

ACKNOWLEDGMENTS

To create a big book like this one, it takes a big crew. So many different people were vital to the production of this book, that this acknowledgments page looks like the credit list at the end of a gazillion-dollar Hollywood movie. Nevertheless, all the people mentioned below deserve a word of thanks, for without their efforts, I could not have begun to tackle a project of this scope.

For their assistance with the acquisition of new power tools and machines for photography: John Crumry, Beaver Power Tools; Bishop Cochran, manufacturer of the rotary-tool plunge-router base; Richard Wedler, designer and manufacturer of Micro Fence; Charles Lamana, Emerson Corp. (Ridgid Power Tools); Jim Swann, Advanced Machinery Imports, Ltd. (Hegner); Dan Sherman at CMT USA; Ernie Frate at Arnold Communications, PR for DeWalt; Bob Hillard at Fein Tools; Peggy Brunet LeMay and Mari Randa at Dremel; Paul Trimble and Michael McGibbon at Tooltechnic Systems, Festool (formerly known as Toolguide, Festo); Jim Brewer at Freud; Kristen Boesch at Hitachi; Kathleen Oberleiter at Colonial Saw, Lamello; Leonard Lee and Wally Wilson, for Lee Valley Tools, Ltd. (Veritas); Ken and Steve Grisley of Leigh Jigs; David Williams at Panasonic; Chris Harm and Ray Venzon at Makita USA, Inc.; David Smith and Terry Tuerk at Metabo; Al Akavan of TNT Virutex Corp.; Brad Witt of Woodhaven; Mark Duginske of FasTTraK; Rich Peterson of Blue Horse, Inc., PR for Milwaukee; Jesse Barragan, owner of Eagle Tools (Inca) and Gary Chin of Garrett Wade (Inca); and Bonny Klein of Klein Lathe. For their incredible support, extra special thanks go to Chris Carlson and John Madden of S-B Power Tool Co.; Mike McQuinn of Ryobi America; and Todd Langston of Pentair, Inc. (Porter-Cable and Delta).

For assistance with the photography of new machinery, I'd like to thank: Charles A. Burback, President, and Tom Sanders, Branch Manager, at C. B. Tools in San Jose, California; Joe Butcher, Mike Bailey, and Bill Roberts at San Lorenzo Lumber in Santa Cruz, California; and Jim Garcia at Post Tool.

For their help with the acquisition of and information about vintage power tools, kudos go to: Steve Sweet of Steve's Used Tools; Gerry Bowden; Gary Benequisto; Steve Johnson; Joel Herzel; Dick Streff; Demitrias Nichols; Paul Richardson, editor of the British magazine *Furniture and Cabinetmaking*; Roger Goad; Matthew J. Prusik Jr.; Jim Schwaub; Joe Johns and his Twisted Knot Woodshop; Jeff Traeger; John Mudd; Keith Rucker; Roberto Rodriguez at the American Precision Museum; and Dan Malouin at Davis & Wells, Inc. Finally, a very special thanks to Keith Bohn, who has probably forgotten more about vintage machinery than I will ever know.

For their assistance with packing and unpacking literally hundreds of power tools and machines, I owe the world to Dick Yount and Steve Robins. For their unqualified support and encouragement: Cliff Friedlander, Peter Bartzack, Larry Rogow, my parents, and my lovely wife Ann Gibb (who has the patience of Job). I'd also like to thank my UPS delivery man, Gary Crossno, for carrying more iron up my driveway for this project than the Marines lugged up Iwo Jima.

On the production end of things, thanks to: Scott Phillips and Laura Bergeron, for keeping me in a steady supply of film; Drew, Lynn, and Randi at Bay Photo for their perfect processing; Paula Schlosser and Mary McKeon in art; Carolyn Mandarano and Jennifer Renjilian, production; and copy editor Suzanne Noel. Last but not least, I'd like to acknowledge the remarkable support of my editor, Helen Albert, who lent crucial inspiration—as well as an ocean of perspiration—to this project.

Contents

PART TWO:
BENCHTOP &
STATIONARY MACHINES

Introduction

If you'd rather find a new tool catalog in your mail box than a love letter, if your pulse quickens when checking out the clever features on a new table saw, if gripping the ergonomic handle of a cutting-edge cordless saw makes you feel like a kid on Christmas morning, then this book has your name written all over it.

The power-tool book you now hold was written and photographed by a hopeless tool junkie: me. The seed for this project was planted many years ago when, as an editor for *Fine Woodworking* magazine, I arranged, edited, or authored dozens of reviews of power tools, machines, and their accessories. The more I learned about how power tools were designed, engineered, and built, the more they fascinated me.

The best power tools are precision-engineered devices capable of performing their cutting, boring, sanding, and planing tasks remarkably well. But power tools and the accessories, jigs, and gizmos that go with them are noteworthy decorative objects in and of themselves—symbols of sophisticated building technology and practice.

This book celebrates power tools for their mechanical, electrical, and electronic achievements and also for how they've changed and improved the ways in which we work, build our projects, and improve or repair our homes. After all, power tools have come a long way. Early machines were heavy, expensive devices made for serious business—small home shops and weekend warriors were few and far between.

After World War II, a new tool market sprang up in the form of homeowners and do-it-yourselfers who wanted to save money by tackling repairs and building projects themselves. This meant creating portable power tools and scaled-down machines that were lighter, easier to use, and more affordable than their industrial-strength predecessors.

Power tools from the 1930s, '40s, and '50s are some of the most exciting ever created. Especially pleasing to the eye, most were constructed with aluminum bodies, which reflected the stylings of the day. Jigsaws and drills often had streamlined, bullet-shaped bodies, which looked like they were developed in a wind tunnel (see the vintage Shop-Mate jigsaw in the bottom photo on p. 47), with raised linear patterns gleaned from Art Deco.

Fast-forward to the dawn of the new millennium. The world of power tools is burgeoning. Space-age alloys have made the heftiest of plunge

routers and worm drive circular saws lighter. New battery-powered tools are being developed for every sort of corded portable. Electronic variable speed and soft start make running a router safer and more comfortable, especially when running a huge bit. Computer-aided cordless power tool chargers with fuzzy logic can optimize a battery's charging potential while increasing its life and preventing damage. Even economy table saws, drills, and rotary tools benefit from the same state-of-the-art electronics that have changed practically every consumer appliance from telephones to floor lamps to toasters. Where will it all end—nuclear-powered table saws?

For the present time, I invite you to unplug your tools, put your feet up, and take an engaging tour through the fascinating world of power drills, circular saws, routers, jigsaws, sanders, table saws, jointers and planers, bandsaws, drill presses, lathes, and more. Besides providing a megavitamin-sized jolt of inspiration, this book offers information that's valuable even to the most seasoned power-tool jockey.

Each chapter will acquaint you with the full range of the tools' variations and permutations. You'll also get a quick anatomy lesson of each basic power-tool type. So that you can see how far tools have come from their first incarnations, I have recounted the colorful past of some intriguing vintage tools. For each major class of tool, I've also picked a classic whose enduring

design has made it so popular that it virtually defines that type of tool.

To help you understand the many tool options, I've pointed out important features and how they benefit the tools' performance. And no discussion of power tools is complete without looking at the parts that actually do the work—the business end: blades, bits, cutters, and abrasives. The sections on accessories give you a taste of all the interesting jigs and add-ons that can make tools safer, easier to use, or expand their range of work.

Finally, I offer a look at the exciting developments in power-tool design, tools that represent ingenious solutions in ergonomic, electronic, or mechanical design. (Just keep in mind that even the best tool occupies the technological high ground only temporarily; new models are coming out every day.)

Whether you use this book to help you decide which tools you need to set up your shop, to study up on the latest in power-tool technology, or just to indulge your love of power tools, one thing is sure: You'll come away with a lot of great power tools and accessories to add to your next birthday or holiday wish list.

PART ONE

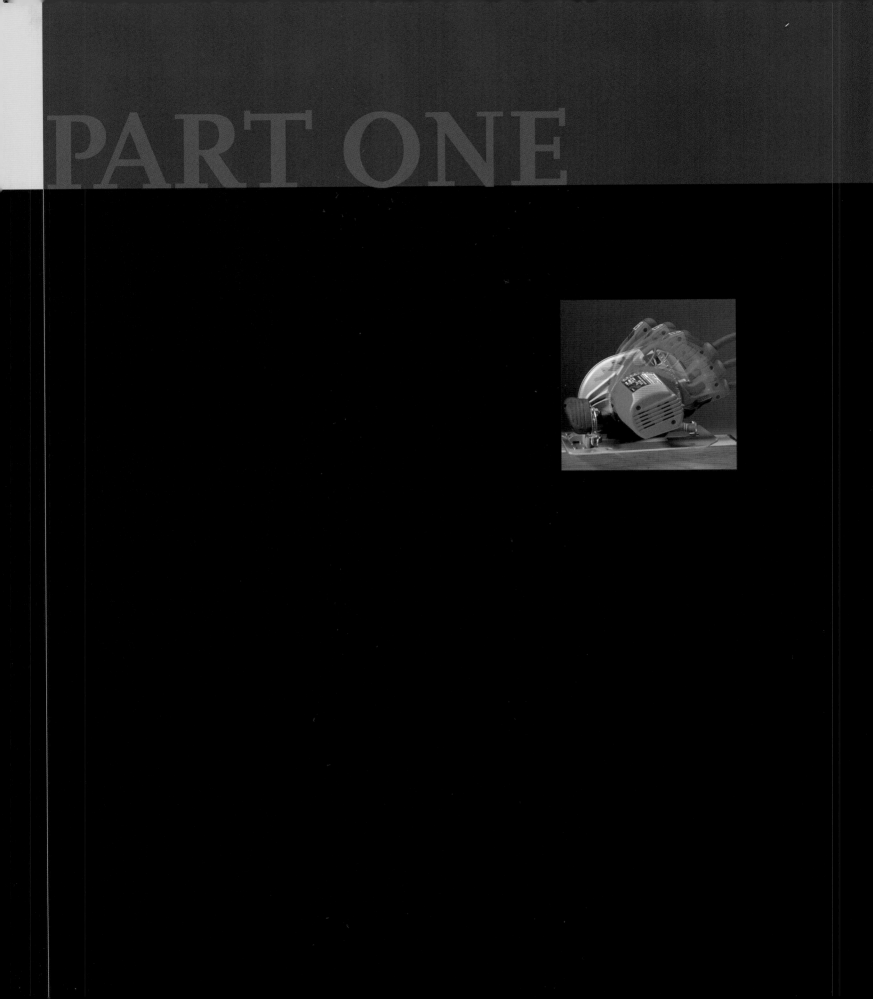

PORTABLE
POWER TOOLS

Compared to other power tools with more polite table manners, portable circular saws are voracious gluttons. That's a good thing if you need to frame a house or build a jungle gym and you need to do it quickly. A sharp-bladed circular saw will furiously dispatch a sizable stack of lumber, cutting studs or posts to length, beveling rafters, and notching joists and headers with the zeal of a hungry teenager devouring a double-crust pizza.

A circular saw is basically a big, round, toothy blade connected to a single-speed motor with a handle. It is made to do one thing and do it well: make straight cuts in wood. Choose a good blade and all you need to do is pull the trigger and keep the blade tracking down the line of cut. If you're adventurous, mount a special dry-cut carbide or diamond-impregnated blade and try your hand at sawing through sheet metal, bricks, or ceramic tile.

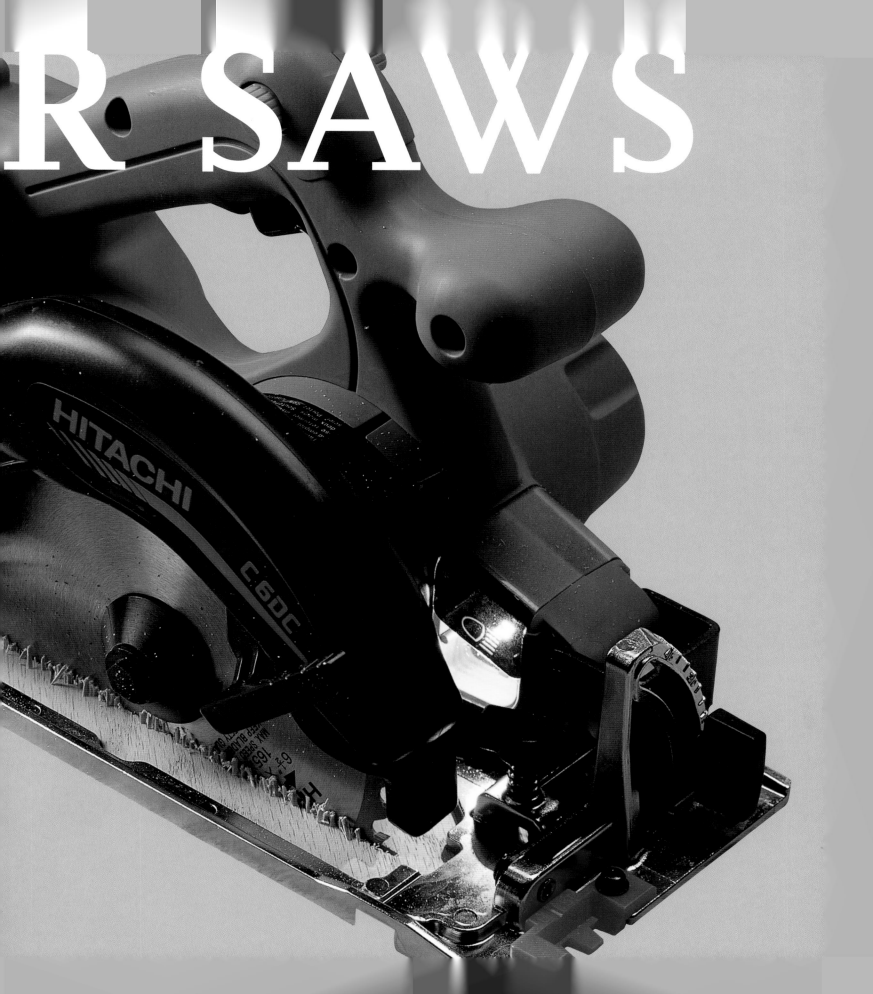

The Classic

SKIL HD77

As a basic component in any contractor's tool kit, a circular saw can cut endless piles of 2x4s for studs, stacks of deck lumber, and acres of plywood. It does its work in all kinds of weather and despite the inevitable job-site bumps and knocks. Any circular saw that gets hard use needs to be tough, reliable, and powerful enough to keep that blade spinning day after day.

One saw has become such a fixture at construction sites that if you ask professional carpenters what kind of portable circular saw they own, they're likely to say, "You mean my Skilsaw?" The basic tool that the Skil Corp. began manufacturing nearly eight decades ago is still the most common name by which both professional and once-in-while carpenters call a circular saw.

The company's model 77 series saws are serious heavy-duty saws preferred by professionals and serious home craftsmen, who value the saws' power and endurance. Interestingly, the choice of circular saw is a regional preference: West Coasters prefer worm drives, while eastern pros favor sidewinder-type saws (for a discussion of saw types, see p. 14).

Skil currently produces several variations of worm drive saw, including the 6½-in.-bladed HD5825 and the magnesium-lightened model HD77M, but its basic bread-and-butter model remains the standard HD77.

SKIL HD77

MOTOR POWER: 13 amps
BLADE DIAMETER: 7¼ in.
BLADE SPEED (NO LOAD): 4,400 rpm
MOTOR DRIVE GEARING: worm drive
MAXIMUM BEVEL ANGLE: 45°
FEATURES: all ball-bearing construction; spindle lock; steel foot

Tools of the Past

THE MOTORIZED MACHETE

Remarkably, it wasn't carpentry that gave rise to the development of a portable circular saw but cutting sugarcane. Developed in the mid 1920s by the Michel Electric Handsaw Co. (later to become Skil), the "motorized machete" had a small 2-in. circular sawblade driven via worm gears and an electric motor at the end of a long handle. Never successful in its own right (can you imagine rambling through high grass with a bunch of other workers armed with motorized blades?), this odd tool gave birth to the portable electric circular saw.

The first Skilsaw was the model E which came out in 1928. It featured aluminum housing, a D-handled grip and trigger, and a worm-driven 6-in. blade. Over the next few decades, the details changed, but the basic design of the saw did not, as witnessed by the '40s-vintage Skilsaw model 825, shown at right.

THE PORTER-CABLE K88 SPEEDMATIC incorporated helical gears into a compact, lightweight design.

THE HELICAL INNOVATION

In 1929, tool designer Art Emmons engineered a new kind of circular saw with the motor mounted transversely to the line of cut: the Porter-Cable model K9. By replacing a worm drive saw's heavy gearbox with helical gears, Emmons created a saw that was lighter and less costly to manufacture. Dubbed the Speedmatic, the K9 was the prototype for the K88, shown above, and other sidewinder-type saws and was quickly adopted by other manufacturers, including Cummins who produced its sturdily built Maxaw in the 1940s.

Circular saws are pretty basic: a single-speed motor that drives a circular blade. Everything is housed in a sturdy frame fitted with a handle that enables the operator to direct the cut.

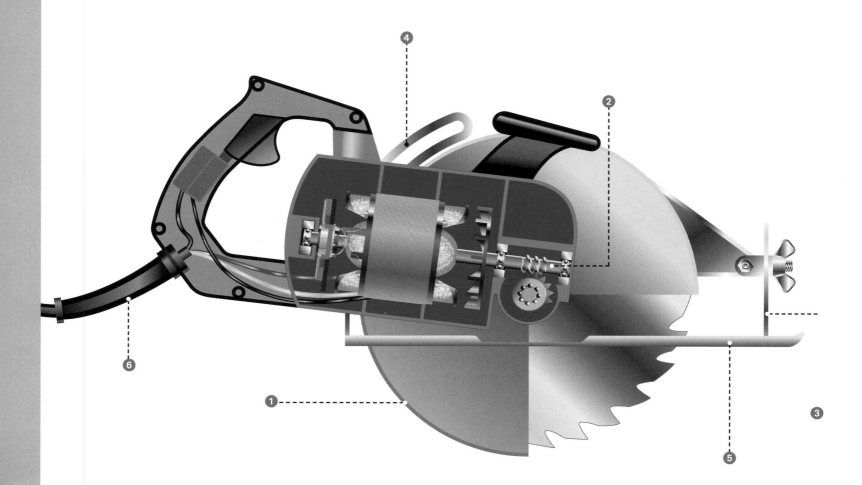

1. A spring-loaded blade guard retracts automatically when cutting, then snaps back to surround vicious saw teeth.

2. A set of reduction gears transforms high-speed motor rotation into slower but more powerful blade spin. Depending on the style of the saw, the gears may be worm, helical, or hypoid.

3. A bevel adjustment allows the saw's motor assembly to be set perpendicular to the foot (for square cuts) or tilted up to 45° to 50° (for bevels).

4. A depth adjustment raises or lowers the blade below the foot, for deeper or shallower cuts.

5. The saw's cast- or sheet-metal foot supports the motor and blade assembly to control the angle of the blade and allow the saw to glide easily across the work.

6. Rubber strain-relief fitting prevents the tool's power cord from fraying or shorting out.

Quick Guide

WORM DRIVE SAWS

- Motor in line with handle
- Mechanical advantage prevents stalling
- Quieter than sidewinders
- Motor placement gives better visibility

SIDEWINDERS

- Lighter in weight than worm drives
- Compact
- Require less maintenance
- More economical

BEAM SAWS

- Designed for cutting heavy timbers
- Large-capacity blades
- Can easily crosscut or miter thick stock
- Can double for general framing work

TRIM SAWS

- Designed for light-duty work
- Excellent for moldings or plywood
- Lightweight and portable
- Easy to handle for fine work

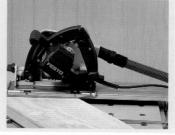

CORDLESS SAWS

- Most portable
- Excel at finish work
- Available in a range of battery voltages
- Heavy-duty models pack plenty of power

Circular-Saw World

WORM DRIVE SAWS

Even to the uninitiated, a worm drive saw has a heft and structure that clearly distinguishes it as a serious tool. Worm drive saws get their name from a pair of gears that transmit power from motor to blade: A worm gear on the end of the motor shaft drives a gear on the blade arbor. The meshed gears run in a crankcase filled with thick oil, which keeps them well lubricated and running cool during long work sessions. This style of power transmission is what gives saws like the Skil HD77M and DeWalt DW378G their characteristic shape, with the motor in-line with the handle and at a right angle to the blade arbor.

Thanks to the mechanical advantage provided by their gearing, worm drives have abundant torque that keeps the sawblade from stalling when it gets pinched in wet or dense lumber. Worm drives are also quieter than most sidewinder-style saws and have their blades to the left of the motor, making it easier for a right-handed user to see the line of cut. But these saws are weighty tools, ranging from 14 lb. to 19 lb.—not for those with puny forearms.

While you can buy a worm drive with a $6\frac{1}{2}$-in. or an $8\frac{1}{4}$-in. blade, most people choose $7\frac{1}{4}$-in.-bladed saws. Although compact, $7\frac{1}{4}$-in. saws can cut through 2x stock with the blade tilted 45°—more than enough for everyday carpentry or home-improvement projects.

SKIL HD77M AND DEWALT DW378G.

SIDEWINDERS

So named because its motor is mounted to the side of the blade, a sidewinder circular saw is more compact and lighter in weight than a worm drive saw. Driven by helical gears that step down the speed of the motor, sidewinders don't have oil-filled gear crankcases and require less maintenance than worm drives. All this, and a lower price, make them an attractive choice for handymen who don't need the fierce torque and durability of a worm drive saw. Traditionally, sidewinders like the Milwaukee 6390 Tilt-Lok and Skil Classic Series 5275-05 have their blades mounted to the right of the motor, making it a little harder for right-handers to see the line of cut. But this arrangement does keep the left hand away from the saw teeth and out of harm's way. Most manufacturers offer a couple of blade-to-left-of-motor models, for righties who like to see what they're doing and don't mind living a little dangerously.

SKIL CLASSIC SERIES 5275-05 AND MILWAUKEE 6390 TILT-LOK.

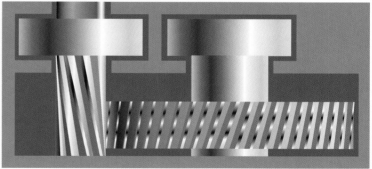

CIRCULAR-SAW GEAR SYSTEMS: worm drive (left) and helical gears (right).

BEAM SAWS

Like a sidewinder on steroids, circular saws with blades 10 in. and larger are sometimes called beam saws, due to their prodigious cutting capacity. For example, the 10¼-in. Skil HD5790 can chomp through nearly 4-in.-thick stock, allowing you to square up the end of a 4x6 header in a single pass. And the Makita 5402A's gigantic 415mm (16⁵/₁₆-in.) blade easily negotiates square cuts in 6-in.-thick stock or cuts angles up to 45° in 4-in. stock. This capacity makes this monster Makita perfect for cutting compound angles on big rafters or slicing through laminated beams or heavy timbers for framing a barn or other sizable structure.

MAKITA 5402A.

TRIM SAWS

They're small. They're cute. But they're not toys. Trim saws pack all the features of a full-sized circular saw into a smaller, lighter package that's much easier to handle. Despite their more petite blades and motors, trim saws have enough power to cut full-sized sheet goods or to zip through door casings, moldings, and other trim. The mightiest of these midget saws is the Porter-Cable 314 with a 4½-in. carbide-tipped blade capable of cutting through more than 1¼-in.-thick stock. Its 4.5-amp motor and worm-gear drive give it enough power to handle even dense hardwoods like maple and oak. But even the most diminutive of trim saws—the 3³/₈-in.-bladed Makita 5090DW—is a versatile tool for trimming light stock or thin paneling. With an optional diamond blade and water-supply kit, the little Makita can even handle glass and ceramic tile.

PORTER-CABLE 314.

CORDLESS SAWS

While there are a lot of features you need in a circular saw, a cord isn't necessarily one of them. Unless you're a whiz with a handsaw, you'll definitely appreciate the convenience of a cordless saw the next time you're far from an electrical outlet and you have a few studs to trim or a sheet of plywood to cut in half. Given their portability and capacity, cordless saws have become a big favorite with finish carpenters.

Like most other batteried power tools, cordless circular saws aren't toys. Even moderate-sized saws sporting 5⅜-in. blades, such as the 18-volt DeWalt DW936K and the 15.6-volt Panasonic EY3531FQWKW, can cut 2x material in a single pass. And saws with full-sized blades, like the 18-volt Makita 5620D, have 6½-in. blades that can bevel-cut a 2x4 at 45°. The biggest 24-volt saws have so much power and capacity that you could probably frame a whole house with one—say, a house in the woods miles from where the power lines end.

ENTERTAINMENT CENTER

Entertain yourself while waiting for your cordless tools to tank up with DeWalt's ingenious DW911, a boom box with a hatch in back for recharging 12-volt to 24-volt battery packs. Besides tools, most cordless toolmakers offer powerful flashlights that use their battery packs, such as the goose-necked DeWalt 18-volt light shown here.

PANASONIC EY3531FQWKW, Makita 5620D, and DeWalt DW936K.

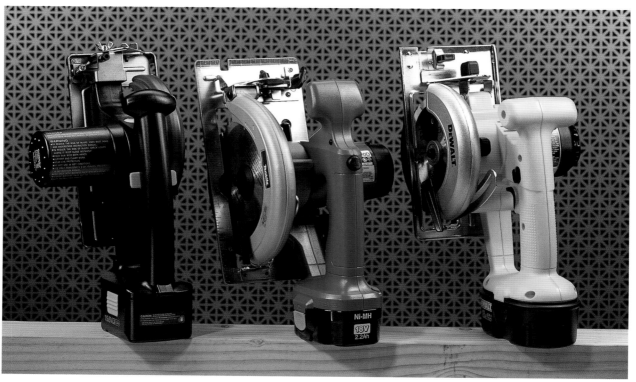

Features

HOUSING AND SOLES

When you're schlepping a circular saw around all day, every ounce counts. By using high-tech composite materials, such as fiberglass-reinforced plastics, and featherweight alloys like magnesium, power-tool manufacturers are making circular saws, belt sanders, and other heavy-duty tools lighter without sacrificing strength or durability.

The magnesium-bodied Skil HD77M is 2 lb. lighter than its traditional partner, the aluminum model HD77, yet uses the same motor. Other circular saws have gone on magnesium diets to reduce weight and save user fatigue, including the Milwaukee 6390, which has magnesium upper and lower blade guards.

SKIL HD77M MAGNESIUM-BODIED SAW.

SOLES

If your circular saw takes a dive more often than a professional wrestler, you'd better hope that it has a sturdy sole. A well-built circular-saw sole, sometimes called a foot or shoe, withstands abuse and survives falls without compromising the accuracy of the saw. Soles on bargain-priced saws are usually made from light sheet metal that gets bent easily. Better models sport cast-alloy soles that take punishment without losing their flatness. Strengthened by reinforcing ribs, the soles of saws such as the Porter-Cable 843K and DeWalt DW378G extend to form a flange that supports the tilt mechanism, enhancing the saws' bevel-cutting performance.

DEWALT DW378G AND PORTER-CABLE 843K.

DEPTH-OF-CUT
ADJUSTMENT

A big blade is just the ticket for slicing through fat planks or broad beams. But when thinner stock needs a trim, it's hazardous to use more of the blade than you need to. For safety's sake, only about 1/8 in. of blade should protrude below the stock—any more and you're taking chances should the saw kick back or your fingers find themselves in the line of fire.

Instead of moving just the blade up and down, like a table saw, a portable circular saw shifts the entire motor/arbor assembly relative to the sole to change its depth of cut. On most saws, the motor pivots from the front of the sole, with a sliding lock at the back for securing the chosen depth setting. The Skil Classic Series 5275-05

has an innovative depth scale located on the back of the blade guard. A pointer attached to the locking knob accurately indicates cutting depth. (The same system is used on the 24-volt Bosch 1660—not surprising since both saws are offered by the same parent company, S-B Power Tool Co.)

SAFE SAWING

Unhappily, the same hunger that drives a circular saw to slice through wood like a voracious termite also makes it one of the most dangerous of all power tools. Make sure you have the depth of the blade adjusted properly for the thickness of the stock. Pay attention to your hand placement when supporting a cutoff. Always use caution, and saw with care—or you might end up learning to point with a different finger.

SKIL CLASSIC SERIES 5275-05.

DUST EXTRACTION

Taming the plume of sawdust thrown by a circular saw might seem like trying to catch the smoke billowing from the stack of a speeding freight train. While other portable tools have canvas collection bags, the prodigious output of a circular sawblade makes a small bag impractical; a bag large enough to handle the chip volume would interfere with operation. A better solution for cleaner cutting is to connect the saw to a portable shop vacuum. A small-dia. hose (1 in. to 1 1/4 in.) has enough capacity to suck chips away yet is flexible enough to allow the tool to move without excessive restriction.

Although few heavy-duty saws have it, newer cordless circular saws have sprouted built-in ports for connecting a vacuum hose. The 19.2-volt Porter-Cable 9845 SawBoss has a dust port atop the guard to capture the stream of chips as they are thrown up by the blade. The 18-volt Makita 5026DWB uses a different strategy: Its trendy translucent-blue plastic guard has deflectors and vents that swirl chips to the back of the guard where the conveniently rear-mounted vacuum hose whisks them away.

DUST-COLLECTION PORTS on the Makita 5026DWB and Porter-Cable 9845 SawBoss.

INNOVATIVE FEATURES

Back in the age when muscles were the main source of tool power, getting a comfortable grip on a saw or an ax meant carving the handle yourself. Thanks to mass production and ergonomics, modern power tools have handles designed to give comfort and control to the majority of users. Contour-molded and/or padded grips, such as the Milwaukee 6390's front grip fabricated from a soft rubbery material, provide comfort and prevent blisters. Ergonomic handles create less stress and strain on hands and wrists, reducing the occurrence of repetitive stress disorders like carpal tunnel syndrome. The Milwaukee's innovative Tilt-Lok D-handle adjusts to eight different positions, allowing you to select an angle to suit your arm position for better cutting control and less wrist strain.

HEADLIGHT on the Hitachi C6DC.

BUILT-IN BRAKES AND HEADLIGHTS

Cordless tools often have cutting-edge features not found on their corded cousins, and circular saws are no different. An electronic blade brake is an important safety device found on few corded saws yet is ubiquitous on cordless ones. It stops the blade a heartbeat after you switch the power off—definitely a good thing when a cut goes awry. An illuminating feature, a built-in lamp on Hitachi's C6DC 18-volt saw, directs a beam of light directly on the line of cut so you can see where you're going even in a dimly lit workspace.

TILT-LOK HANDLE on the Milwaukee 6390 adjusts to eight positions.

BATTERIES AND CHARGERS

BATTERIES AND CHARGERS for cordless tools incorporate high-tech electronics and chemistry.

As much convenience as they offer, not all is free and easy in the world of cordless power tools. Unlike most battery-powered radios, flashlights, cameras, etc., you can't just throw a new set of D batteries in a cordless saw, drill, or biscuit joiner to get it back up and running. Power-tool battery packs are rechargeable units assembled from a number of separate 1.2-volt cells wired together to create a higher voltage. It takes 15 cells to make an 18-volt battery, 20 for a 24-volt pack. A higher-voltage pack lets a saw cut more 2x4s before a recharge but is heavier and less compact than a lower-voltage pack.

Battery technology is keeping pace with the growth in popularity of cordless power tools. Recent developments include high-performance nickel-metal-hydride (NiMH) batteries, currently featured in many Makita cordless tools. These have a much longer running time than standard nickel-cadmium (NiCad) batteries, are more environmentally friendly, and have no memory

effect. DeWalt battery chargers have a tune-up mode that equalizes the individual NiCad cells in the battery pack, enabling them to retain their peak capacity after repeated chargings. Another advance is the development of batteries with built-in charge gauges: Panasonic now produces battery packs with a series of LEDs that light up to show you how much juice is left in the battery.

EACH POWER-TOOL MANUFACTURER has its own dedicated battery packs and chargers.

EACH TO HIS OWN

To make cordless life more confusing, each power tool brand has its own proprietary battery packs and chargers. Even cordless tools of the same brand require different battery packs for different voltages, although most chargers will recharge batteries of multiple voltages.

Regardless of its make and voltage, a battery pack needs proper treatment to perform athletically and endure years of spirited use. Early packs contained nickel-cadmium batteries that were constrained by their memory: If recharged before they were nearly empty, they tended to remember that charge level and would lose charging capacity. Modern NiCad packs are better but still shouldn't be recharged before they're at least partially spent.

HEAT BUILDUP

Quick battery chargers that can top up a battery in as little as 15 min. save time, but repeated rapid charging creates heat that can damage expensive battery packs. Computerized chargers, such as the Bosch BC012 with "fuzzy logic," sidestep this problem by monitoring the battery and carefully regulating the charge to avoid heat damage. Such chargers also include an indicator light to warn you if a recently discharged battery is too hot to immediately recharge. If you go through batteries faster than growing children go through shoes, keep several batteries on hand: one to run, one to charge, and one to let cool after heavy tool use.

A LOOK INSIDE the Bosch BC012 battery charger, where "fuzzy logic" keeps the battery from overheating during a charge.

The Business End

CIRCULAR SAWBLADES

1. **Steel-tooth general blade (Makita).**
2. **Teflon-coated carbide blade (Freud).**
3. **Antikickback blade (Porter-Cable).**
4. **Ultrathin-kerf carbide-tooth blade (Makita).**
5. **Heavy-duty framing blade (DeWalt).**
6. **Decking/framing blade (Freud).**
7. **Antiwarp Enduro (Milwaukee).**

It's that set of voraciously sharp teeth that makes a circular saw the tiger of the power-tool jungle. But just as Nature gives creatures different kinds of teeth adapted to tearing and/or chewing various kinds of food, sawblades are designed with different teeth depending on the material being cut and the type of job. Choose the right blade and all you need to do is pull the trigger and keep the blade tracking down the line of cut.

BLADE TYPES

Old-fashioned steel saw teeth are good for general work and are easy to resharpen. The chisel-toothed Makita blade (1) rips and crosscuts quickly when freshly sharpened. But steel blades just don't hold up like high-quality carbide-tipped blades, which have teeth that stay sharp longer and slice nimbly through a variety of materials. The teeth on the yellow-rimmed 20-tooth DeWalt Series 20 blade (5) are supported by tall shoulders that stand up to heavy-duty construction work, such as remodeling and house framing. For really difficult cuts in wet, dense, or pressure-treated lumber, the Freud TKR103 decking/framing blade (6) has a friction-reducing Teflon coating and has cooling slots to

dissipate heat buildup. The raised bumps behind the carbide teeth of these blades, as well as the general-purpose Milwaukee Enduro (7), limit the rate at which the teeth gobble up stock, to help prevent overfeeding and dangerous kickbacks.

The more teeth, the smoother the cut, so the black Teflon-coated Freud TK001 (2) fine-trim blade has 36 teeth packed around a $4^{3}/_{8}$-in.-dia. body, to deliver clean cuts in plywood or lumber. And special thin-kerfed carbide blades, such as the blue-colored Makita 5026DWA (4), have narrow teeth that remove less stock and hence use less motor power and battery energy.

SPECIALTY BLADES

Fitted with a special blade, a circular saw can actually cut brick, concrete, tile, fiberglass, sheet metal, and even mild steel! Bonded abrasive blades provide an inexpensive way to grind through masonry or metal but wear down quickly. Higher-quality metal-bodied blades have carbide teeth specially formulated to handle specific materials. The Irwin Fibercut blade (bottom in the photo at left) zips through concrete board and thin masonry. The DWL Steel Pro blade (top) dry-cuts mild steel without the need for lubricating oil. The $7^{1}/_{4}$-in. DeWalt blade (center) has a serrated rim impregnated with tiny diamond flakes that slice through tile and brick quickly and cleanly.

SPECIALTY BLADES for cutting concrete, tile, and even mild steel.

STEEL PRO

FIBERCUT™
Saw blade • Lame de scie • Hoja de sierra
ROTATION
6 Tooth Dents Dientes
7 1/4"
184 mm
5/8"
16 mm
WARNING: DO NOT USE BLADE TO CUT MORE THAN
ADVERTISSEMENT: NE PAS UTILISER
ADVERTENCIA: NO UTILICE

Accessories

CUTTING STRAIGHT AND SQUARE

Most people think of a portable circular saw as a tool that's used freehand. True, accurately crosscutting a 2x4 doesn't take much more than a square pencil line and a steady hand. But making a longer cut (say, crosscutting a full sheet of plywood) can create problems. If the sawblade doesn't stay parallel in the kerf, it can bind up and kick the saw back toward the user (talk about getting a tiger by the tail!) That's why cutting guides are such a good idea.

BOSCH 1660 CIRCULAR SAW
fitted with its rip fence.

RIP FENCES

Unless you've got a hand steadier than Wyatt Earp, you'll appreciate how much easier it is to rip a board in half or cut a narrow strip off the edge of a sheet of plywood with a rip-fence attachment. Mounted in a slot or groove in the sole of the circular saw, a rip fence adjusts in or out to set the width of cut. A small shoe at the end of the fence arm rides on the edge of the stock to guide saw travel. Rip fences, like the one shown on the Bosch 1660 24-volt cordless saw, are usually proprietary, designed to fit a specific brand and model of saw.

PORTER-CABLE 48083
protractor gauge.

CROSSCUT AND MITER GUIDES

For quick, accurate crosscuts or miters in construction lumber or trim, the handiest tool to use is a portable cutting jig, like the Porter-Cable 48083. With the angle of cut set on a protractor-like gauge and the tool butted up against the straight edge of the stock, a fence bar guides the edge of the saw's sole for a straight, precise cut. A step up from the portable crosscut guide, the M.A.C. miter board is a stationary guide useful for square crosscuts in panels up to 18 in. wide or for 45° miters in stock up to 8 in. wide. By adjusting its plastic guide rails, the M.A.C. works with any circular saw. By tilting the saw, you can also cut compound miters, for crown moldings and trim up to 1⅝ in. thick.

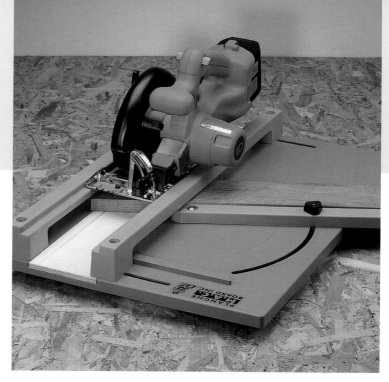

M.A.C. MITER BOARD.

BEAM-SAW ATTACHMENT

Who would imagine that a simple accessory could transform a standard circular saw into a super beam-slicing monster? The Prazi PR-7000 beam cutter is essentially a chainsaw attachment that mounts to a 7¼-in. or 8¼-in. worm drive circular saw. The Prazi's long bar protrudes down through the blade opening in the sole and gives the saw an impressive 12-in. cutting capacity. That's enough to take on tough carpentry chores, like crosscutting, notching, or even ripping heavy girders and laminated beams or cutting logs and planks for timber framing. A kerf-splitting bar is mounted directly behind the chain bar to protect the user and prevent binding and kickback.

PRAZI PR-7000 BEAM CUTTER.

The Cutting Edge

FESTO AFT55 E-PLUS

MOTOR POWER: 1,200 watts

BLADE DIAMETER: 6¼ in.

BLADE SPEED: 2,000–4,800 rpm

MAXIMUM CUTTING DEPTH:
90°: 2³⁄₁₆ in.; 45°: 1⁷⁄₁₆ in.

WEIGHT: 10.6 lb.

ACCESSORIES: rip fence; guide rail
(32 in., 55 in., 95 in., or 118 in.); stop adapter; table (sole) extension; false joint set

FESTO AFT55 E-PLUS

From the country that brought the world fine automotive marques such as BMW, Porsche, and Mercedes comes the German-made line of Festo (now known as Festool) portable power tools, including the innovative AFT55 E-Plus circular saw. While comparable to standard sidewinders in its arrangement of motor and handles, the Festo saw has a host of distinguishing features including the ability to plunge cut. Another unique feature is the saw's continuously variable speed control, which allows optimal speed settings for cutting materials besides wood, including plastics and aluminum.

The AFT55 E-Plus's advanced electronics offer soft start, constant speed under load, and overload protection that monitors both the motor's temperature and current draw. But the plucky Festo's most remarkable feature is its plunging blade: Hold down a button on the handle and you can plunge the 6$\frac{1}{4}$-in. blade into the stock, great for cutting slots or making pocket cuts. A spring brings the blade back up after each cut and a riving knife behind the blade prevents kickback.

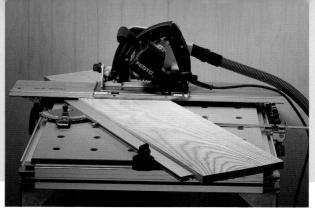

FESTO TOOLS, which include routers and jigsaws as well as circular saws, are designed to work with common accessories: a portable guide rail, a work table, and highly efficient dust collection.

For accurate crosscuts and miters, Festo has another innovation: the MFT800 multifunction table. Usable with both Festo routers and circular saws, the table has sturdy folding legs and an aluminum apron, with channels that mount its guide-rail system.

The guide rail's rib mates with a groove in the saw's sole, thus steering the saw in a straight line. Two height-adjustable supports hold the rail, allowing it to be lowered onto the workpiece. This table helps a portable saw do the work of a radial-arm or sliding compound miter saw—taking wide crosscuts, miters, and compound-angle cuts. An angle stop, adjustable from 45° to 90°, positions the work relative to the guide rail. The stop mounts to the table surface via handscrews set through holes in the medium-density fiberboard (MDF) top. A length stop allows accurate repeat cuts.

To protect the tool, Festo has elevated the concept of tool cases to a whole new level. Its Systainer plastic tool cases provide a clever and effective method of storing and protecting circular saws and other Festo portables. Any number of Systainers can be interlocked for transporting several tools to and from a job site.

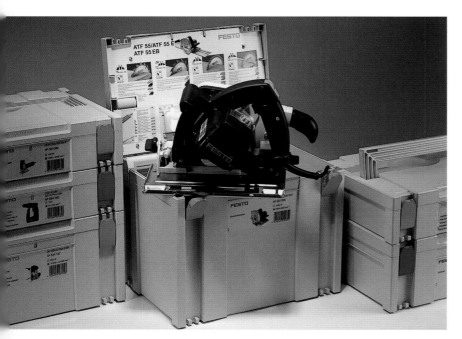

FESTO'S SYSTAINER TOOL CASES are designed to stack and interlock, for ease in transporting them to a job site.

RECIPRO

Sporting the right blade, a reciprocating saw can tap-dance through wood, metals, and plastics or can perform tricky cuts, straight or curved, in tight, cramped spaces. A reciprocating saw's simple in-and-out blade action belies a sawing versatility unmatched by other portables. In the hands of a skilled user, a reciprocating saw excels at demolition tasks, such as removing walls; rough-in work, such as cutting rough openings for skylights or cutouts for running plumbing or heating ducts; and even gardening jobs, such as pruning fruit-tree branches.

Unlike wood-eating circular saws and jig-saws, a reciprocating saw isn't on a strict diet: A bimetal-bladed saw will happily munch through a nail-infested board or eat a metal-lath-and-plaster sandwich for lunch. Such versa-tility makes it an indispens-able tool for contractors and home remodelers alike.

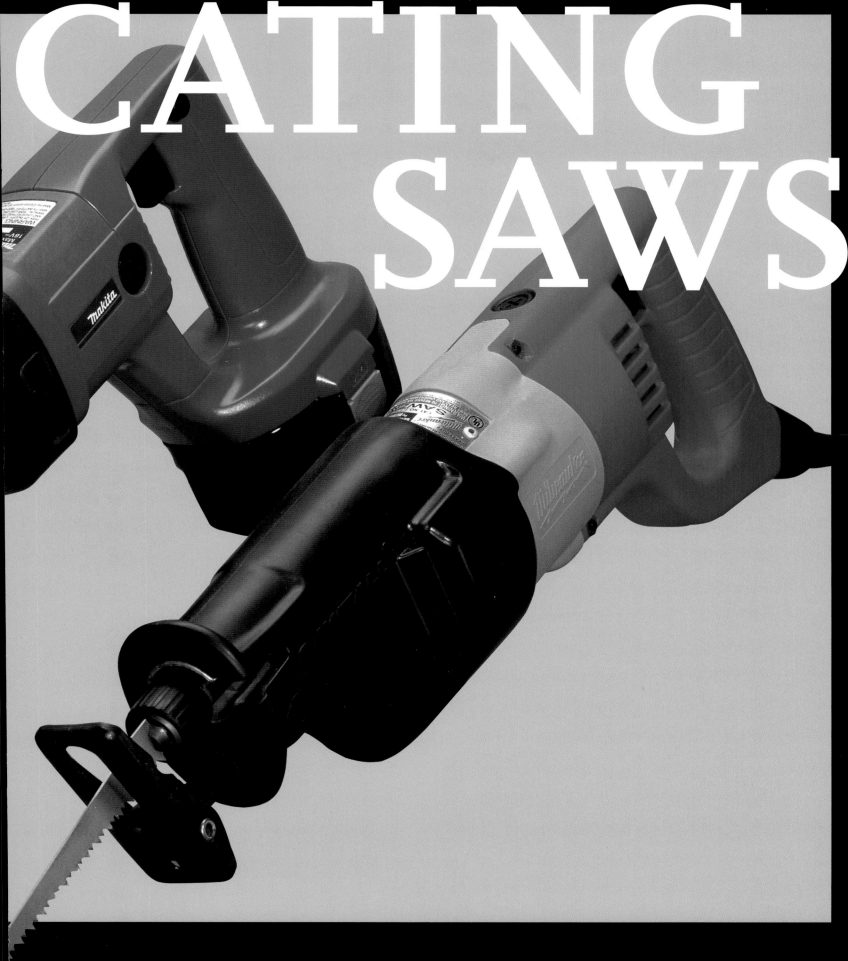

CATING
SAWS

The Classic

MILWAUKEE 6509 SAWZALL

Most old-timers call their reciprocating saw a Sawzall, just as many people call facial tissues Kleenex and colas Coke. While several other power-tool companies now manufacture reciprocating saws, Milwaukee invented the tool and introduced it to the building trades in the early 1950s.

Over the decades, the Sawzall's versatility and sturdy construction have made it a highly prized tool for house remodelers, plumbers, HVAC (heating, ventilating, and air-conditioning) installers, and other professional workmen. Today, Milwaukee produces more than half a dozen Sawzall models. But its basic workhorse—the affordable, no-frills model 6509—is still a favorite among carpenters and home-project craftsmen alike.

MILWAUKEE 6509 SAWZALL

MOTOR POWER: 6 amps

BLADE SPEED: 0–2,400 strokes per min.

STROKE LENGTH: ¾ in.

WEIGHT: 6.75 lb.

OVERALL LENGTH: 16 in.

FEATURES: variable speed; Quik-Lok tool-less blade clamp

ACCESSORIES: carrying case

A Look Inside

The heart of a reciprocating saw is a mechanism that converts the motor's rotation into rapid in-and-out action.

1. A pivoting shoe braces the saw against the work during cutting. Adjusting the position of the shoe in or out helps distribute wear along the length of the blade.

2. A keyless blade clamp allows quick blade changes without the need for a wrench or screwdriver.

3. A rubber boot covers the front of the saw to protect it during heavy cuts and when working in dirty and wet conditions.

4. The reciprocating mechanism converts the rotation of the motor into the in-and-out action that moves the blade.

5. Special counterbalance action found on some models reduces vibration created by the reciprocating mechanism.

6. The heavy-duty motor is powerful enough to drive the blade through thick materials.

7. Large D-handle gives user better control of the saw in difficult cutting conditions.

Reciprocating-
Saw World

CORDED RECIPROCATING SAWS

For demanding jobs like sawing holes for pipes through several layers of flooring or hacking through cast-iron sewer pipe, you can't beat the power of a corded reciprocating saw. The heavy-duty saws with high-amperage motors—like the Porter-Cable 9737 Tiger Saw, Hitachi CR13VA, and Milwaukee 6521 Super Sawzall—are the champs of high performance.

Despite their beefy motors, these saws' reinforced plastic and alloy bodies make them relatively light—a decidedly good thing when you're perched precariously atop a ladder, trying to single-handedly cut out a hole for a ceiling fixture. Whether large or small, a reciprocating saw should be high on your wish list if you've just gotten your contractor's license or if you've taken two weeks off work to remodel your garage or turn the basement into a family room.

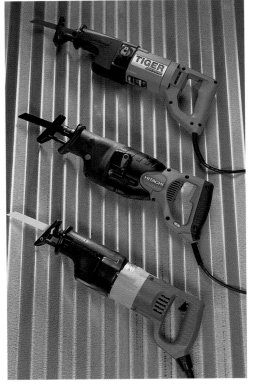

PORTER-CABLE 9737 Tiger Saw, Hitachi CR13VA, and Milwaukee 6521 Super Sawzall.

DETACHABLE POWER CORDS make storing the tool easier.

DETACHABLE POWER CORDS
Except for the flow of current that they conduct to power tools, power cords are mostly a nuisance. To make cord stowage tangle-free, Milwaukee has put detachable cords with twist-locking plugs on many of its power tools. By fitting an optional longer power cord, you don't need an extension cord when working far from an outlet.

CORDLESS RECIPROCATING SAWS

Few are the craftsmen who haven't sung the praises of cordless power tools. (Even the electricity-eschewing Amish use them, with the help of non-Amish services to keep their batteries charged.) But those who sing the loudest are surely the plumbers, contractors, and handymen who have experienced the joy of using a cordless reciprocating saw.

Handy and maneuverable, you can tote this tool to the farthest reaches of an attic or basement with no worry about dragging a long, cumbersome extension cord along. Although they don't pack as powerful a punch, cordless saws—such as the Makita JR180DZ, DeWalt DW938, and Milwaukee 6515—have most of the features of the corded models, plus an electronic brake that stops blade action in a heartbeat, to prevent accidents and broken blades.

MAKITA JR180DZ, DeWalt DW938, and Milwaukee 6515.

AN EARLY "SAW TO REPLACE ALL SAWS"

Another type of tool that employed reciprocating-blade action was the general-purpose shop saw, like the Wen Zipp Saw and the All Saw. Wen manufactured the two-speed All Saw in the 1960s and early 1970s and modestly claimed that it was "the one saw to replace all saws." In truth, the odd-looking tool's ample 6-amp motor, 1-in.-long stroke, and large assortment of blades (including the whopping 6-in.-long blade shown here) enabled it to perform a variety of straight and curved cuts in wood and metal with reasonable aplomb. The All Saw tilted for bevel cuts and came with a fence that doubled as a circle guide.

Features

ORBITAL AND SWING ACTION

Moving the blade in an orbit, rather than just up and down, makes a jigsaw cut more like a tiger than a kitten. What works for jigsaws also works for reciprocating saws, and several brands have orbital action among their list of features. A selection lever on the Porter-Cable 9737 Tiger Saw lets you choose between a linear back-and-forth blade motion—best for cutting tough stuff like steel—and orbital action. Orbital action, which pulls the blade through the material, makes cutting more aggressive without demanding more motor—or muscle—power.

The Hitachi CR13VA employs a variation of orbital action it calls "swing action," which moves the rear section of the reciprocating shaft up and down along the slope of a swinging rail mounted in the gear case. Intended to offer a smoother cutting motion than orbital-action designs, swing action works equally well with the blade mounted upside down during flush-trimming operations.

TAMING THE RECIPROCATING BEAST

The laws of physics dictate that every action produces an opposite and equal reaction. In the case of reciprocating saws, the rapid back-and-forth movement of the blade creates an undesirable reaction, namely vibration. A difficult cut in thick or dense material can produce so much

ORBITAL-ACTION SWITCHES on the Porter-Cable 9737 Tiger Saw and Hitachi CR13VA.

bone-jarring vibration that you can almost feel the fillings in your teeth loosen. But clever engineering can simmer down a bucking reciprocating saw: A counterbalance mechanism found in several models moves a counterweight in opposition to the blade shaft to reduce vibration and user fatigue.

COUNTERBALANCE reduces vibration. (PHOTO BY ANDREW WORMER, COURTESY *FINE HOMEBUILDING* MAGAZINE, © THE TAUNTON PRESS, INC.)

SPEED CONTROL

By controlling the number of blade strokes per minute, you can slow down a reciprocating saw's cutting speed when you hit a nail or knot and can speed it up when you're ready to sail through clear lumber or plywood. Saws like the Super Sawzall and Hitachi CR13VA have a variable-speed dial that sets the upper speed limit of the motor. By pressing the trigger gently, you can start cuts slowly, to prevent the saw from bucking or the blade from bending.

DIAL- AND TRIGGER-CONTROLLED variable speed: Hitachi CR13VA and Milwaukee Super Sawzall.

ADJUSTABLE SHOE

No matter how long your reciprocating saw's blade is, a small number of teeth end up doing most of the work. To increase their blades' bites, most reciprocating saws feature an adjustable shoe. As teeth on one part of the blade wear out, you can reposition the shoe to let teeth on a fresh section of the blade go to work. This extends blade life dramatically, especially when you're hacking through thin but tough-to-cut materials like cast iron and stainless steel. The means of adjusting the shoe range from effortless to irksome, depending on the saw. The Makita JR180DZ and the Milwaukee Super Sawzall have shoe-adjustment levers that are among the easiest to use.

SHOE ADJUSTMENT on the Makita JR180DZ and the Milwaukee Super Sawzall.

The Business End

BLADES OF EVERY LENGTH AND TYPE

Even the burliest, most powerful reciprocating saw won't cut well without the right blade. What's right depends on what material you're cutting, how thick it is, and how fast you plan to zip through it. The construction of the blade and the tooth style are designed for specific types of materials. The overall length of the blade and the number of teeth per inch (tpi) affect both maximum cutting depth and the fineness or raggedness of the cut edges. Bimetal construction, which bonds hard-steel teeth to a flexible steel body, is used in many types of blades, including general-purpose blades that are good for everyday work. For faster cuts, choose a blade with 3 tpi to 6 tpi; blades with 6 tpi to 10 tpi cut slower but leave a smoother finish.

Incidentally, the blades on all reciprocating saws can be reversed in the blade chuck so that the teeth point up instead of down, which makes it much easier to plunge-cut into the middle of a wall or panel.

TOOL-LESS BLADE CHANGE

Taking rough cuts with a reciprocating saw makes broken blades a regular occurrence. When you're working on a rooftop or ladder, you'll appreciate the convenience of tool-less blade changes. The Porter-Cable Tiger Saw and many others have finger-operated blade chucks that twist to release the blade, while the DeWalt DW938 liberates its blade with a flip-up lever.

BLADES COME IN A WIDE VARIETY of lengths, shapes, tooth configurations, and number of teeth, to suit the many uses of a reciprocating saw.

BLADE-CHANGE MECHANISMS on the DeWalt DW938 and the Porter-Cable Tiger Saw.

From left to right:

1. A versatile bimetal blade with special teeth developed by DeWalt specifically for cordless reciprocating saws.

2. An 7-in. Hitachi all-purpose blade, long enough for deep cuts in lumber or rough-in remodeling work.

3. Skil's The Ugly blade has coarse teeth and enough length to tackle pruning, branch trimming, and timber work.

4. Tungsten-carbide grit embedded on the edge of this blade cuts through cast iron, cement board, ceramic tile, fiberglass, and epoxy or polyester plastics.

5. A fine-tooth Makita high-speed steel blade cuts metal pipe, sheet metal, and rubber or hard-plastic parts cleanly.

6. The wide-blade body on this Milwaukee bimetal demolition blade keeps it from bending when plunged into walls and lumber.

7. Sharp teeth on this bimetal blade quickly cuts through wood while still standing up to embedded nails.

8. Special teeth on this bimetal plaster blade cut in both directions for faster, more aggressive cuts, even in walls with embedded metal lath.

Accessories

VERSATILITY PLUS

As if the reciprocating saws weren't versatile enough, manufacturers have come up with a few ingenious devices that allow these saws to do even more tricks, including offset sawing and pipe-cutoff work. Given the tool's growing popularity, we're likely to see more accessories introduced for these saws in the near future.

OFFSET BLADE ADAPTER

Sometimes you just can't get close enough to something. In the case of a reciprocating saw, cutting right up flush to a surface can be down-right impossible—unless you fit the saw with an offset blade adapter. This accessory replaces the tool's blade holder and supports the blade off axis so that its teeth are slightly above the tool's body. With the adapter, you can saw right up against a wall or into a corner without tilting the saw.

A CLAMP HOLDS PIPE for straight, square cuts.

PIPE CLAMP SYSTEM

Getting a straight, square cut through a cylindrical pipe with a reciprocating saw is tough enough with the pipe clamped to your workbench. But making that same cut while lying on your back in the crawl space beneath your house makes you want to cry out for help. That help comes in the form of a special pipe-cutting clamp made by Milwaukee for its Sawzalls. A stud on the device fits in place of the reciprocating saw's shoe, and a chain-style pipe clamp wraps around pipes up to 4 in. in diameter. A pivot between the stud and clamp keeps the saw square to the pipe and gives you leverage and control to make cuts easier, especially in tough materials like cast-iron sewer pipe.

MILWAUKEE OFFSET BLADE ADAPTER lets you saw right into corners.

The Cutting Edge

BOSCH 1640VS FINECUT

Muscle-driven reciprocating action is what we use to power a handsaw through a plank or panel. Bosch has replaced muscles with a motor and created a very different kind of reciprocating saw. Its Finecut power handsaw isn't designed for rough cuts and remodeling work but rather for accurate cuts for finish carpentry and cabinetmaking.

Unlike a standard reciprocating saw's narrow blades, which are designed primarily for rough work, the Finecut uses any one of three wide, handsaw-like blades, each designed for straight, accurate cuts. Used freehand with a fine-tooth blade, the in-line-motored tool will handily cut dovetails or tenons. With its offset blade, the tool trims dowels or pegs flush and easily pares the bottom of door casings in preparation for a new floor.

Fitted into its FS2000 miter-table attachment, the Finecut becomes a stationary cutoff and miter saw, ready to tackle trim carpentry or furnituremaking with speed and precision.

BOSCH 1640VS FINECUT

MOTOR POWER: 3.5 amps

STROKE LENGTH: ⅝ in.

STROKES PER MINUTE (NO LOAD): 2,000–2,800

CUTTING CAPACITY:
wood: 2½ in.
plastic: ¾ in.

LENGTH: 11⅞ in.

WEIGHT: 3.5 lb.

ACCESSORIES: kit 1640VSK includes three sawblades, miter-table attachment, clamps, and plastic case

---

THE MITER-TABLE attachment turns the Finecut into an accurate cutoff saw for trimwork.

JIGSAWS

With its narrow blade that cycles up and down like a carousel horse, a jigsaw can cut all kinds of curves and circles—square or beveled—as well as scroll cuts fanciful enough for any gingerbread decoration. Sometimes called a sabersaw, a jigsaw can also tackle the occasional straight cut, but serious rips or crosscuts should be left for a circular saw.

The variable speed and orbital-blade action found on most jigsaws make them extremely versatile tools capable of cutting cleanly and accurately a wide range of materials, including wood, metal, plastics, cardboard, and leather. One particularly handy jigsaw trick is plunge cutting into a surface to start a cut in the middle of a panel—say, to saw out an electrical outlet in a wall or to cut out a countertop for a kitchen sink. To add to its versatility, you can pick a jigsaw that's powered by household current, batteries, or compressed air. Or you can choose a bayonet saw that's compact and powerful enough to tackle the most demanding carpentry chores.

The Classic

BOSCH 1587AVS

I was pretty happy with the little jigsaw my dad bought at a department store in the 1960s. It pounded its way through plywood and soft lumber, though the blade scorched the wood and broke or bent as often as it didn't. But in the mid '70s, some Swiss-made jigsaws came along that changed my expectations of what a jigsaw could do. A review from that time said that the Bosch jigsaw "ran like a sewing machine and cut like a chainsaw." Built like a Swiss watch, the powerful Bosch saws had sophisticated features including orbital-blade action and electronic motor feedback.

A lot of improvements have come along since I bought my first Bosch jigsaw, the D-handled model 1578. (To date, Bosch has produced more than 20 million jigsaws worldwide.) Bosch's latest top model, the 1587AVS incorporates its tool-less Clic blade-change system. To swap blades, you simply pull up the black top handle and turn it, to loosen or tighten the blade clamp (my old Bosch required a long, skinny screwdriver for blade changes). Another popular feature is the variable-speed dial on the trigger, which sets the maximum blade speed; slowly pulling the trigger gradually ramps up the blade speed for better control and less tearout at the beginning of the cut.

THE AUTHOR'S BOSCH JIGSAW, a model 1578 purchased in the 1970s, is still going strong.

BOSCH 1587AVS

MOTOR POWER: 5 amps

STROKE LENGTH: 1 in.

STROKES PER MINUTE (NO LOAD):
500–3,100

CUTTING CAPACITIES:
wood: 3⅜ in.
plastic: 1¼ in.
aluminum: ¾ in.
mild steel: ⅜ in.

LENGTH: 10⅝ in.

WEIGHT: 5.5 lb.

A Look Inside

A jigsaw motor's rotary motion not only drives the blade up and down but can orbit the blade for more aggressive cutting.

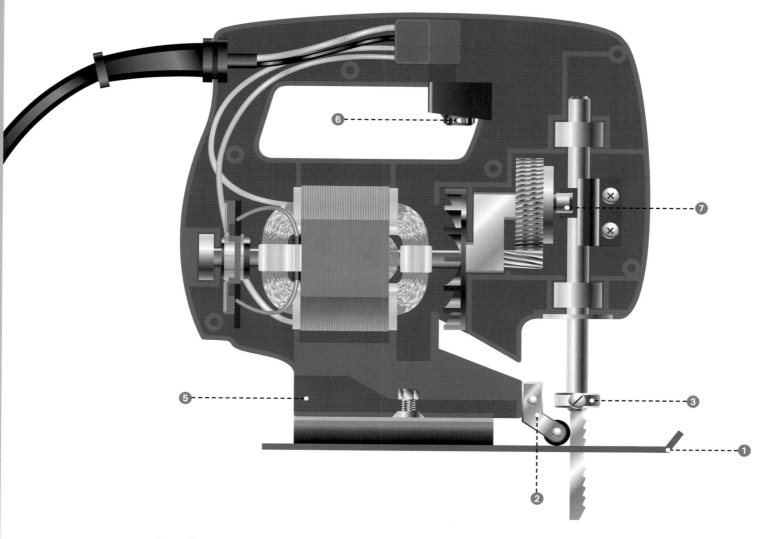

① A tilting baseplate keeps the saw square to the work or allows it to tilt for beveled cuts.

② The blade guide prevents the blade from deflecting, to keep it running straight up and down.

③ The blade holder locks the blade on the end of the reciprocating arm. On most saws, the holder allows tool-less blade changes.

④ A dust-collection port connects the saw to a shop vacuum hose.

⑤ The variable-speed dial allows you to select the best top blade speed for the material being cut.

⑥ The gear case translates the rotary action of the motor into the reciprocating action of the blade.

Tools of the Past

GETTING AROUND THE CURVES

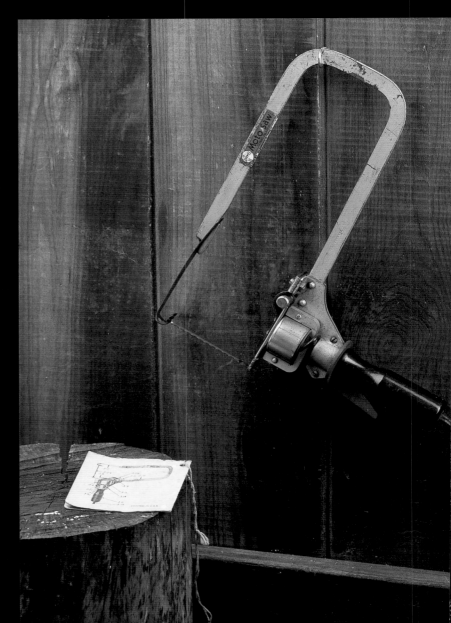

THE DREMEL MOTO-SAW bears little resemblance to today's jigsaws. It's simply a motorized coping saw.

In the early days, when woodworkers wanted to cut out fancy fretwork—say, for the surround on a Chippendale desk—they had to rely on their skill with a coping saw. One of the earliest powered versions of this basic tool is probably the Dremel Moto-Saw, a wacky-looking coping saw with the addition of an electric vibrator, which oscillated the blade up and down rapidly. The length of stroke was adjustable using a small screw atop the vibrator coil. The tool turned on and off with a rudimentary switch, made from a triangular piece of fiberboard slotted into the base of the handle.

RECIPROCATING ACTION

A much more useful portable saw was developed in the late 1940s by Scintilla, a Swiss company that later became part of Bosch. Early Scintilla jigsaws linked a powerful electric motor with a reciprocating mechanism, which propelled a blade vertically through a flat baseplate (the inspiration for these early saws was the sewing machine). By not suspending the blade at both ends, the jigsaw made it possible to cut closed shapes and fretwork without having to unhook the blade and thread it through a starter hole.

THE SWISS SCINTILLA, developed in the 1940s, was the world's first portable jigsaw.

THE GOLDEN AGE

As a class of portable power tools, jigsaws hit full stride in the 1950s and 1960s when dozens of brands became available to American craftsmen, including the Sears Craftsman, the PowerCraft (sold by Montgomery Ward), and the ShopMate. Most of these jigsaws were stoutly constructed, with heavy cast-aluminum bodies (the Shop-Mate's Art Deco-influenced body looks like a futuristic spacecraft). Although none of these saws has orbital-blade action or quick-change blade holders, they do sport some useful features: The massive PowerCraft has variable-speed control, and the ShopMate has a built-in light located above the blade.

VINTAGE JIGSAWS FROM THE 1950S AND 1960S: the Sears Craftsman, the PowerCraft, and the ShopMate. All sport heavy cast-aluminum housings, popular in that period.

Jigsaw World

CORDED JIGSAWS

The modern corded jigsaw is a sophisticated curve-cutting machine with a multitude of features that enable it to accomplish all kinds of cuts in all kinds of materials. The most powerful corded jigsaws can cut wood up to $2\frac{3}{4}$ in. thick, $\frac{3}{4}$-in.-thick aluminum, and even $\frac{1}{4}$-in.-thick mild steel. The biggest difference among corded saws is their body/grip style. Barrel-grip saws, preferred by Europeans, such as the Bosch 1584AVS and the Fein Aste 638, are held by wrapping one hand around the motor housing; top-gripped D-handled saws, such as the DeWalt DW321 and the Porter-Cable 9543, are preferred by American craftsmen.

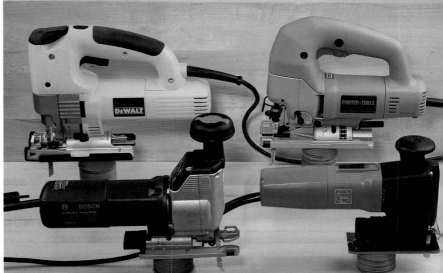

CORDED JIGSAWS (clockwise from left): DeWalt DW321, Porter-Cable 9543, Fein Aste 638, and Bosch 1584AVS.

CORDLESS JIGSAWS

Snip the power cord from a traditional jigsaw, fit a battery, and you have a truly portable saw. Now you can cut rounded shingles for your daughter's treehouse or cut a shapely curve on your sailboat's transom without long extension cords or the worry of electrocution. Although they're less powerful than corded saws and need recharging, cordless saws, like the Makita 4332DZ, pack some impressive features. The 14.4-volt Makita sports variable speed, a tilting baseplate, a blade-orbit selector, and an electronic brake that stops the blade the instant the trigger is released.

MAKITA 4332DZ cordless jigsaw.

PNEUMATIC JIGSAWS

While air tools are fairly common among portable sanders, it's a fairly new concept among jigsaws. Connected to a good-sized compressor, the Bosch 7561 118 is just as versatile and cuts just as powerfully as similarly featured corded models but weighs about a third less. Lacking a cord also makes it safe to use in wet or damp places, where running an AC-powered tool would be unsafe. The pneumatic Bosch is activated by a paddle-trigger air control beneath its narrow barrel-grip body.

BOSCH 7561 118 PNEUMATIC JIGSAW.

BAYONET SAWS

PORTER-CABLE 548 BAYONET SAW.

Developed in the mid 1950s by Porter-Cable, the bayonet saw is a slightly different animal than the other jigsaws featured in this chapter. The low-profile Porter-Cable 548 saw uses a worm gear to transfer power to the blade-reciprocating mechanism. The saw's sturdy, nontilting base and large 7/16-in. blade orbit make it great for square cuts in metals, plastics, thinner woods, and laminates.

Features

QUICK-RELEASE BLADE CHANGE

To make blade swapping quicker and less tedious, the best jigsaws incorporate some kind of quick-release blade-changing device, which does not require any tools to operate. To change blades on models like the Skil 4470 and Porter-Cable 9543, you simply press or pull a lever or flange located on the end of the blade carrier itself. The blade-changing mechanism is more integral on jigsaws like the Bosch 1584AVS and DeWalt DW321; the top handle on both saws rotates to lock or unlock the shanked blade below. Even though the Fein Aste 638 jigsaw doesn't have tool-free blade change, it offers a great time-saving feature: The saw's top handle unscrews to reveal an Allen wrench that is used to lock or loosen the blade.

SKIL 4470 AND PORTER-CABLE 9543.

BLADE WRENCH in the top handle on the Fein Aste 638.

BOSCH 1584AVS AND DEWALT DW321.

BLADE ACTION AND SPEED CONTROL

Inexpensive jigsaws that simply thrust their blades up and down get the job done, but they don't cut aggressively and they wear their blades down quickly. Premium jigsaws offer varying degrees of blade action: straight line or orbital. Orbital action uses an oscillating mechanism to move the blade in a slight circular motion as it reciprocates. The blade moves forward on the up stroke (the direction the teeth cut in), helping it to cut more quickly and aggressively, then moves back on the return stroke, keeping the teeth clear of wear. Since different kinds of cuts in different types of materials require varying degrees of orbit, jigsaws such as

FREUD FJ85 allows variable orbital action.

the Freud FJ85 have a selection lever to let you choose the amount of orbit: more for straight, super-fast cuts or energetic cuts in porous materials; less for curved cuts, tight scroll work, or slower cuts in dense materials like metals.

ELECTRONIC VARIABLE SPEED

For a jigsaw to wear its crown of versatility, it must cut many different materials with the same alacrity. Variable speed is as important to that goal as choosing the right kind of blade. Deep cuts in dense hardwoods require high speed, while hard steel demands much slower blade reciprocations. The Fein Aste 638's variable-speed control is at the end of its motor housing, while the Bosch 1581AVS has a dial mounted on the trigger itself.

SPEED ADJUSTMENT on the Fein Aste 638 and the Bosch 1581AVS.

BASES

While a jigsaw's blade spends much of its time set square to its base, most saws allow the saw to be tilted for bevel cuts. Typically, loosening a single screw allows the base to tilt up to 45° in either direction. While many saws provide an on-board Allen wrench for base adjustments, the DeWalt DW321 and Porter-Cable 9543 do one better: A built-in lever loosens and tightens the base to allow tilting. The bases on these saws slide back and forth and lock at 45° or 90°, eliminating the need for a square or protractor to set these commonly used angles. And by sliding the bases backward and locking them, you can saw right up to a wall or other vertical surface—handy when working inside a cabinet or closet. Many premium saws also have a smooth plastic cover or insert on the metal baseplate that won't scratch delicate surfaces, such as veneers or plastic laminates.

BASE TILT CONTROL on the Porter-Cable 9543.

ANTISPLINTERING INSERT

Although many jigsaw owners use their saws to cut metal, plastic, rubber, leather, and even paper, most use their saws to cut wood. Because a jigsaw cuts on the up stroke, it has a tendency to tear out wood fibers on the top side of the cut. This is bad because it obscures the line of cut and results in a rough, splintery edge. Therefore, better-quality jigsaws like the Festo PS2 E-Plus have a slot at the front of the base for mounting an antisplintering insert. Made from plastic, the removable, replaceable insert fits close to the cutting edge of the blade, thus supporting the wood fibers at the point of cut and significantly reducing tearout.

ANTISPLINTERING INSERT on the Festo PS2 E-Plus.

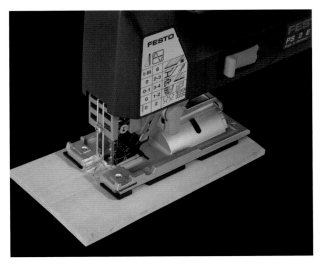

BLADE GUIDES

When it comes to
cutting thick mate-
rials without twist-
ing or bending, the
narrow reciprocating blade of a
jigsaw can use all the help it can get.
Many models offer help in the form of
a blade guide: a grooved disk that supports the back edge of the blade. This
keeps the blade running straight and helps it
resist deflection, which improves the accuracy of
the cut and reduces blade bending and breakage.
On orbital jigsaws like the Makita 4332DZ, the
blade guide serves a double duty: The arm to
which the guide disk is mounted swivels back
and forth, thus initiating the orbital action.

MAKITA 4332DZ BLADE GUIDE provides
orbital action.

SCROLLING FEATURE

Cutting out a curvy pattern, say for Victorian fretwork, usually
means rotating the saw or the workpiece. But some saws have
a scrolling feature that lets the blade rotate all the way around
while keeping the jigsaw itself pointed in the same direction.
The same lever on the Skil 4470 that selects blade orbit also
engages the scrolling feature, which is controlled by the saw's
front handle. By rotating the knob as the cut progresses, you
can turn tight corners and cut out fancy shapes with a lot less
wrist-twisting effort.

Accessories

BLADES

The failing of many early jigsaws were cheap blades that compromised the saws' cutting performance. Fortunately, modern jigsaw blades employ as much advanced technology as the jigsaws themselves. The shape, size, and spacing of teeth on a blade affect its performance as well as the material from which it's made. Good general-purpose wood-cutting blades, such as the Metabo and Bosch blades (far left and far right in the photo at right), have precisely machined taper ground teeth, while the DeWalt cobalt-steel blade (second from left) has a reinforced tooth design. Bosch's savage-looking Progressor blade (second from right) features a variable tooth size, for aggressive cutting and less splintering. The Bosch bimetal blade (center) has hardened carbon-steel teeth bonded to a high-speed-steel back. The durable teeth stay sharp while the flexible blade body resists breakage, making bimetal blades ideal for demanding tasks.

BLADES (left to right): Metabo taper ground blade, DeWalt cobalt-steel blade, Bosch bimetal blade, Bosch Progressor, and Bosch taper ground blade.

RASPS

Did you think sawing and slicing were the only things a jigsaw could do? Mount one of these specially designed rasps in a jigsaw, and you're ready to trim the edge of a cutout, shape a slot, or fair the fit between two irregular parts. Both the half-round and flat rasps (made by Bosch) have teeth that cut only on the up stroke and have shanks that mount in a standard single-tang blade holder.

STATIONARY TABLE

Routers aren't the only portable tools you can mount in a table. When inverted and attached to a stationary table, a jigsaw is very useful for sawing small or delicate workpieces. Made from cast aluminum, the Bosch stationary jigsaw table conveniently clamps to the edge of a table or benchtop. A pair of cleats and a locking plate secure the jigsaw to the underside of the table but allow quick removal when it's needed for portable duties.

CAN'T AFFORD A BANDSAW? Turn your jigsaw into a stationary tool with a table accessory.

EDGE GUIDE AND CIRCLE JIG

Because they are light and portable, jigsaws excel at freehand cutting of curvy parts. Still, there are times when a jigsaw is the best tool for making a straight cut. To assure an even rip or square crosscut, fit the saw with an edge guide. Like other jigsaws, the edge guide on the Metabo STE105 Plus attaches near the front of the baseplate, adjusting in or out to set the distance between the fence and the blade. By flipping the edge guide over and mounting a pivot knob, the Metabo's guide serves double duty as a circle jig, here used to radius the end of a redwood plank.

THIS METABO DEVICE is both an edge guide and circle jig.

DUST CONTROL

All the jigsaws and other electric portables with built-in dust collection have spawned a whole generation of sophisticated shop vacuums designed to work in tandem with power tools. The German company Festo offers an entire line of compact shop vacuums, with natty green-striped hoses that connect directly to their portables. The fine dust–trapping Festo CT 33 E vacuum has a built-in electrical outlet for the power tool and circuitry that turns the vacuum on and off automatically in concert with the tool.

THE EFFICIENT FESTO VACUUM works with an entire line of nearly dustless power tools, including jigsaws.

DUST BLOWING

Getting chips and dust out of the way not only makes using a jigsaw a cleaner proposition—it's essential if you're trying to see the line you're cutting! Early jigsaws often kept the sight line clear with a built-in dust blower that piped a small stream of air in front of the blade. Nowadays, premium jigsaws have built-in dust collection, which pulls air from behind the blade to draw vision-obscuring dust away from the line of cut. To enhance collection and to block chips from flying into your eyes, the Metabo STE105 Plus encloses the blade in a transparent, removable plastic guard. Chips are drawn through the base of the saw to a vacuum hose, which attaches to a port at the rear of the motor housing.

METABO STE105 PLUS chip deflector and chip guard.

The Cutting Edge

BOSCH 3294EVS

Resembling a reciprocating saw as much as a jigsaw, the Bosch 3294EVS in-line jigsaw is designed to go "where no jigsaw has gone before"—not outer space, but into tight spaces where a conventional jigsaw can't reach. Instead of a solid baseplate, the blade of the 3294EVS is flanked by a pair of metal rails that braces the saw against the work surface and keeps it square during cutting.

Like other Bosch jigsaws, the 3294EVS has adjustable orbital-blade action, variable speed, and tool-less quick blade change via a pull-out lever on the underside of the body. A long

BOSCH 3294EVS

MOTOR POWER: 3.6 amps

STROKE LENGTH: ⅝ in.

STROKES PER MINUTE (NO LOAD): 300–3,800

LENGTH: 13½ in.

WEIGHT: 3.2 lb.

paddle-like trigger makes the barrel-grip tool comfortable to operate. To bolster its versatility, the 3294EVS accepts rasps (see the sidebar on p. 54) and wire brushes, for power shaping parts and cleaning metal parts.

ROUTERS

The router is the undisputed king of power-tool versatility. It can shape, joint, plane, trim, carve, drill, and slice wood. It's tops for cutting joinery ranging from simple to fanciful. Want to shape an edge or make a molding? With even a small selection of shapely router bits, you can create nearly an infinite number of variations. You'd need a whole chest full of molding planes just to create all the shapes you can with a single router and a box of bits. A router can follow a pattern to create perfectly identical multiple parts. You can use a router to cut mortises for hardware, to joint and trim lumber, to create recesses for decorative inlays, and to do so much more that it boggles the mind.

The incredible versatility of this machine has spawned some useful variations: regular fixed-base routers for everyday tasks; plunge routers that let you change bit depth on the fly; mini routers to trim laminates; and heavy-duty routers and air-powered routers for demanding production work.

The Classics

PORTER-CABLE 690

Early success with small routers gave Porter-Cable an advantage that led to the development of a model that's been in continuous production for decades. With its stout-yet-lightweight construction, simple design, and reliable features, the Porter-Cable 690 router is truly a classic among fixed-base models. A single-speed, $1\frac{1}{2}$-hp workhorse, this little router will go on shaping edges and routing grooves and dadoes mile after mile. It features a releasing collet that prevents the bit from seizing and comes with both $\frac{1}{4}$-in. and $\frac{1}{2}$-in. collets.

PORTER-CABLE 690

MOTOR POWER: 10 amps

RATED HORSEPOWER: $1\frac{1}{2}$

SPEED: 23,000 rpm

WEIGHT: 8 lb.

COLLET SIZES: $\frac{1}{4}$ in. and $\frac{1}{2}$ in.

CONSTRUCTION: aluminum motor housing and base

FEATURES: auto-releasing collets; micrometer depth-of-cut adjustment; motor fits plunge and D-handled bases

ELU/BLACK & DECKER 3337

In the mid 1980s, American furniture and cabinetmakers were treated to a new type of portable shaping machine: the plunge router. Although most early models came from Japan, it was the bold design and precision construction of the Swiss-made Elu 3337 that really got American woodworkers excited about a router that could plunge a spinning bit to safely accomplish mortise and inlay work. One reviewer wrote: "In the comparison of the three top-rated Japanese machines, they [the Elu plunge routers] so far surpassed anything else I tested as to redefine the standards." Baltimore-based Black & Decker was also impressed and quickly licensed Elu routers for the American market, adding Elu's name to the moniker to bolster Black & Decker's image. A similar version of the 3338 (the 3337's variable-speed brother) is still in production today as the yellow-clad DeWalt DW625.

ELU/BLACK & DECKER 3337

MOTOR POWER: 12 amps

RATED HORSEPOWER: 2¼

SPEED: 20,000 rpm

WEIGHT: 11.25 lb.

COLLET SIZES: ¼ in. and ½ in.

PLUNGE DEPTH (MAX.): 2⁷⁄₁₆ in.

CONSTRUCTION: plastic-and-aluminum motor housing; aluminum base

FEATURES: auto-releasing collets; magnifying cursor on depth scale; large edge guide; universal guide bushing adapter

Tools of the Past

A CIRCUITOUS ROUTE

Although the forerunner of today's router was invented around 1905, these versatile machines didn't find widespread use until the 1930s. Like all portable power-tool prototypes, the earliest routers were only "portable" in the hands of the muscular. The most powerful early routers weighed in at 35 lb. and could only produce about $1^{1}/_2$ hp, about what a lightweight modern "starter" model puts out today.

THIS ROCKWELL ROUTER from the 1970s features a versatile D-handle.

PORTER-CABLE PRODUCED a successful line of power tools under the Guild brand.

COMMON ANCESTORS

Routers were first mass-produced during World War I. Carter Electric, based in Syracuse, New York, was one of the earliest manufacturers. Sold to Stanley Tools in 1929, the Carter router, by way of Stanley's improvements, also became the foundation for today's Bosch routers.

The earliest Porter-Cable router dates back to 1906, the ancestor of what was to become a long-lived dynasty. The Guild model 1100 was one of a whole line of power tools Porter-Cable produced under the Guild brand. Although its dome-topped motor housing doesn't lend itself well to bit changes—it won't stand on the bench upside down—its visual attractiveness still pleases woodworkers today in the modernized form of the Porter-Cable model 100.

In 1950, Porter-Cable introduced the Speedmatic line, which today includes the 3¼-hp production workhorse found mounted under router tables across America. During the 1960s, Porter-Cable was purchased by Rockwell, who continued to produce most of the tools that were in the company stable, including routers. The handsome aluminum-bodied Rockwell Speedmatic D-handled router is one of the gems produced during that period.

THE GUILD MODEL that set the standard for many of today's fixed-base routers.

A Look Inside

A basic plunge router is a fairly simple machine, consisting of a universal motor that spins a cutter. A mechanism raises and lowers the cutter to set the depth.

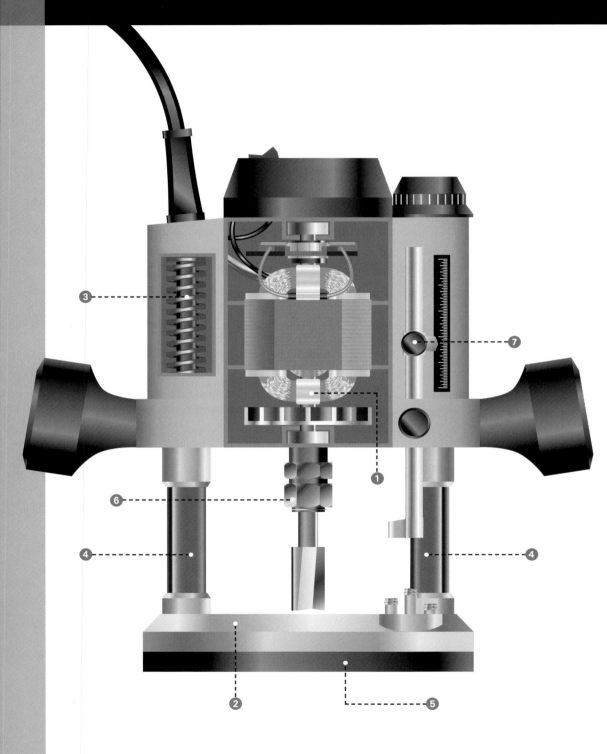

1. A motor unit has an internal cooling fan and is mounted on sturdy ball bearings (necessary because of the unit's high rpm).

2. A base and columns support the motor vertically.

3. Sturdy springs inside the body help retract the router bit from the work after plunging.

4. Plunge rods allow the motor unit to be raised or lowered to set the depth of cut; a thread system is used on fixed-base routers.

5. A slick subbase allows the router to glide easily across the work surface. The subbase is also removable, allowing accessories or custom subbases to be fitted.

6. A collet secures the bit on the end of the shaft. Modern collets are auto releasing, meaning that they pull the bit out when loosened, which prevents the shank from getting stuck.

7. A depth-stop rod and cursor help user set the final plunge depth of the bit. Many models have a rotating turret beneath the stop rod so user can quickly choose between several settings; some models have a top-mounted dial, for fine adjustment of depth.

Quick Guide

FIXED-BASE ROUTERS
- Economical, basic machines
- Good for top-side work
- Highly portable
- Often available in D-handled styles

PLUNGE ROUTERS
- Ability to plunge into the work
- Easy to set multiple depths
- Feature precise depth adjustment
- Most versatile routers for joinery

PRODUCTION ROUTERS
- High horsepower for heavy work or router-table use
- Offer variable speed
- Fixed-base, plunge, and pneumatic models
- Heavy and clumsy for top-side routing

LAMINATE TRIMMERS
- Specially designed for flush trimming
- Lightweight and highly portable
- Can function as light-duty general routers
- Handy for small projects or fine work

Router World

FIXED-BASE ROUTERS

The router in its most basic form puts a universal motor in a convenient holder that allows the chuck and bit to be adjusted up and down. A flat, slick base keeps the bit square to the work and allows the router to glide with ease. The rapidly spinning bit generates amazing torque, so sturdy handles are essential to give you a good grip and to keep the router from leaping out of your hands.

While fixed-base routers aren't as versatile as plunge models, they still have plenty of utility. Smaller models are eminently portable, enabling you to do edge treatments with ease, even on assembled work. When used with specially designed jigs, fixed-base routers are great for cutting dovetails. On large projects, such as bed rails or architectural members, their portability makes them the tool of choice for joinery and decorative effects.

FIXED-BASE ROUTERS come in all shapes and sizes.

THE BEST OF BOTH WORLDS

Can't decide whether to buy a plunge router or a fixed-base model? Consider buying a Porter-Cable router with two bases. The 693PK kit features a classic 690 series motor that quickly slips into either a plunge or fixed base. (You can even buy a D-handled base for the router—to get the best of all possible worlds.)

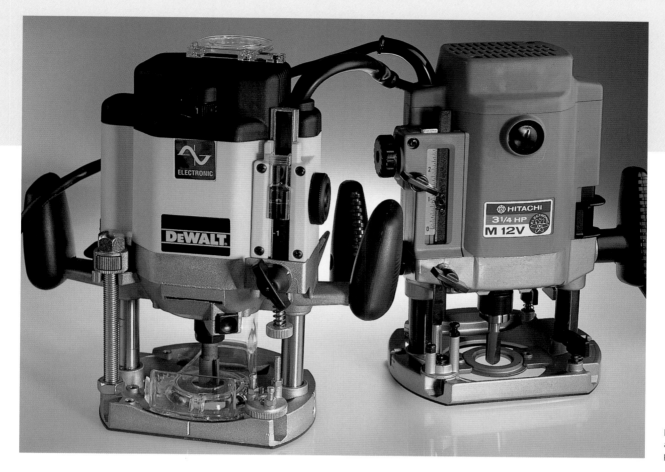

DEWALT DW625
and Hitachi M12V
plunge routers.

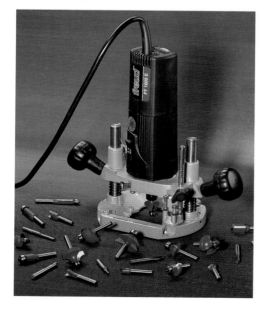

FREUD FT1000EK.

PLUNGE ROUTERS

By freeing the motor from its fixed base and putting it in a spring-loaded carriage that moves up and down, a plunge router lets you lower a spinning bit into wood safely and accurately. Special depth-setting and adjustment features provide a means to accurately plunge to the same depth time after time—to chop a bunch of mortises in frame members for a picnic table or to plow deep grooves or cut rabbets in a series of successively deeper passes, lowering the bit by a prescribed amount each time. Although most plunge routers have large universal motors just like their fixed-base counterparts, Freud's FT1000EK motor is tall and narrow, making it resemble a plunge laminate trimmer.

PRODUCTION ROUTERS

When you're raising panels for dozens of doors or milling miles of molding, you're likely to challenge the stamina of a small router. Large bits (over 1½ in. dia.) should be run at low speeds for safety. (It's also best to use a router table for this kind of work. See "Router Tables" on p. 80.) Adjustable speed is a common feature in big routers over 2½ hp, and these bruisers are meant for sustained, heavy-duty work. They can be fixed-based routers, like the classic Porter-Cable Speedmatic; plunge routers; or industrial air-powered routers. The common denominator is power for the long haul, usually 3 hp or more.

THE PORTER-CABLE Speedmatic is a popular model for router-table use.

ULTIMATE VERSATILITY

Laminate trimmers, such as the Bosch 1608, have bodies designed to detach from the standard base and mount on any one of several special bases, including a tilt base, flush-seam base, and a corner-routing base. The latter requires that the trimmer's chuck be removed and fit to an arbor offset at the corner of the special base; a drive cog mounted on the motor shaft drives the arbor via a toothed belt.

LAMINATE TRIMMERS

Although designed for a specific purpose—namely to trim thin plastic countertop materials—laminate trimmers are also extremely handy as mini routers. Why strain to heft a big router when all you need to rout is a shallow V-groove? A compact unit, like the Porter-Cable 310 production laminate trimmer, has more than enough power to get small jobs done, and its single-hand size and light weight let you work deftly and without muscle strain.

Capable of accepting only $1/4$-in. shanked bits, trimmers are perfect for delicate work, like cutting small grooves to inlay decorative banding or chopping shallow mortises for jewelry-box hinges. They do these jobs deftly, with little user fatigue and less effort than it takes to schlep a full-size router.

PORTER-CABLE 310.

LAMINATE TRIMMERS from Bosch, Porter-Cable, Hitachi, Ryobi, and DeWalt.

Features

FIXED-BASE ROUTER-HANDLE STYLES: Bosch 1617EVS, Sears 17506, Makita 3606.

HANDLES AND BASES

HANDLES

The bigger and more powerful a router is, the more important it is to have big, comfortable handles to hold onto, especially when tackling tricky routing jobs, like carving signs or cutting dovetails. Handles on contemporary routers run the gamut: from the round retro wood knobs on the Bosch 1617EVS to the shapely elongated handles on the Makita 3606 to the ergonomic pistol grips on the Sears 17506, which conveniently incorporate an on/off trigger.

Long a staple in production shops and factories, D-handled routers are just like fixed-base models but with a small but important difference: A D-shaped handle, much like one you'd find on a portable circular saw, replaces one of the knobs. The D-handles on routers, like the Makita 3601B or the Bosch 1618EVS, offer what many woodworkers consider to be a superior grip and control of the router. Many pros even use D-handled models single-handedly; for example, the Festo OF1000 E-Plus plunge router has a large pistol-grip handle and trigger that allows single-handed operation. A handle-mounted trigger lets you turn the router on and off without the slightest hesitation or fumbling for a switch.

D-HANDLED ROUTERS: Makita 3601B and Bosch 1618EVS.

SUBBASES

A router's plastic subbase provides a slick surface that glides over the workpiece. Remove the stock subbase, and you can attach special-purpose subbases that work with jigs and accessories or allow the router to quickly mount in a router table. Buy ready-made subbases or make your own from sturdy plastic, such as phenolic or polycarbonate.

ROUTER SUBBASES.

DUST COLLECTION

Routers fling chips and belch dust in every direction when they cut, turning your work area into a pigpen in a hurry. Unless you really like sweeping up the floor, think of buying a router with built-in dust collection. Many router manufacturers have incorporated dust collection into their more recent models. Some, including the Sears 17506, use a simple bag system; others, such as the DeWalt DW621, have ports for connecting to a shop vacuum. Dust trapped by a plastic enclosure around the bit travels up the DW621's hollow plunge guide rod, the top of which connects to a hose. Dust collection can also be used when edge-routing stock: The Porter-Cable 39690 mounts to the underside of the router's base to capture chips as they're flung sideways by the bit.

BAG DUST COLLECTION
on the Sears 17506.

DEWALT DW621.

PORTER-CABLE 39690 dust-collection
accessory.

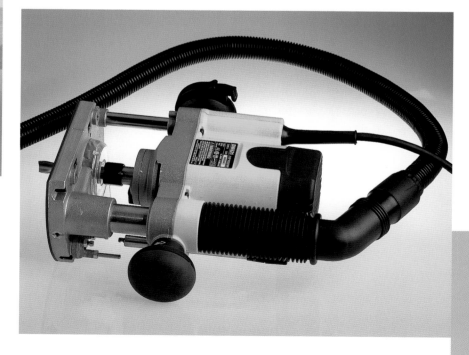

DEPTH-SETTING MECHANISMS

The way to change the cutting depth of the bit varies among different router types, makes, and models. On many fixed-base routers, such as the Porter-Cable 690 series, you rotate the entire motor housing to raise or lower the bit. To guide the motion, tabs on the cylindrical housing ride in spiraling grooves in the base. On routers like the Ryobi RE185, the entire motor housing is threaded; turning a large ring changes the depth of cut. The D-handled Bosch 1618EVS features yet another depth-setting arrangement: The body screws up and down for coarse settings; a small knob allows incremental fine depth adjustments.

PORTER-CABLE 690.

BOSCH 1618EVS.

RYOBI RE185.

Regardless of the mechanism's design, once the depth is set, a lever or handscrew solidly locks the motor into the base. Routers like the Makita 3606 have a scale built into the base, to show how far cutting depth has been adjusted up or down.

MAKITA 3606.

PLUNGE DEPTH STOPS: DeWalt DW625 and Hitachi M12V.

PLUNGE DEPTH STOPS

Because their motors ride up and down on guide rods, plunge routers usually don't get set and locked at a fixed cutting depth before they're switched on (unless they're inverted and used in a router table). Instead, their depth of cut is regulated by a depth stop. The depth-stop rod (or bar) protrudes down from the motor assembly and strikes a turret mounted to the base, thus limiting downward travel and establishing cutting depth. After switching on the router and plunging the bit to the set depth, you engage a lever or, on some models, use one of the handles to lock the carriage and maintain that cutting depth.

Most routers have an adjustable depth scale and cursor that work with the stop rod. The DeWalt DW625 and the Hitachi M12V have adjustable cursors, allowing you to accurately guage the final plunge depth of the bit.

DEPTH-STOP TURRET

So that you're not limited by setting just a single cutting depth, plunge routers have another small but significant feature: an adjustable multi-position turret. Instead of just one point for the stop rod to contact, turrets on routers like the Porter-Cable 7538 and the Bosch 1613EVS have three, four, five, or more different contact points.

By setting the plunge depth with the stop rod touching the shortest turret contact point, you can reduce the plunge depth by rotating the turret so that the rod hits a taller point. This makes the routing of deep recesses easier: You remove a little wood on each pass, rather than trying to hog it all out at once.

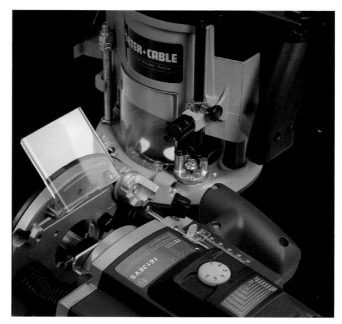

TURRET STOPS on the Porter-Cable 7538 and Bosch 1613EVS.

FINE DEPTH ADJUSTMENT

Another card that a plunge router has up its sleeve is a fine depth adjuster. This adjustment knob, found atop the guide rod on routers like the Porter-Cable 7529, allows you to tweak the final cutting depth of the bit after the router has been plunged. A small scale around the knob lets you change cutting depth by increments as small as $1/128$ in.! This adjustment feature is especially handy for router-table use. On the Festo OF1000 E-Plus, cutting depth is finely adjusted by turning a knob (calibrated in tenths of a millimeter), which moves the stop rod up and down.

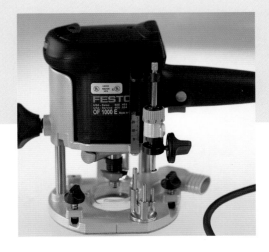

FINE-ADJUSTMENT KNOB on the Festo OF1000 E-Plus.

PORTER-CABLE 7529.

VARIABLE SPEED AND SOFT START

Because the collet is mounted directly to the end of the motor shaft, a router bit spins at the same high rpm as the motor. Slip a really big cutter in the collet, like a $3\frac{1}{2}$-in.-dia. panel raiser, and things get really scary in a hurry (the speed of the outer rim of such a bit actually approaches the speed of sound!). The way to keep your router from becoming a hovercraft is to reduce the motor rpm with variable-speed control. Depending on the make and model of router, motor speed is set with either a selection switch or a continuous dial.

So powerful are the motors in big routers ($2\frac{1}{2}$-plus hp) that switching them on generates enough torque to challenge your grip. Fortunately, many variable-speed models also feature a soft start. The same electronics that regulate motor speed ramp up the rpms gradually when the router is switched on, making startups smooth and safe.

SPEED ADJUSTMENT on the Hitachi M8V and Porter-Cable 7539.

COLLET/ARBOR LOCK

A LOCKING COLLET requires only one wrench.

Instead of having an adjustable chuck, like a drill does, a router simply uses a collet to hold the bit securely. Collets come in different sizes, each designed to hold bits of a specific shank diameter. Collets that are $\frac{1}{4}$ in. and $\frac{1}{2}$ in. are most popular, since most bits made for the American market have shanks in those diameters. Routers of, say, $1\frac{1}{4}$ hp or less are limited to $\frac{1}{4}$-in. collets, while bigger routers can use either size: Simply screw the larger or smaller collet into the end of the motor shaft as needed. Smaller European routers use metric-size collets and bits with 8mm-dia. shanks. To make bit changes easier, routers like the Ryobi RE600 (left) have spring-loaded buttons or levers to lock the motor arbor, so that only one wrench is needed to tighten or loosen the collet.

QUICK-RELEASE CHUCK

Tired of fumbling with wrenches every time you want to change a bit? One solution is to remove your router's stock collet and replace it with a wrenchless collet. Jacobs's version of this innovation features a large outer flange that tightens or releases the collet inside. Slip a bit into the end and push down on the flange to secure the bit; pull up to release it. Even the largest bits are held firmly and safely; it would take telekinesis to change bits more quickly!

JACOBS'S WRENCHLESS COLLET.

The Business End

A FOREST OF BITS
FOR EVERY PURPOSE

Think of a shape: for a molding or trim, on the edge of a chair leg, around a tabletop. There's almost certainly a router bit that could produce that shape. Or cut the joinery for a door, drawer, or box. Or create a recess for an inlay or piece of hardware.

The endless variety of router bits, represented here by a modest selection, includes bits for cutting roundovers, coves, beads, chamfers, countertop bullnose, cope-and-stick joints, dovetails, raised panels, finger pulls, crown moldings, locking miter joints, decorative moldings, and slots; as well as bits for flush trimming; pattern rout-

ing; and mortising. Most of these bits are carbide tipped for durability and longevity. The shapely and colorful bodies of most bits are large enough to support the brittle carbide close to their cutting edges and also to limit the rate at which those edges can gobble wood (or other objects they encounter), for safety's sake.

STRAIGHT AND FLUSH-TRIM BITS

A straight cut for making a dado, groove, or mortise might seem like the simplest thing a router can do. But whether you end up with a clean cut or a splintery mess depends a lot on the kind of

ROUTER BITS for every purpose—edge treatments and moldings, cope-and-stick joints, panel raising, joinery, flush trimming, pattern routing—as well as dedicated bits for cutting keyholes and finger pulls.

SPIRAL BITS come in up-cut and down-cut styles; both slice wood fibers efficiently.

CMT HORIZONTAL AND VERTICAL PANEL-RAISING BITS.

straight bit you use. Spiral bits have cutting edges that curve around them like spiral stair-cases. They cut wood more cleanly and with less tearout than regular straight bits because their edges slice rather than chop wood fibers. There's another twist to spiral bits: They come in up-cut and down-cut varieties. The edge of a spiral up-cut bit pulls chips up and out of the cut, great for deep mortises or inverted pin routing. Down-cut bits keep pressure at the edge of the cut to reduce tearout, making them a great choice for routing splintery woods or delicate materials.

Take any straight bit and put a ball bearing on the end (or on the shank) with an outside diame-ter the same as the bit, and you've got a flush-trimming bit. The bearing rides on a fence or on the edge of the stock, which guides the cut. The trickiest flush-trim bits are made by Woodhaven. These have two sets of spiral cutting edges—one up-cut, one down-cut. When routing plywood, this arrangement cleverly prevents chipping and tearing out the face veneers on both edges!

RAISED-PANEL BITS

Unless you have a shaper handy, a big router strapped to the underside of a router table is your best bet when you've got a demanding job to do, like shape the raised panels for a set of kitchen doors. But woodworkers are often skittish when it comes to using those really huge router bits designed for panel raising (see the bit on the left in the top right photo). It can be scary to run a big bit like this, especially if your router doesn't have variable speed (see "Variable Speed and Soft Start" on p. 74). Fortunately, there's another choice: The bit shown on the right is a vertical panel-raising bit. These bits come in the same range of shapes as the big horizontal panel rais-ers do, but because they run vertically, they are smaller in diameter and can be run at higher rpms. The only catch is that you can't rout curved or arched-top panels with a vertical bit; you'll have to brave a horizontal bit for that task.

MAXIMUM SAFE SPEEDS

Bit diameter	Maximum rpm
1 in.	24,000
1¼ in. to 2 in.	18,000
2¼ in. to 2½ in.	16,000
3 in. to 3½ in.	12,000

Accessories

EDGE GUIDES

Unless you're routing freehand or using a bit fitted with a pilot bearing, a router's path of cut must be guided to produce consistent results. An edge guide does the trick, providing a fence below the base that rides against a clamped-on straightedge or the edge of the work itself, guiding the router along a straight path (you can also rout circles and regular arcs). Most manufacturers produce edge guides for their routers, either as accessories or standard equipment. The edge guide for the Festo OF1000 E-Plus plunge router features a clear plastic enclosure that rides below the router's subbase. Connected to the Festo's built-in dust collection, the guard deflects and collects chips during edge routing.

An aftermarket edge guide, like the precision-made anodized-aluminum Micro Fence, fits practically any router or laminate trimmer. A precisely calibrated adjustment knob lets you set the distance between the guide's fence and the bit with thousandth-of-an-inch accuracy. A circle attachment with optional vacuum-powered center pivot lets you rout out disks of exact diameter or cut arcs for circular inlays.

Another kind of edge guide that's used with laminate trimmers is the ball-bearing guide, shown on the Hitachi TR6. The guide's bearing rides directly below the bit and is the same diameter as the bit, for flush trimming wood veneers or plastic laminates.

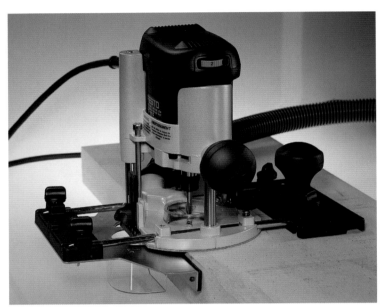

FESTO EDGE GUIDE.

THE MICRO FENCE EDGE GUIDE fits a wide range of routers and laminate trimmers.

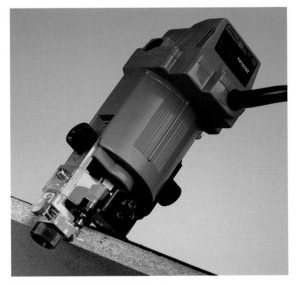

HITACHI LAMINATE TRIMMER with a ball-bearing edge guide.

JIGS

DOVETAIL JOINERY JIG

Routers are great for cutting all types of joints, including dovetails. The only trouble with router dovetail templates is that they usually create boring looking joints, with pins and tails all the same size. But adjustable dovetail jigs, like the Leigh jig, change all that by giving you full control over the size and spacing of elements on a dovetail joint. Workpieces—box or chest sides, drawers, etc.—are secured to the jig with cam-action clamps. A series of user-arranged metal fingers steer the guide bushing attached to the base of the router as pins and tails are cut for either through or half-blind dovetails. The jig also cuts sliding dovetails and, with additional templates, finger joints and multiple mortise-and-tenon joints.

For something truly different, mount one of Leigh's unique Isoloc templates on the jig. Each template creates a decorative corner joint with interlocking shapes that look like waves, ellipses, bear ears, and more. To take care of flying chips, Leigh designed the RVA1 vacuum attachment, shown here mounted to a Festo OF1000 E-Plus plunge router.

WOODHAVEN OVAL-CUTTING JIG.

OVAL-CUTTING JIG

There are lots of different ways to cut a circle with a router, including replacement subbase attachments and accessories for edge guides and homemade jigs. But routing an oval is a special challenge that takes a special jig. The push-and-pull action of the Woodhaven oval-cutting jig guides the router in an elliptical path, allowing you to rout ovoid grooves and create oval moldings and picture frames. By changing the position of the two dovetailed sliding guides and the router mounting plate on the extruded aluminum bar, you can change both the size and proportions of the oval.

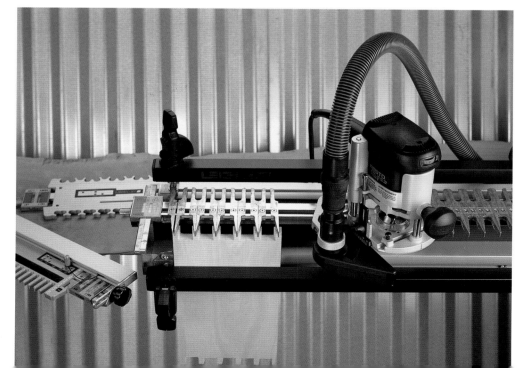

LEIGH JIG and Festo router with vacuum attachment.

ROUTER TABLES

If you don't have a router table, you're missing half the fun of owning a router! While you can cobble up a router table by drilling a few holes in the top of a fruit box, your routing chores will be made easier and more efficient if you mount your router to a well-designed table. A nice example is Rockler's router table, which features a sturdy laminated top and an adjustable fence with a plastic safety guard. The most significant feature of this table is the unique Rout-R-Lift center insert. Beneath its handsome blue anodized-aluminum top plate is a movable lower plate to which the router mounts. A hole atop the plate accepts a handle, which turns an ingenious mechanism via a toothed belt that cranks the lower plate—and router—up and down, to make bit depth-of-cut adjustments easy and accurate.

ROUT-R-LIFT ROUTER-TABLE INSERT.

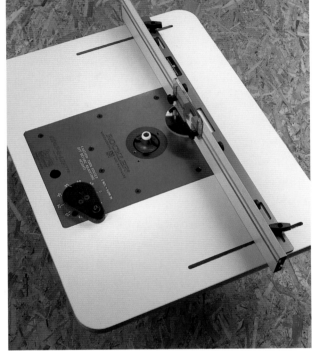

ROCKLER ROUTER TABLE.

PIN-ROUTING SETUP

A pin router is an expensive stationary tool that few part-time woodworkers can afford—or have the space for. But you can now transform any ordinary router table into a versatile pin router by mounting an accessory pin-routing arm. The Veritas pin-routing kit includes a beefy cast-alloy arm, which fastens to the corner of a router table. A spring-loaded, interchangeable pin in the end of the arm centers over the bit. In use, the pin engages a template (cut to the desired shape of the part you wish to rout) mounted temporarily to the top of the work.

VERITAS ROUTER TABLE and micro-adjusting fence.

ROUTER-TABLE FENCE

Unless you're totally into freeform work, anytime you use an unpiloted bit in a router table, you need a fence to guide the workpiece. The Veritas router table sports an excellent fence that's as versatile as it is accurate. The extruded-aluminum fence channel has T-slots on all sides. The slots attach the fence to the tabletop and secure a pair of wooden fence faces, which adjust side to side to suit the diameter of the bit as well as the accessories, including hold-downs and safety guards. To help you fine-tune the distance between the fence and the bit, the Veritas fence features a micro-adjuster with a micrometer-style screw dial.

HORIZONTAL TABLE AND ANGLE BASE

Whether handheld or in a router table, a router bit spins vertically. This is fine for most work, but there are times when it's easier to lay the workpiece flat and run the bit horizontally. That's exactly what a horizontal router table does: The router is mounted to a vertical panel butted to a flat work table. On Woodhaven's horizontal table, the depth of cut is adjusted by turning a crank, which moves the panel to which the router is mounted up or down. This setup is great for cutting tenons or, when fitted with a vertical panel-raising bit, shaping raised panels for cabinet doors. When is a bullnose router bit not a bullnose? When it cuts at an angle and produces a slanted slot, such as on the integrated wood pulls commonly found in Euro-style kitchen cabinets. Woodhaven's Angle-Ease replacement router base is just the tool for putting a different slant on your bits.

WOODHAVEN HORIZONTAL ROUTER TABLE and Angle-Ease replacement router base.

ROUTER-TABLE BIT JACK

A plunge router can be just as effective in a router-table setup as a fixed-base one. However, you can't easily plunge it to change the bit's depth of cut. That is, unless the router is fitted with a Veritas router bit jack. The bit jack replaces the plunge router's threaded pull rod with a piston-action lever, which quickly raises or lowers the router on its guide rods. A separate fine-setting knob lets you tweak the depth of cut after the lever is locked. By fitting a pull chain and foot pedal to the bit jack, you can elevate the bit with the touch of a toe. The foot pedal also makes it possible to plunge a spinning bit up into the workpiece, as needed with the pin-routing attachment described in the sidebar on p. 80.

VERITAS BIT JACK.

QUICK-CHANGE GUIDE BUSHINGS

One way to guide the cut of an unpiloted router bit is a guide bushing: a short cylindrical sleeve mounted to the underside of the router's sub-base. The bushing bears against a template, fence, or the edge of the work itself and guides the bit, which protrudes through the bushing. Bosch produces a very handy, interchangeable guide-bushing system for their routers: A holder in the router's base accepts special bushings that have keyed flanges. A spring-loaded lever in the holder locks or releases the flange, allowing guide bushings to be fitted or changed on the fly, as the task dictates.

BOSCH QUICK-CHANGE GUIDE BUSHINGS.

The Cutting Edge

VIRUTEX FR98H

Not really a router in the conventional sense, Virutex calls its model FR98H a "motorized hand shaper." Unlike a regular router with a motor and chuck that spin the bit vertically, the FR98H has a pair of cutters that rotate horizontally. A V-shaped sole supports and guides the tool on the edge of the stock. The FR98H is specialized for shaping edges; no surface routing is possible. Here's the really interesting part: Besides adjusting up and down for setting the depth of cut, the machine's sole adjusts side to side. Most styles of the changeable, replaceable cutters have several different profiles along their length, so by adjusting the position of the sole, the same cutters can create a variety of different shapes. For example, the ogee cutter set (see the photo below) can cut Roman, classical, and inverted ogees as well as an ogee with fillet or a multiple ogee, for a fancy crown molding.

INTERCHANGEABLE CUTTERS mount in an arbor and can be set for a multitude of different shapes.

VIRUTEX FR98H	
MOTOR POWER: 1,100 watts	
CUTTERHEAD SPEED (NO LOAD): 23,000 rpm	
CUTTING CAPACITY: 40mm wide, 20mm deep	
WEIGHT: 10.8 lb.	
ACCESSORIES: optional knife sets for different profiles	

Drills can do an amazing number of tricks, from boring clean holes and driving screws to stripping off old paint and buffing your car. No wonder their ranks have swelled, and today you can find home-center shelves bulging with all manner of drills. These range from compact models with small chucks to heavy-duty machines that look like jackhammers.

The variations on the theme now include right-angle drills that can bore holes in tight places and hammer drills that pound their special bits through concrete and masonry. And drills aren't just for drilling anymore: Most drill chucks accept bits for driving screws of every configuration, hole saws that cut perfect circles, and sanding drums that smooth curves. Drills have also spawned offspring that look like drills but are only for driving screws, including screw guns and power screwdrivers. Given their incredible versatility, drills may just be the most useful power tool you can have around the house or shop.

DRIVERS

The Classic

MILWAUKEE 75TH EDITION MAGNUM DRILL

Whether you're boring holes, driving screws, or running a sanding drum, you'll want a solidly made drill that's easy to use and delivers enough power for the job. Milwaukee drills have been part of contractors' tool kits for generations. The red and aluminum colors and the lightning-bolt company logo are recognized by both pros and serious do-it-yourselfers. One of the reasons these tools have been around so long is that they're well designed and tough. They seem to last for generations, requiring only an occasional tune-up and the replacement of a worn-out power cord.

The Milwaukee Electric Tool Co. began manufacturing tools in 1924. To celebrate its 75th anniversary in 1999, Milwaukee issued a special edition of its 1/2-in. Magnum drill: the Milwaukee 0236-75. The tool is compact, well balanced, and is ergonomic. Like most corded drills, it has a grip that allows the user to hold the tool in line with the bit. The tool's 5½-amp motor delivers a lot of power, so the body has a socket for an extra handle to give the user a two-handed grip when boring big holes in tough materials.

MILWAUKEE 0236-75

MOTOR POWER: 5½ amps

RPM: 0–850

WEIGHT: 4 lb. 3 oz.

GEARCASE: aluminum

SPEED CONTROL: variable-speed trigger

REVERSING: yes

CHUCK: ½-in. keyed industrial chuck

FEATURES: removable brush-cartridge system; polished aluminum motor; steel carrying case

Tools of the Past

DRILLING DOWN TO THE PAST

At the turn of the 20th century, if you wanted to drill a hole, you had the choice of using either a brace-and-bit or drill press. Then, around 1915, Duncan Black and Alonso Decker Sr. patented the first pistol-grip electric drill in America. Among the early portables offered to consumers were the Goodell-Pratt Toolsmith Series drills. Hardly more than a motor with a chuck at one end and a rudimentary handle on the other, the Toolsmith's chuck has only an $1/8$-in.-dia. capacity and the aluminum-bodied tool lacks a trigger.

THE DEATH RAY

Early electric drills with big chucks and motors strong enough to bore holes in thick wood and metal were two-handed tools that were so heavy and cumbersome that only the strongest workers could operate them effectively. The cast aluminum–bodied Thor drill, made by the Independent Pneumatic Co., is an example of this kind of heavy-duty drill. Its industrial styling makes it look more like a death ray Buck Rogers would wield than a utilitarian device for boring holes!

THE GOODELL-PRATT TOOLSMITH DRILL offers a surprising feature: variable speed activated by a tubelike transverse lever made of Bakelite.

THE CAST ALUMINUM–BODIED THOR DRILL required heavy lifting.

WORLD WAR II–ERA WORKERS put the new portable drills to work building ships and planes. (PHOTO COURTESY MILWAUKEE ELECTRIC TOOL CO.)

DRILLS HELP WIN THE WAR

Around the end of World War I, Henry Ford asked tool manufacturer A. H. Petersen to create a lighter, more portable electric drill. Petersen created the Hole-Shooter, a 5-lb. drill with a heavy-duty Westinghouse motor. The Hole-Shooter was the tool industry's first lightweight, one-handed drill capable of handling heavy-duty workloads. Petersen was joined by A. F. Siebert to found the Milwaukee Electric Tool Co. in 1924. During World War II, Milwaukee Hole-Shooters were used extensively by the U.S. Navy to build warships and airplanes.

THE DESIGN OF THE THOR reflects industrial styling.

A Look Inside

What makes up a great basic drill? Whether it's corded or cordless, strip off
a drill's outer skin and you'll find many of the same basic components.

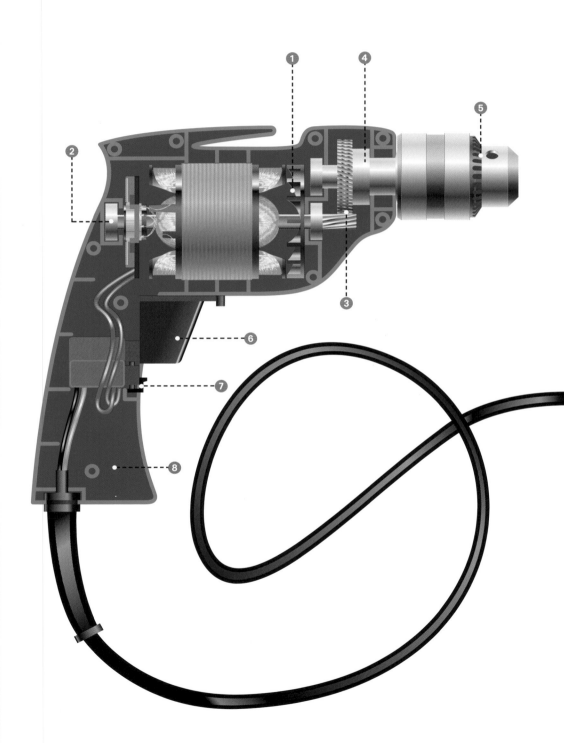

1. The motor armature and cooling fan assembly is supported at either end on bearings.

2. Bearings may be ball or needle bearings (less expensive drills use bronze bushings or a combination of bushings and bearings).

3. A gear at the end of the motor's arbor transmits power to helical gears or, in a two-speed drill, a transmission comprised of a series of gears. The gears step own the rotational speed of the motor to give the drill more torque at the bit.

4. A slower-spinning arbor shaft supported by heavy-duty bearings is the mount for the drill's adjustable chuck or, on a screw gun or screwdriver, the bit holder.

5. The adjustable chuck uses a geared key to tighten its three jaws securely around the shank of the bit.

6. A trigger assembly turns the drill/driver on and off or provides variable-speed control.

7. A lever or button (usually located near the trigger) reverses the drill's direction of rotation.

8. A body housing is made from injection-molded plastic or cast alloy.

CORDED DRILLS

- Lightweight but powerful
- No recharging, just plug it in
- In-line drilling helps accuracy
- Wide range of power, speed options, and chuck types available

HEAVY-DUTY CORDED DRILLS

- Pack lots of power to tackle tough jobs
- Durable materials and electricals mean longer life
- ½ in. or larger chucks handle big bits
- Gearbox selects high speed or increased torque

CORDLESS DRILLS

- The ultimate in portability
- Adjustable clutch a standard feature
- Power depends on battery voltage and capacity
- T-handled design helps balance battery weight

HAMMER DRILLS

- Pulsing action specially suited for masonry work
- Geared for power and low speed
- Choice of rotary action, pulse action, or both
- Specialized handles for good tool control

RIGHT-ANGLE DRILLS

- Specifically designed for working in tight spaces
- Heavy-duty corded joist drills bore big holes
- Compact cordless models handy for installing hardware
- Useful in specialized drilling situations

SCREW GUNS

- A driver, not a drill, dedicated to driving screws
- A special head holds driver bits
- Especially well suited to drywall work
- Automatic models feed screws like a machine gun

CORDLESS SCREWDRIVERS

- Dedicated to driving screws
- Compact and lightweight
- Wall-mountable chargers
- Heavy-duty models available

Drill World

CORDED DRILLS

Balancing power with agility is a trick all Olympic athletes strive for. Portable electric drills are compact tools that are easy to grip yet pack loads of wrist-wrenching torque at the end of their power cords. Drills with high-efficiency motors offer the greatest power output, and some manufacturers use extrathick insulation on motor windings to make the motors longer lasting and more resistant to overheating and short circuits. Although not as handy as their cordless offspring, corded drills are lighter and more powerful.

While the majority of drills are fitted with strong ³⁄₈-in.-dia.-capacity chucks, heavier-duty models often feature ¹⁄₂-in. chucks. Chucks of either size are commonly available in keyed or keyless type (see "Chucks" on p. 99).

DRILLS WITH TAILS (clockwise from bottom): Hitachi, Metabo, DeWalt, Milwaukee, Makita.

THE REDI DRILL

The Sears Craftsman cordless Redi Drill has a special chuck with a "tunnel" through which bits are inserted from the rear. A rotary-loading mechanism atop the body of the drill (like a torpedo-loading device on a submarine) keeps four bits—any combination of drill or driver bits—handy. After loosening the drill chuck, the current bit is withdrawn and stored in its slot in the loading mechanism. The user then rotates a lever to choose another bit and pushes it forward to slide it into the chuck.

CORDLESS DRILLS

Cordless drills have become such important home-workshop staples that it's hard to believe that the first consumer cordless model was introduced by Black & Decker as recently as 1961. Cutting the cord can set you free to do a whole range of drilling and driving tasks more easily and quickly. Want to screw a light-fixture mounting plate to the ceiling? Need to drill holes for a planter box you're building outside? A cordless drill lets you work on top of a ladder or on damp ground safely, without the worry of cord tangles or the chance of electric shock.

Cordless drills come in many different voltages, from 9.6 volts to 24 volts. The tradeoff is that the lower-voltage drills are lighter but can't handle the hard drilling and driving of the heavier, higher-voltage models. Modern chargers have computerized circuitry that gets batteries charged in a hurry and helps to extend battery life (see p. 22).

AN ARSENAL OF CORDLESS DRILLS with power from 9.6 volts to 24 volts (from left to right): Black & Decker FireStorm, Festo, Hitachi, Dewalt, Porter-Cable, Bosch.

HEAVY-DUTY DRILLS

When it's time to bore fist-sized holes for which a regular corded drill doesn't have the power, it's time to bring out the big dog and let him eat. Heavy-duty drills are built as big and sturdy as Humvees. They have the capacity and power to handle big bits and not bog down, even when boring through a stack of 2x4s.

Not only do heavy-duty drills have large chucks that will take $\frac{1}{2}$-in.-shank bits but also mighty motors that pump out oodles of power via reduction gearing. The rate at which a drill spins its bit is a tradeoff between speed and power, or (more accurately) torque. Higher rotational speed turns the bit at a higher rpm but with less oomph; if the bit hits a knot or gets stuck exiting the cut, the drill can stall. Gearing down the speed of the motor makes the bit spin slower—around 500 rpm in most machines—but gives it a lot more torque or slow-speed power to get through tough stock.

These bruisers are perfect for propelling large multispur bits, Forstner bits, and hole saws. To control boring depth, models such as the Hitachi D13VB2 offer an adjustable stop rod; boring stops when the rod hits the surface of the work.

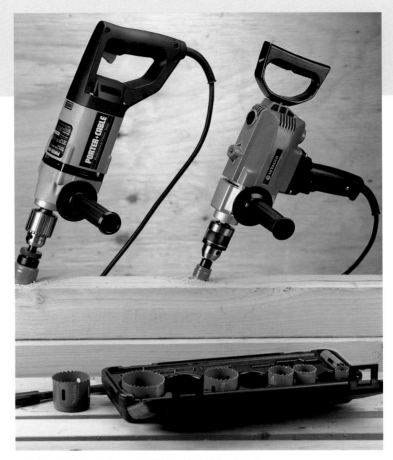

BIG GUNS FROM PORTER-CABLE AND HITACHI deliver power for drilling large holes.

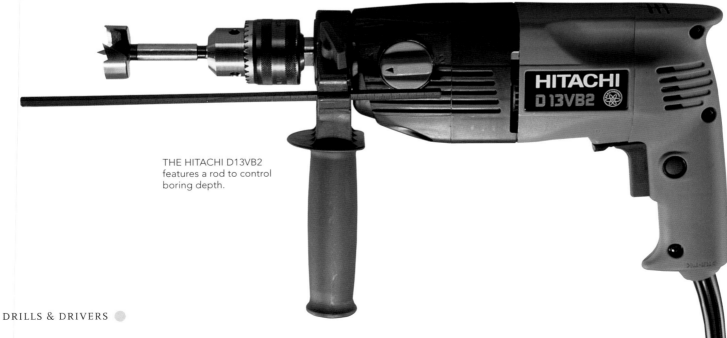

THE HITACHI D13VB2 features a rod to control boring depth.

HAMMER DRILLS

A spinning bit and a little elbow grease is usually enough when boring holes in most materials. But concrete and other masonry materials are so dense and abrasive that they're a lot tougher to penetrate. Hammer drills are specially designed to both rotate the bit and apply a pulsing pressure (hammering) that breaks through masonry neatly yet much faster and easier than with rotary action alone. Like heavy-duty drills, hammer drills are built big and tough and are geared for low speed and the power required for masonry drilling.

To make hammer drills more versatile, most models have a lever that offers the selection of rotary action alone or rotary combined with hammer action. By selecting hammer action alone (allowed on some models), a stone chisel fitted in the drill's special splined chuck punches through rock, brick, or concrete for light demolition work (you can rent a real pneumatic jackhammer if you want to tear down skyscrapers).

THE PANASONIC CORDLESS hammer drill has an accordion-like pleated cuff, which mounts around the chuck, to contain dust produced by the bit.

A SWITCH ALLOWS YOU TO CHOOSE either rotary action or rotary plus hammer action.

HAMMER DRILLS from Bosch and Panasonic can drill right through concrete.

RIGHT-ANGLE DRILLS

Ever see one of those cool spy cameras that shoots photos around corners? It lets a hard-working secret agent snap his nemesis while staying concealed and out of the line of fire. In similar fashion, a right-angle drill lets you reach around a corner or into a confined space and bore a hole or drive a screw. Large, heavy-duty right-angle drills (also known as joist drills) are designed to bore large holes in cramped quarters, through house framing for pipes and electrical wiring. These heavies can generate enough torque to twist the arms off a professional weightlifter. Therefore, each model gives you two or more large handles to choose from, so you can put your leverage in the right place when you need to.

HEAVY-DUTY RIGHT-ANGLE DRILLS from Makita and DeWalt.

Compact right-angle drills, of both corded and cordless varieties, are great for smaller jobs, like drilling pilot holes for hardware or driving screws inside a cabinet carcase. In addition to variable speed, cordless models, such as the DeWalt DW965, offer a two-speed transmission: fast for drilling and slower for driving screws.

MILWAUKEE ⅜-in. reversing "Close Quarter" drill.

CORDLESS right-angle drills from DeWalt and Hitachi.

AUTOMATIC SCREW GUN

The Gatling gun of the carpenter's arsenal, the automatic screw gun can drive a handful of screws faster than you can say "Phillips head." In addition to a clutch, these tools have a driving mechanism that, when pressed down against the stock, feeds a screw into the path of the driver bit, ready to be driven. Special screws attached to a plastic strip facilitate automatic loading.

MAKITA 6825TP and Metabo SE5040R+L.

SCREW GUNS from Metabo, Hitachi, and Makita.

SCREW GUNS

While driving screws is only half the duty of a drill/driver, some drill-like portables are designed only for that purpose. Portable screw-driving tools, known as drywall screwdrivers or screw guns, look like standard corded/cordless drills, with an important exception: Instead of a chuck, guns such as Metabo SE5040R+L and Makita 6825TP have a dedicated screw-driving head. This head houses a regular driver bit (usually a Phillips head) controlled by a clutch and depth-control mechanism.

You put a screw on the driver bit, press it against the stock, and drive it. When the screw is driven, the clutch automatically disengages the driver bit, so the head of the screw doesn't strip out. By adjusting a depth mechanism, you can set how deep the head of the screw is driven into the stock. Drywallers love these tools since they can drive drywall screws consistently (with the heads just below the surface yet not too deep to tear the paper). Screw guns are also great for cabinetmakers, remodelers, deck or house builders, or any woodworker who drives lots of screws. If you drive bushels of screws, you'll speed up the task considerably by using an autofeed screw gun.

CORDLESS SCREWDRIVERS

Even if you'll never build anything, it's hard to get through domestic life without driving a few screws now and then: to mount a mirror, remove a license-plate frame, assemble a bicycle. A cordless screwdriver makes these jobs go much faster and easier than using a regular screwdriver. Even if you have the hand strength of a child, a cordless driver lets you install, tighten, or remove screws like a pro.

These compact tools are only slightly bulkier than "manual" screwdrivers and come with a reversible tip, to handle slotted or Phillips fasteners. While most models live in their wall-mountable chargers, ready for use, more serious cordless screwdrivers have small removable battery packs, like their bigger drill/driver cousins, which provide hours of power for big jobs.

CORDLESS SCREWDRIVERS come in many sizes, shapes, and voltages.

REMOVABLE BATTERY PACKS provide power for heavy-duty cordless screwdrivers, like the Panasonic EY6225.

Features

CHUCKS: TO KEY OR NOT TO KEY

KEYED CHUCKS are more secure, but keyless chucks are more convenient.

A keyed chuck's advantage is that it doesn't take a firm grip to tighten and loosen the chuck jaws, even around a giant bit shank. And if the bit jams in the chuck, a little persuasive force on the key loosens the jaws every time. For this reason, the majority of ½-in. drills have keyed chucks.

On the downside, it takes time to tighten and loosen. (Technically, you should always tighten the chuck in at least two of the three locations where you can insert the key for secure, even jaw clamping around the bit.) Also, keys tend to be scarce when you need them. Without a key, no one short of Superman can remove a bit from a properly tightened chuck.

THE KEYLESS ADVANTAGE

Keyless chucks are easier to use than the keyed kind: All it takes is a quick turn on the chuck's outer sleeve to tighten its grip around a bit's

shank. A turn in the opposite direction releases the jaws, making bit changes lightning fast. Most keyless chuck users employ the spinning drill itself to tighten and release the bit, holding the chuck sleeve while revving the motor slowly (but if the bit jams in the chuck, it can take a grip of steel to turn the bit loose).

If you're after an all-purpose kind of drill for around-the-house drilling and driving duties, a keyless chuck is a good choice. For rugged use, choose a drill with a steel-clad chuck rather than one with a glass-filled nylon shell, which is more susceptible to wear.

CUTAWAY VIEW of a Jacobs keyless chuck. (COURTESY JACOBS TOOL CO.)

GETTING A GRIP:
HANDLE STYLES

Lacking a big battery, most corded drills favor a pistol-grip style, which allows the user to hold the tool in line with the bit for better control. The triggers on models like Milwaukee's 0235-20 have evolved from the index finger–fired triggers found on early pistol-grip drills (here, an early 1960s-vintage Fury drill) to longer triggers that are easier to control with the ring finger and/or pinkie—a more convenient arrangement when gripping the drill in-line.

Most cordless drills have a T-handle design, which balances the weight of the motor with that of its hefty battery pack. One exception is the D-handled Festo CDD 12 ES, which achieves balance with an L-shaped pack mounted ahead of the grip. To lend cordless tools better control, grips are molded ergonomically and often have soft padded inserts to make them more comfortable to hold. The big D-handles, spade handles, and/or adjustable side handles found on heavy-duty machines help you heft and control them.

PISTOL-STYLE GRIPS of corded models allow in-line drilling.

T-HANDLED GRIPS on cordless drills balance the battery weight.

SPEED CONTROLS AND CLUTCH MECHANISMS

SPEED-CHANGE LEVER on cordless drills for Makita, Hitachi, and Festo.

Like their modern corded cousins, cordless drills sport variable speed, controlled by a finger on the trigger. A small lever or push button sets the direction of rotation, which is handiest when located near the trigger and can be operated by the user's trigger finger or thumb. For greater versatility, most cordless drills have two speed ranges: a slower one for greater torque when running big bits and a faster one for quicker driving or spinning small bits. Speed change is accomplished mechanically, with a slide lever that engages a set of gears inside the drill.

CLUTCHES

One of the most important features found on virtually all cordless drills is an adjustable clutch. The clutch lets you select the degree of force applied to the bit before power is disengaged or shut off. This makes a cordless drill better in two ways: It keeps the DC motor from stalling and overheating, which can also damage or ruin the batteries, and it lets the drill drive screws and tighten fasteners to the degree you choose. The second feature turns an everyday cordless drill into a versatile drill/driver. Say you need to mount small cabinet hinges with short #4 screws without stripping them. By setting the drill's clutch to a low setting, say 1–3 (clutch setting

scales vary among models), all screws are driven to the same degree of tightness. Choosing the right setting also prevents screw heads from getting stripped or, more annoying, shanks from getting snapped off. Most clutches have an off setting for supplying full power during tough drilling jobs, like punching holes through thick sheet metal.

FORWARD/REVERSE BUTTON on the Black & Decker FireStorm drill.

CLUTCH-SETTING RINGS on Bosch and Panasonic cordless drills.

The Business End

BITS, DRIVERS, AND DRUMS

When it comes to portable drill/drivers, the price of versatility is high: A complete assortment of high-quality bits, drivers, and other chuckable accessories can set you back two or three times the price of the tool itself! Depending on the kind of material you're working with and the size of the holes you need to bore, there's no shortage of choices in drill bits.

Just having a complete collection of twist drill bits may require a special shelf in your tool cabinet. These would include: fractional bits ($\frac{1}{16}$ in. to $\frac{1}{2}$ in.), letter bits (A–Z), large-numbered bits (1–60), and small-numbered bits (61–80), the latter including drills barely bigger than human hairs! To keep bits organized and protected, each set should be in a foldout index box.

SETS ARE A GOOD WAY to acquire a wide range of sizes needed for drilling tasks.

DRIVER ATTACHMENTS allow for quick change, easy reach into tight spaces, and even driving at an angle.

WOOD BORING BITS

1. Auger bit (not for power boring).
2. Hole saw.
3. Spade bit.
4. Brad-point bit.
5. Multispur bit.
6. Tapered bit.
7. Forstner bit.
8. Beaver drill saw.
9. Speed-bore bit.

METAL BORING BITS

10. Bullet-point twist bit.
11. Titanium nitride-coated twist bit.
12. Standard twist drill.
13. Stepped sheet-metal drill.
14. Split-tip twist drill.

MASONRY BORING BITS

15. Carbide-tipped masonry bit with special splined shank (for hammer drill).
16. & 17. Small and large carbide-tipped masonry bits.
18. Masonry bit with titanium nitride-coated tip.

THE FESTO CORDLESS DRILL has a clever and convenient hiding place for drivers.

When bits dull, a sharpening device, such as the compact Drill Doctor, restores the keen edges at each tip.

When it comes to installing or removing fasteners, the right driver bit turns a screw gun, cordless screwdriver, or just about any power drill into a muscle-saving screw-driving machine. Once you've picked the size of slotted, Phillips, Torx, or Robertson (square-drive) driver bits you need, it doesn't hurt to fit them into a quick-change bit holder rather than into the chuck itself. As its name implies, a quick-change holder lets you swap bits as quickly and as often as the job demands. The Festo CDD 12 ES cordless drill has a compact caddy that snaps on to the base of the handle to keep driver bits handy.

In case you think the usefulness of your lowly $1/4$-in. or $3/8$-in. drill ends at punching holes and spinning screws, behold a small sample of the incredible array of devices designed to chuck up in an ordinary drill: wire wheels, sanding drums, flap sanders, power rasps, rubber and plastic abrasives, buffing wheels, and more.

VINTAGE DRILL KIT

Tools that do it all fascinate us. Just consider the success of Swiss army knives and multipurpose tools like the Leatherman. That spirit was alive and well when the John Oster Manufacturing Co. (producers of Osterizer blenders) made the Cummins model 3052 Home Workshop drill set in the mid 1950s. Besides the accessories that one would expect to find in such a drill kit (including a sanding disk; wire, grinding, and buffing wheels; and a set of small drill bits), the metal clamshell–boxed kit included a nifty drill stand and one device that didn't survive into our litigation-crazed times: a circular saw accessory. Although it looks like something Rube Goldberg might have invented, the 4-in.-dia. sawblade actually cuts pretty well—as long as you don't expect a kerf that's too straight or too smooth.

SPECIALTY ATTACHMENTS allow you to sand, polish, and grind with your drill.

Accessories

BEYOND THE BASICS

Drills may have been designed for a limited set of duties, but manufacturers always find ways of stretching those duties with inventive accessories.

MINI DRILL PRESS

If you want the control of a drill press in a more portable arrangement, consider the Portalign drilling fixture. Mounted between the drill and the chuck, the Portalign's two steel columns and cast-alloy base allow drilling of perpendicular holes with ease—great for boring stock too large to put under a drill press. Springs on the Portalign's columns retract the drill after boring, and a locking collar allows hole depth to be set. You can extend the columns slightly beyond the base for angled holes; the base has a straight edge on one side for greater stability during angled drilling.

Hitachi's drill-press accessory allows a big portable drill to behave like a stationary one. It provides a sturdy mount for its heavy-duty drill (it also fits a number of other models) and has all the basic features you'd expect to find on a small drill press: a depth-stop mechanism, an adjustable head on a column, and a spring-loaded press arm.

PORTALIGN drilling fixture.

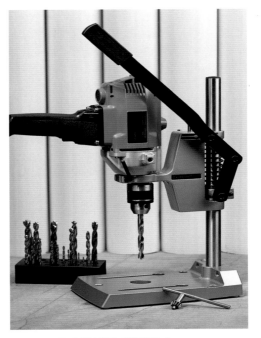

HEAVY-DUTY DRILLING FIXTURE that turns your portable drill into a drill press.

QUICKDRIVE auto screw-feeding accessory.

QUICKDRIVE

You can convert just about any drill into an autofeed screw gun with the aid of a Quickdrive. This light-weight accessory, made of durable plastic, mounts in your drill's chuck and locks to the drill body. The Quickdrive's head works like a lighter-duty version of the autofeed mechanisms on dedicated auto screw guns: Special screw strips thread into the head, where a spring-loaded driver runs them into the work, one after the other. You can spend the weekend using it to screw dry-wall or sheathing to walls, then remove it so that your drill can resume its more mild-mannered everyday tasks.

A SHELF HOLE–DRILLING JIG from Woodhaven.

PERFECT ALIGNMENT

To ease the chore of drilling long rows of holes for adjustable shelf pins in the sides of bookcases or cabinets, team your drill with a shelf hole–spacing jig, such as the one made by Woodhaven. Accurately spaced holes in the jig position the head of a special spring-loaded drilling bit. An oversized collar on the bit engages the holes in the jig while the bit drills down into the work. To create a row of holes longer than the jig, an index pin aligns one end of the jig to the last hole drilled. Spacers on the edges of the jig align it to the workpiece so holes are parallel to the edge.

The Cutting Edge

THIS DECEPTIVELY SMALL SWITCH is the gateway to powerful pulsing action.

METABO PLUS SERIES

One tool that's stretching the cutting edge of drill/driver tool technology is Metabo's Plus Series of cordless drills. In addition to all the features a modern cordless drill should have (keyless chuck, adjustable clutch, dual-speed range, and electronic variable speed), these drills have a unique "Impuls" feature: A small switch at the back of the motor housing activates circuitry that electronically revs the motor as if you were flicking the switch on and off rapidly. This pulsing action helps you start bits in hard materials, such as tile or sheet metal, without center punching first and prevents the bit from "walking" out of a newly started hole.

A GERMAN "IMPULSE" PURCHASE

When driving screws, the Impuls feature helps the bit seat in the screw head. It's also great for driving out stubborn screws, even if their heads have stripped. Switch Impuls off, and the Metabo behaves just like a regular cordless drill. Metabo's Impuls and Plus Series drills all have dual-range variable speed and come in regular or hammer drill/driver versions.

The German-based Metabo Corp. began building high-quality hand tools in 1924, and it initially focused on *metallbohrdreher* (drills for metalworking), an abbreviation of which lent the company its name. Each drill is hand-assembled from Metabo-manufactured parts, including high-capacity electric motors contained in metal housings for strength and durability. To get Metabo drills and other cordless tools charged in a hurry, there's an optional fast battery charger available. Using microchip-control technology pioneered by Metabo, the fast charger replenishes a drained battery in as little as 10 to 20 minutes.

A LOOK INSIDE THE METABO DRILL reveals its high-capacity electric motor, contained in a metal housing for strength and durability.

METABO BST 15.6 PLUS

CHUCK CAPACITY (MAX.): ½ in.

BATTERY VOLTAGE/CAPACITY:
15.6 volts/2.4 Ah (amp hours)

NO-LOAD SPEED:
dual range: 0–450 rpm and 0–1,600 rpm

TORQUE (IN./LB.):
maximum: 484

continuous: 211

with Impuls: 246

MAX. HOLE-DRILLING CAPACITIES:
mild steel: ½ in.

soft wood: 1³/₁₆ in.

LENGTH: 9¼ in.

WEIGHT: 4.2 lb.

SANDERS

Sanding wood is one of the most tedious parts of building a new cabinet or chair or removing an old finish from a garage-sale antique. Yet, with the right power tools, the sanding process can change from exhausting to exhilarating. Okay, maybe not exhilarating, but at least by using a modern power sander, you can bring your project to a smooth finish easily and quickly so you'll have time to get out and do something fun and exciting.

Whatever kind of shaping, smoothing, or polishing job you need to do with sandpaper, there's a modern power tool that's made for the job. Part of the reason that abrasive power tools are burgeoning is that, compared to bladed power tools like routers and circular saws, power sanders are far less intimidating to use and are much safer. So set your hand-sanding block on the shelf and get ready to delve into the smooth world of portable powered sanding machines!

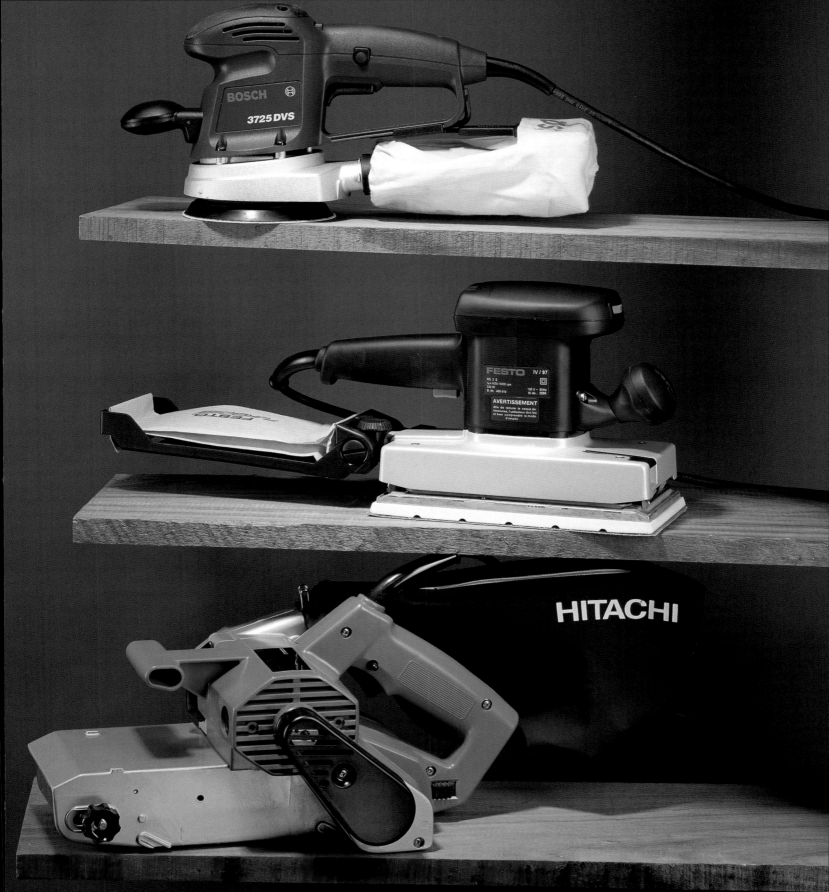

The Classics

PORTER-CABLE 504 BELT SANDER

When I was around 11 years old, I asked a neighbor if I could borrow a sander to smooth the floor of a tree fort I was building from an old shipping crate. Never having seen a belt sander before, my eyes must've popped out of my head when I saw the sleek aluminum tool he offered to loan me: a Porter-Cable 504 belt sander. Known as "Takeabout" sanders when they were made by the Guild Tool Co. (Porter-Cable's earlier incarnation), the model A2, shown at right above, was one of a long line of belt sanders. The modern 3x24-belted 504 is still as sleek and

powerful as the bullet train it resembles: a worm drive sander with lots of amps on tap for getting some serious sanding done.

PORTER-CABLE 504 BELT SANDER

MOTOR POWER: 9 amps

BELT SIZE: 3 in. by 24 in.

BELT SPEED, SFPM (SURFACE FEET PER MINUTE): 1,500

LENGTH: 16 in.

WEIGHT: 15½ lb.

PORTER-CABLE 330 SPEED-BLOC

The Porter-Cable model 330 Speed-Bloc palm sander is a tool I would call the Volkswagen of orbital sanders. The ¼-sheet-sized 330 has been around for decades and embraced by generations of power-tool users.

Pros and novices alike appreciate the tool's compact size, ample performance, and rugged construction. The Speed-Bloc's signature feature is its shapely body, which tapers near the top knob to form a grip that's comfortable for just about any size human hand.

PORTER-CABLE 330 SPEED-BLOC ORBITAL SANDER

MOTOR POWER: 1.2 amps

PAD SIZE: 4½ in. by 5½ in. (¼ sheet)

PAD SPEED, OPM (ORBITS PER MINUTE): 14,000

ORBIT DIAMETER: $\frac{5}{64}$ in.

HEIGHT: 4½ in.

WEIGHT: 4 lb.

Tools of the Past

SANDING HEAVYWEIGHTS

Invented in the 1920s by Art Emmons, the same man who developed the sidewinder-style circular saw (see p. 15), the first belt sander, the B3, looked like the undercarriage of a train car with a domed motor housing rising up in back and a single vertical handle sticking up at the front. The locomotive-like Porter-Cable belt sanders that evolved from the B3 were of an in-line design embraced by other manufacturers, including Skil, who minted the impressive-looking model 323 SkilSander in the 1940s. The 323's heavy-duty aluminum castings and stout construction are beautiful but add up to a tool that weighs more than 23 lb.!

THREE-ROLLER DESIGN

The Art Deco–styled Craftsman model 207.2230 belt sander is as odd as it is handsome. Lifting the cover off its toaster-like outer body reveals not two but *three* rollers around which its nonstandard-sized 3-in. by 27-in. belt travels. The third roller allows a longer belt to be used, thereby increasing the effective amount of abrasive without lengthening the tool substantially. This layout puts the motor at the center of the tool, keeping its center of gravity low and balance admirable.

NOT A TOOL FOR THE TIMID, the big Skil 323 runs an odd-sized 4½-in. by 26-in. belt powered by its big 12-amp motor.

THE THIRD ROLLER at the top front of this Craftsman model 207.2230 is spring loaded and tensions the belt.

IMPRESSIVE BUT NOT EFFICIENT

Electric sanders of the 1950s, unlike modern orbitals, simply vibrated the pad, creating a sanding action that, while useful for its time, wasn't very effective. With a cage-like aluminum housing that looks more like the cylinder head of a motorcycle engine than a power tool, the Dremel model 2000 used a pair of electromagnets to vibrate its small (2⅞-in. by 6½-in.) pad back and forth. Although it more closely resembles a modern orbital, the handsome Sears Craftsman model 110.7600 uses a similar electromagnetic mechanism to propel its ⅓-sheet-sized pad. While not a great performer, this Craftsman is a miser when it comes to electricity, only drawing 2 amps!

THE CRAFTSMAN 110.7600 and the Dremel model 2000 are the ancestors of today's pad sanders.

Belt sanders are relatively simple power tools: a continuous loop of sandpaper spun between two wheels by a motor, plus a pair of handles.

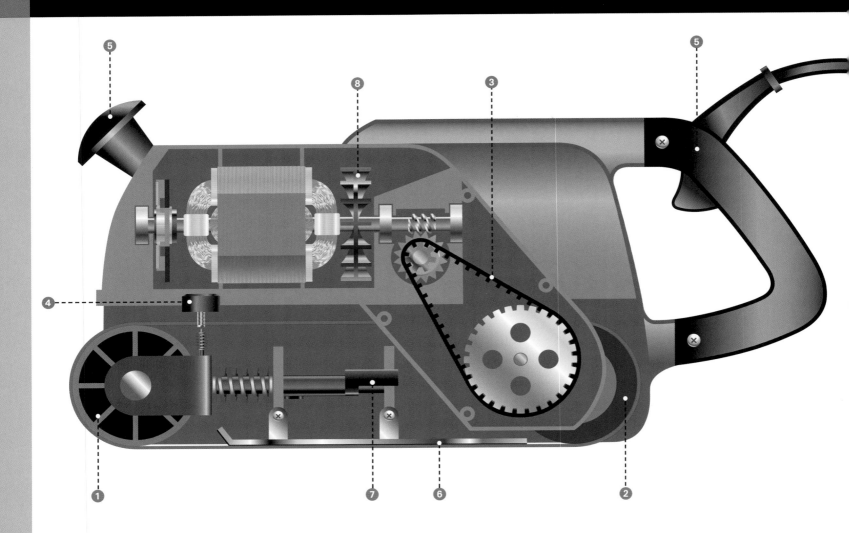

1. Front idler roller is crowned to keep the belt centered.

2. Rear drive roller has a rubber covering to grip and propel the belt.

3. Drive belt or chain transfers motor power to drive roller.

4. Tracking knob changes angle of front roller to keep belt running straight and centered.

5. Front and rear handles are for hefting and controlling the tool.

6. Platen provides a flat contact patch between the belt and the work.

7. Belt-release lever disengages spring tension so belt may be removed.

8. Motor-driven fan sucks dust from the rear of sander and expels it into dust bag or hose.

BELT SANDERS

- Heavyweight and powerful
- Aggressive stock removal
- In-line and transverse motor styles
- Range of sizes to fit the job

NARROW-BELT SANDERS

- Sand in tight spots
- Easier to maneuver than large-belt sanders
- Can be mounted for stationary sanding tasks
- Not effective on wide surfaces

RANDOM-ORBIT SANDERS

- Aggressive sanding with few scratches
- Can sand across grain
- Use hook-and-loop or PSA (pressure-sensitive adhesive) disks
- Electric and pneumatic models available

ORBITAL SANDERS

- Accept regular-sheet sandpaper
- Square pad sands inside corners
- Lightweight and easy to handle
- Good for general finish work

DOUBLE-DUTY ORBITALS

- Do orbital and detail sanding
- Useful for general sanding
- Nose can get into tight spots
- Alternative to buying two sanders

DISK SANDERS

- Aggressive stock removal
- ariety of pad sizes available
- Leave visible scratches
- Powerful heavy-duty tool

DETAIL SANDERS

- Specifically designed for tight spots
- Variety of sanding mechanisms
- Accessories extend versatility

PROFILE SANDERS

- Can sand profiles or details
- Wide variety of shapes available
- Eliminate tedious sanding on moldings
- Not useful for general sanding tasks

Sander World

BELT SANDERS

Unlike a handplane, which requires a sharp blade and equally sharp user skills, a belt sander can produce impressive results even in the hands of an inexperienced user. This powerful tool can remove squeeze-out from a glued-up panel, level a tabletop, or even trim a tenon to better fit its mortise. Fitted with a coarse-grit abrasive, a belt sander can grind down the bottom edge of a door or can trim an uneven frame almost as quickly as a portable power plane.

Models with dual or variable speed are most versatile. By slowing the belt down, you reduce sanding aggressiveness without the need for switching to a finer-grit belt. Lowering belt speed also lets you sand nonwood materials—metal, plastic, painted surfaces—more efficiently.

DEWALT DW431 and Porter-Cable 362VS belt sanders.

PILOTING A BELT SANDER

Running a big belt sander over a surface is like steering a big boat (just don't follow the example of the *Exxon Valdez*). Just guide the tool with a steady hand and let its weight do the work. Keep it moving, and don't dally too long in one place or you might end up with a wavy surface instead of a flat one.

Belt sanders come big or small, to suit sanding jobs of any scale. The smaller sanders that use 3-in. by 21-in. belts are maneuverable and compact enough to work inside cabinets or to be used single handedly to smooth rough plaster on walls or ceilings. The big brutes run 3-in. by 24-in. or 4-in. by 24-in. belts and have enough motor power to make quick work of flattening a glued-up butcher-block countertop or removing tool marks and scratches from a multipanel door. If you can't decide between a 3x21 or 4x24, don't toss a coin—toss a sack of coins to your local tool dealer and buy both!

NARROW-BELT SANDERS

When it's time to take on a big job with a belt sander, wider is better. But even the most compact 3x21 unit is too big to get into the kinds of nooks and crannies that sometimes require thorough sanding. In such situations, a narrow-belt sander is just the tool to turn the trick. Also known as a power file, Makita's 9031 narrow-belt sander runs a 21-in.-long belt that's only 1⅛ in. wide—slender enough to sand between louvers or notches on wood or metal surfaces. Running a band of abrasive only 1½ in. wide and 12 in. long, the Bosch 1278VSK Compact belt sander has a small front roller that brings the leading edge of the belt nearly to a point, allowing it to sand down into tight slots and mortises. Mounting the Bosch to its accessory bench stand turns it into a handy stationary tool for trimming or shaping small parts like dollhouse components or wheels for toy cars.

BOSCH COMPACT BELT SANDER in its accessory bench mount.

MAKITA 9031 NARROW-BELT SANDER and the Bosch 1278VSK Compact belt sander.

RANDOM-ORBIT SANDERS

The way an RO (random-orbit sander) runs is the key to its ruthless sanding efficiency: Its pad spins like a disk sander yet, at the same time, moves in a circular orbit, like an orbital sander. The spinning action tears through wood grain like crazy; the orbital action tones down the effect of the spinning disk a bit, so it doesn't leave glaring cross-grain scratches. Sanding action is aggressive, yet the tool is relatively easy to control and comfortable to handle (especially if you slow down the sanding action with variable speed).

Unlike a sanding belt or disk that creates definite, directional scratches, a random-orbit sander attacks the wood at all angles, allowing you to sand in any direction across a board or panel—even over corners where wood meets cross-grain. (ROs are terrific for getting out cross-grain scratches left by a belt sander across cabinet-face frame rails and stiles.) Slow-speed sanding with a variable-speed model is tops for sanding metals and plastics or for buffing and polishing finishes.

SCRATCHLESS SANDING

Like any power tool, ROs aren't foolproof. You can and will end up with visible scratches if you press too hard (remember, let the weight of the sander do the work!). For best results, move the sander slowly (about an inch a second), and take care to remove all coarser-grit scratches before switching to a finer-grit disk.

BOSCH 3725DVS and DeWalt DW423 random-orbit sanders.

A Look Inside

Like a doomed planet spinning out of control, a random-orbit sander's mechanical design spins its disk in an eccentric orbit.

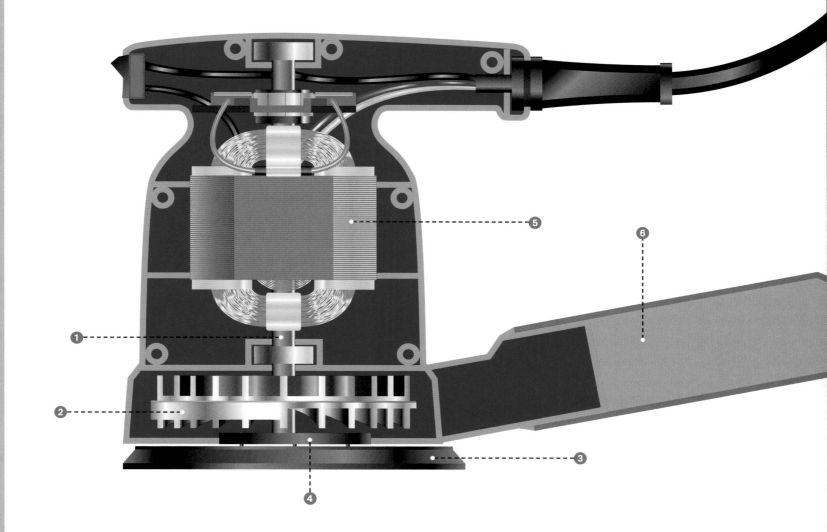

① Eccentric shaft creates the pad's circular orbit.

② Balance weight reduces vibration caused by orbiting disk.

③ Sanding disk mounts to a rubber- or foam-backing pad.

④ Pad brake keeps disk from spinning at excessive speed; slows disk after power is shut off.

⑤ Direct-drive motor powers orbiting mechanism and backing pad.

⑥ Dust extraction pulls fine wood powder through holes in sandpaper disk and backing pad and blows it to a dust bag or vacuum port.

PNEUMATIC ROs

Although corded random-orbit sanders are now ubiquitous, they didn't start out as electric tools. The earliest RO sanders were air-powered workhorses, used in auto body shops for smoothing Bondo-filled fenders and sanding primer and paint. Although they're often cheaper to buy than their electric counterparts, the cost of the sander is only part of the picture: You need the air output of a fairly large compressor, say 5 hp or more, to run them efficiently.

Because of their extremely compact size and eccentric sanding action, pneumatic ROs, such as the Sioux model 690, are known as "doodle bugs." In-line pneumatics, such as the Campbell-Hausfeld dual-piston TL1016, also come from automotive work but are great for woodworking as well. Their in-line back-and-forth action is great for sanding dense, straight-grained woods, like maple, that show swirl marks easily. They're also a tool of choice for leveling a finish (sanding out irregularities left from brushing or spraying).

SIOUX 690 and Campbell-Hausfeld TL1016 air-powered sanders.

DISK SANDERS

SEARS CRAFTSMAN 11504 and Makita GV5000.

Even though it's capable of removing stock quicker than an orbital or a random-orbit sander, a disk sander is a very simple machine: a flexible disk held in a chuck or arbor that's rotated by a motor. Disk sanders come in pistol-grip and right-angle types. You can purchase a dedicated pistol-grip model, like the Makita GV5000, or buy an accessory sanding disk and mount it in the chuck of an electric drill. A right-angle sander is very much like an angle grinder fitted with a hard rubber or fiber disk (see the Sears Craftsman 11504 in the photo at right). In fact, a regular angle grinder fitted with a sanding disk can be pressed into service quite nicely.

ORBITAL SANDERS

To produce an affective sanding motion, an orbital sander's electric motor spins an eccentric weight mounted directly above its pad. Its sandpaper-covered pad is propelled into small circular orbits, and the abrasive scours the surface of the work in all directions. Although easy to handle, perfect results aren't guaranteed with an orbital sander: It takes a light touch to get a smooth surface that's free of swirl marks (little semicircular scratches that result when abrasive particles cut across the grain of wood). Swirl marks are most apt to show up when sanding dense, fine-grained hardwoods such as maple and cherry, and show most after the surface is finished with a penetrating oil finish, like Danish oil, or water-based finish.

PORTER-CABLE 330 and Makita 9046 orbital-pad sanders.

DOUBLE-DUTY ORBITALS

Buying a power tool that does twice as much work for the same amount of money is definitely something that will help keep your wallet from going on a diet. Double-duty orbital sanders, such as the Makita BO4562 and the Sears Mouse, are just such animals. Both have pads large enough to handle everyday sanding jobs, smooth surfaces, or soften sharp edges and corners. And both have a pointed front edge that will sand into tight corners and recesses. While the pads of both models are designed for hook-and-loop paper, the Makita's pad accepts a $1/4$-sheet-sized square *and* a triangular-shape standard detail sander paper; the Mouse uses special proprietary hook-and-loop paper that fits the shape of its three-sided curvy backing pad.

MAKITA BO4562 and Sears Mouse double-duty sanders.

DETAIL SANDERS

If God is in the details, then surely a detail sander is the most divine of all portable sanders. Its small triangular pad has tips pointy enough to reach into corners or get between obstructions—say, when smoothing oak stair treads around balusters.

With long, sleek bodies that are easy to grip, different brands of detail sanders look very similar. But, depending on the brand, the mechanicals that drive the oscillation of the head are of two distinct types. Detailers such as the Bosch 1294VSK and Festo DX93 E-Plus have an eccentric driveshaft and counterweight that orbit the pad much like a regular orbital sander. In contrast, the Fein MultiMaster uses a pivot drive that moves the pad in a small arc, like the windshield wipers on a car. Both drive systems work: The pivot action is more apt to produce cross-grain scratches than the orbital action but allows the use of special attachments—a scraper, to remove paint or finishes, or even a small sawblade, here shown on the Fein MultiMaster.

As if they weren't handy enough, accessory pads and scraper blades for detail sanders allow you to reach deep into slender crevices or scrape off old finishes. If metalwork is the order of the day, mount a plastic abrasive or steel-wool pad, and you're ready to clean up rusty parts or polish shiny metal surfaces.

DETAIL SANDERS from Porter-Cable and Festo.

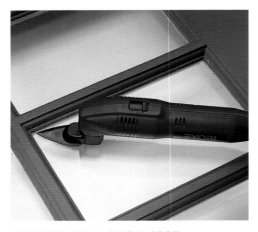

OUTFITTED WITH A SPECIAL FOOT and a scraper blade, this Ryobi power detailer extracts dried-up and cracked window-sash putty.

THE FEIN MULTIMASTER accepts a small semicircular sawblade for flush trimming.

PROFILE SANDERS

A profile sander is the power tool of a thousand faces. That's because it has a head designed to accept a myriad of sanding attachments. Most profilers, including the Porter-Cable 9444VS, have a detail-sanding head for sanding flat surfaces in tight quarters. But their specialty is sanding smooth a multitude of shapely profiles. By choosing from a selection of rubber cauls—including coves, roundovers, slots, and V shapes—a profile sander can handle moldings, raised panels, and

THE PORTER-CABLE 9444VS is both a detail sander and a profile sander.

DREMEL 6000 profile sander.

shaped wood edges. For complex molding shapes, several different cauls need to be used on different parts of the profile. The Porter-Cable sander comes with a head that holds two profiles at the same time. The cauls are angled so that tipping the tool one way or another lets you use each separately. In contrast to the Porter-Cable's solid-rubber cauls, the Dremel 6000 profile sander's cauls are hollow, which allows them to better conform to slightly irregular surfaces.

A SELECTION OF CAULS for profile sanding can handle a wide variety of molding and other curved work.

Belt Sander Features

DRIVING AND TRACKING THE BELT

A belt sander rides on a small area where the platen presses the belt against the workpiece. If the tool isn't well balanced, controlling the sander can be tricky. In an in-line belt sander, such as the Bosch 1274DVS, the motor is oriented with the length of the tool, centering the motor's weight over the platen. Some in-lines have a flat-topped rectangular body, which makes them easier to mount upside down for stationary work.

In transverse-style belt sanders, such as the Porter-Cable 362VS, the motor sits perpendicular to the tool's length. Because of the length of the motor's armature, fan, and belt-drive pulleys, the housing overhangs the body and can throw the side-to-side balance of the tool. However, different models vary considerably in balance, even within the same belt-size and motor-power range, so test-drive a few before you buy one.

BELT TRACKING

Because sanding belts aren't perfect, they tend to wander off to one side of the roller, either scraping the inside of the sander or jumping off entirely. That's why all belt sanders have a built-in belt-tracking adjuster. Turning a small knob (or lever) changes the angle of the front roller slightly, thus changing the position of the belt on the rollers. A slight adjustment is usually all it takes to get the belt centered.

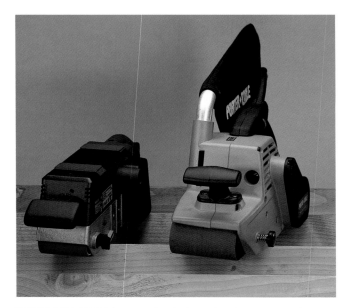

THE BOSCH 1274DVS is an in-line belt sander. The Porter-Cable 362VS has a transverse-mounted motor.

TRACKING CONTROL on the Hitachi SB10T and the Porter-Cable 504.

DUST COLLECTION

DUST BAGS on DeWalt, Milwaukee, and Ryobi belt sanders.

The sheer volume of fine wood powder a belt sander spits out makes it the undisputed over-lord of dust demons. Therefore, all belt sanders have integral dust-collection ports to which canvas bags attach. A fan on the motor armature blows dust from where it's sucked up at the back of the belt into the bag. Even so, a significant amount of dust doesn't make the trip. The best way to increase the efficiency of this system is to retire the bag and plug a flexible hose into the port (a hose-converter fitting may be necessary), and use the power of your shop vacuum to suck up the dust.

BELT-RELEASE LEVERS

BELT-RELEASE LEVERS.

There's a lever on every belt sander that's small but is your best friend at belt-change time. A single pull on that lever releases the spring tension that keeps the belt taut and running smoothly, thus loosening the belt for removal. That's the idea anyway. Unfortunately, not all belt-tension release levers are created equal: Some are hard to pull and have pressed-steel handles with sharp edges. Better-designed levers made of cast plastic or alloy are engineered with enough mechanical advantage to release and re-tension the belt with very little human effort required.

THE PLATEN

The bigger the platen on a sander, the more rubber on the road (or more accurately, the more grit on the wood). Even within the same belt-size sanders, platens vary in size. Bosch extended the platen on its in-line 3x21 closer to the front wheel, giving it more sanding surface area. Most platens are a thin stainless-steel sheet over cork. The cork layer underneath gives the platen a bit of give, which actually helps the belt sand more aggressively.

Random-Orbit Sander Features

GRIP STYLE

The first thing you'll notice about electric random-orbital sanders is that they don't all look alike. Palm-style ROs, such as the Porter-Cable 333VS, have a rounded, cylindrical body and single-hand grip located directly above the pad for excellent balance. You can grip the knob atop the sander or hug the body itself while you steer the tool around the workpiece.

In-line random-orbit sanders, such as the Ryobi RS200, feature a pair of handles: A rear, pistol-grip handle has the tool's on/off trigger while the overhanging front grip is removable for sanding close into corners. You can hold the tool single-handed or using two hands, for better control and less fatigue.

Right-angle ROs are designed like small angle grinders, with models such as Festo's RO150 E-Plus equipped with powerful motors to drive their sanding pads. The Festo's motorcycle-handlebar-grip front handle screws into either side of the head to make it usable for righties or lefties.

GRIP STYLES (clockwise from the top): the body and handlebar grip on Festo's RO150 E-Plus, the handle grip on the Ryobi RS200, and the palm grip on the Porter-Cable 333VS.

SPEED AND ORBIT ADJUSTMENT

Variable speed is included on many different brands and models of random-orbit sanders, enabling the user to adjust the aggressiveness of the sanding action to suit the job: slower for delicate work, faster for heavy stock removal. But the electronic circuitry in ROs, such as the Metabo SXE450, also performs another valuable function: to keep the selected speed constant even when sanding gets tough. Simply put, when the spinning disk is working hard and bogs down a bit, an electronic sensor detects the reduced motor speed and provides feedback, thus supplying the motor with higher voltage that brings the speed of the rotating disk back up to par. The feedback controller constantly monitors disk speed and automatically adjusts motor voltage as required in order to maintain constant speed.

ORBIT ADJUSTMENT

One of the cutting-edge features you'll find on a select few random-orbit sanders is orbit adjustment. A red push button on the base of the Metabo SXE450 selects a larger or smaller orbit diameter of the pad. Choosing an $1/8$-in. orbit produces a better finish-sanding action, while the $1/4$-in. orbit is better for fast stock removal. The green selector lever on the right-angle Festo RO150 E-Plus random-orbit sander performs a slightly different function. Turning the lever one way disengages the drive that spins the randomly orbiting pad, thus producing a less dynamic sanding action—much like that of an orbital sander. Turning the lever the other way engages the Festo's full random-orbit action for more aggressive stock removal.

THE METABO SXE450 uses electronic feedback circuitry to keep its disk speed constant.

ORBITAL ADJUSTMENT is a premium feature found on the Metabo SXE450 and Festo RO150 E-Plus.

PAD SIZE

ROs are sized by the diameter of their round sanding pads. Pads of 5 in. dia. and 6 in. dia. are by far the most common. Palm-grip sanders and in-lines like the Makita BO5021K favor the smaller 5-in. pads, while the 6-in. pads often appear on right-angle sanders, such as the DeWalt DW443. At the extremes are Metabo's SKE400 orbital sander with its small-but-handy 3⅛-in.-dia. pad and the giant of the lot, the Fein MOL1200E, which spins an enormous 8-in.-dia. pad. Larger pads put more abrasive grit to wood and thus sand big surfaces faster. But they weigh more and take more muscle to control (be sure to hang on tight if you put the Fein's big pad to rough wood!).

RANDOM-ORBIT PAD SIZES range from the huge 8-in. Fein MOL1200E to the tiny 3⅛-in. pad on the Metabo SKE400; 5- or 6-in. pads are most common.

DISK HOLES

The madly whirling disk at the heart of a random-orbit sander can kick out choking quantities of dust. Fortunately, all ROs have some kind of built-in dust collection. On most models, a fan just above the pad pulls up dust through holes in the sandpaper disk. A dust cuff at the bottom of powerful right-angle ROs, including the Fein MOL1200E, helps collect dust around the perimeter of the pad and direct it to a shop vacuum hose.

DUST CUFF on the Fein MOL1200E makes vacuuming away the dust more efficient.

DUST BAGS AND MORE

Some ROs sport bags or canisters that are cleverly designed to help make dust disposal easier. Paper disposable bags attach snuggly to the rear dust port on the Bosch 3725DVS. A clip on the underside of the sander's handle holds the bag in place while a rubber gasket keeps dust from leaking around the port. Made from a canvaslike fabric, a round canister attached to the rear of the DeWalt DW423 is supported by a coil spring inside, keeping the bag resilient while making it easy to empty.

Ryobi's RS200 5-in. in-line model has a wedge-shaped dust bin that's snuggly set below its rear handle. The bin's plastic frame is covered inside with a durable plastic mesh that filters and traps fine dust. The seemingly solid plastic Sand-trap canister protruding from the side of the 6-in. pad Porter-Cable 335, which looks like a muffler on a dirt bike, is actually cast from a porous plastic so air escapes while dust doesn't.

DUST BAGS AND CANISTERS: Bosch 3725DVS, DeWalt DW423, Ryobi RS200, and Porter-Cable 335.

Orbital Sander Features

SANDPAPER SIZE

The square or rectangular sanding pad on an orbital sander reflects the portion of a standard 9-in. by 11-in. sheet of sandpaper it uses: $\frac{1}{4}$-, $\frac{1}{3}$-, and $\frac{1}{2}$-sheet sanders are the most common. Unlike a round-disk RO, the square-edged pad of an orbital can sand right into tight inside corners. Just be careful not to bump adjacent sides, as the hard edges of the vibrating metal pad support can leave nasty dings and dents.

The $\frac{1}{4}$-sheet-sized Hitachi SV12SF (shown left in the photo at top right) is a palm-style sander that's light and easy to use single handedly. Palm sanders are great for rounding edges and smoothing smaller parts. The $\frac{1}{3}$-sheet-sized Skil 7390 (center) has an in-line handle with trigger and a small front grip. This size is good for smoothing medium-size panels as well as general sanding duties. The big Festo RS2 (right) takes a $\frac{1}{2}$ sheet of sandpaper. Its big handle and front grip are needed to control the tool's aggressive sanding action. Half-sheet orbitals are best reserved for sanding large parts or panels, cabinet sides, and tabletops.

ORBITAL SANDERS ARE SIZED by the fraction of a standard sandpaper sheet that fits its pad.

PAPER CLAMP MECHANISMS: Makita 9046, Porter-Cable 505, and Metabo SR358.

WITH A SANDPAPER PIERCING PLATE, there's no charge for the dust-extraction holes.

EASY-CHANGE PAPER CLAMPS

Most modern orbital sanders are designed to use either special pressure-sensitive adhesive (PSA) or hook-and-loop sandpaper. But just in case you run out unexpectedly (or aren't willing to pay a premium for the convenience of those special papers), most models are fitted with paper clamps. These special holders grasp the ends of a flat sheet, so you can use regular-sheet sandpaper. The trio of ½-sheet orbital sanders shown in the bottom photo on the facing page all have paper clamps, although each works in a slightly different way. The Porter-Cable 505 (center) has a conventional notebook-clip clamp that's powerful but must be held under pressure while the ends of the paper are inserted. In contrast, both the Makita 9046 (left) and Metabo SR358 (right) have lever-operated clamps, which stay open while sandpaper ends are inserted or removed.

SANDPAPER PIERCING PLATE

When you buy a doughnut, the hole is included in the price. But when you purchase special perforated disks for dust-collecting random-orbit sanders, you have to pay for the holes! Luckily, many orbital sanders use a more economical solution: Orbitals like the Bosch 1293D come with a special piercing plate that punches holes in regular-sheet sandpaper to match the pattern of dust-sucking perforations in the tool's backing pad. Simply attach the paper to the sander, and press it down over the plastic plate. Voilà, free holes!

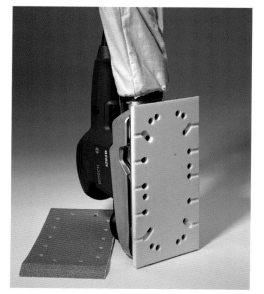

BOSCH 1293D.

The Business End

THE NITTY-GRITTY

All sandpaper starts its gritty life in a big way, first manufactured into leviathan cylinders known as jumbo rolls. The abrasive-grit-coated paper, cloth, or film is then cut into standard 9-in. by 11-in. sheets, punched into disks or detail-sanding triangles, or fabricated into belts, drums, spindles, flap wheels, and more.

Most sandpaper products are made in a range of grit sizes. For example, sanding belts are available in grits ranging from extrafine 320 grit to a lunar-crater-coarse 24 grit.

Once you've picked the grits you need, there are other choices to make. When buying sandpaper sheets or belts, the kind of abrasive particles (aluminum oxide, silicone carbide, garnet, ceramic, etc.) affect sanding performance. The paper backing of sheet sandpaper comes in different weights (A, C, and D), which affect how durable or flexible the backing is. Disk backings are covered either with PSA or hook-and-loop treatments. Sadly, the pattern of prepunched holes for dust collection isn't standardized across various brands of sanding disks.

ABRASIVES COME IN all types, shapes, and sizes to suit a wide range of different power sanders and all the various smoothing, cleaning, and polishing tasks they're capable of.

How do you know which sanding products are best for you? Aside from getting more information (for example, from my book *The Woodsanding Book*, published by The Taunton Press), a practical method is to try several different types and brands and see which ones work best for you. Some styles of sandpaper cut more aggressively than others and wear out less quickly. As a general rule, you get what you pay for. For example, a sanding belt that costs twice as much as a cheap one may last 4 to 10 times longer.

PSA VS. HOOK-AND-LOOP SANDPAPER

Who would have thought that a major decision when buying a random-orbit or orbital sander would be over what kind of sandpaper it uses? The issue is whether the sander's backing pad is designed to accept paper coated with PSA or covered with a fuzzy fabric for hook-and-loop mounting.

Which type should you choose? Sanders that use PSA papers are great if you sand a lot of material at one time with one grit of paper—say, sanding a whole slew of cabinet doors or production items. Once the sticky-back paper is spent, it's done. Hook-and-loop paper easily rips off the backing pad and can be used again and again, until the abrasive wears out.

If you just can't decide which sandpaper system to go with, choose a PSA model; you can always retrofit the backing pad with an accessory stick-on pad cover, thus adapting it for hook-and-loop paper.

PUTTING A SHINE ON IT

Just because you bought a variable-speed random-orbit sander for your woodshop doesn't mean it can't help you out the next time you want to wax and polish your car, RV, or boat. By mounting a special polishing pad or bonnet, the sander quickly and safely buffs automotive paint—or colored fiberglass finishes—to a sparkling shine (just be sure to turn the RO's variable-speed dial down to about half of maximum). You can also fit the sander's pad with a convoluted-foam applicator pad, as shown on the Makita BO5021K, and use your sander to rub out a finish or to apply wax or polishing compounds to your motorscooter's fenders.

HOOK-AND-LOOP PAPER is easily reusable, but PSA paper is cheaper.

Accessories

STANDS AND FRAMES

Although they're not available for every model, a bench stand transforms your portable belt sander into a small stationary model, just right for trimming or shaping small parts. A stand-mounted sander can also sharpen the edges of steel-plane blades and chisels. Most accessory stands can be clamped in either a horizontal or vertical position, as demonstrated by the stands for the Bosch 1274DVS and DeWalt DW431 3x21 belt sanders.

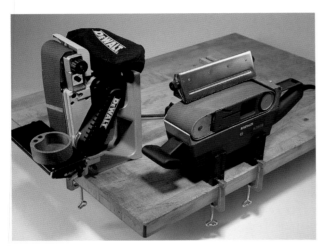

CLAMP-ON STANDS for the Bosch 1274DVS and DeWalt DW431 belt sanders turn them into handy stationary tools.

A SMOOTH RIDE

A sanding frame lengthens the footprint of a belt sander so you can smooth a big tabletop or door panel and produce a surface that's truly flat. Purchased for a specific brand and model of sander, a sanding frame attaches and detaches from the sander via special brackets or recesses on the sander's body. The bottom of a sanding frame is either covered with smooth plastic or short tufts of bristle to reduce friction and help the large frame glide easily over the work surface. An adjusting knob on the frame lets the user raise or lower the belt in relation to the frame, thereby setting a lighter or heavier cut.

THE BRISTLES ON THE BOTTOM of a Bosch sanding frame allow the sander to glide smoothly over a large wood surface.

The Cutting Edge

PORTER-CABLE 121

Just when you thought you had every type of portable electric sander known to humankind, a new breed makes its abrasive presence known: Porter-Cable's new model 121 portable oscillating spindle sander. Like benchtop oscillating spindle sanders (see p. 258), this new portable has interchangeable spindles with diameters ranging from $\frac{1}{2}$ in. to 2 in. But unlike stationary machines, the model 121 lets you to bring the tool to the work, rather than forcing you to lift large, heavy materials onto a stationary machine. This makes the 121 handy for shaping sink cutouts or sanding the curved corners of stair treads.

The model 121's innovative design includes integral dust collection and three ergonomically designed handles to make controlling the heavy tool easier. The tool's 6-amp variable-speed motor oscillates the sanding spindle up and down $\frac{1}{2}$ in. and creates between 40 and 60 oscillations per minute, to produce much smoother results than you could get with a drum sander.

For smoothing straight, square edges, a fence attaches to the baseplate to control the sanding action. One side of the fence is adjustable like a jointer's in-feed table, allowing you to fine-tune the amount of material that's sanded from the edge in a single pass. With a special mounting plate, the model 121 also may be inverted in a router table for stationary use.

A FENCE ATTACHMENT allows the Porter-Cable 121 to sand edges smooth and square.

PORTER-CABLE 121

MOTOR POWER: 6 amps

SPINDLE SPEED (NO LOAD): 2,400–2,600 rpm

SPINDLE OSCILLATIONS PER MINUTE: 38–60

HEIGHT: 8 in.

WEIGHT: 10 lb.

After years of scrimping and saving, you've hit every sale and Internet special and managed to assemble a respectable collection of portable power tools: A circular saw; drills, both corded and cordless; a jigsaw; a belt sander, random-orbit sander, and finish sander; and a router (or maybe two). However, your tool kit still doesn't feel complete. What's next for your Christmas wish list?

Special-purpose tools may not be part of a basic complement of tools, but having them around can make getting the job done a lot easier. You could trim a long edge with a router and a straight fence. And with the right jig, a router can be pressed into service as a slot cutter or even as a board surfacer. But in this fast-paced world, who has the time to fool around trying to make tools perform tasks they weren't designed to do? Sometimes it's just smarter to have that special tool around when you need it.

RTABLES

Plate Joiners

QUICK-AND-EASY JOINERY

Many woodworkers who once proudly used mortise-and-tenon joints or cut dovetails have gone on a diet of biscuits. Plate joinery biscuits, that is: football-shaped wafers made from compressed wood. A water-based adhesive (white or yellow carpenter's glue) makes the biscuit swell until it's wedged tightly into the slot. Biscuits not only strengthen the mitered members or parts joined edge to edge or edge to surface, but they keep them aligned during assembly.

These specialized tools have a horizontal blade and sliding-motor assembly. Place the face of the tool against the surface you want to join, press the handle forward to plunge the blade, and voilà: you've created a semicircular slot just the right size for a biscuit.

CLOCKWISE FROM BOTTOM: Lamello Top 20, Porter-Cable 557, Makita 3901, DeWalt DW682K, and Virutex AB11C.

CLOCKWISE FROM LEFT: 100mm standard blade, 2-in. blade for Porter-Cable proprietary FF biscuits, and a 78mm blade for the smallest standardized #H9 biscuits.

A small circular blade is at the heart of every plate joiner. The standard blade is basically a miniature sawblade 100mm ($3^{15}/_{16}$ in.) in diameter with half a dozen carbide teeth, which cut a 4mm ($5/_{32}$-in.) kerf. This blade cuts slots for a variety of different biscuit sizes and recesses for several types of hardware. By mounting a special, smaller 78mm- ($3^{1}/_{16}$-in.-) dia. blade, any plate joiner can plunge slots for the smallest standardized #H9 biscuits.

SWISS PRECISION

Although most Americans haven't used biscuit joinery for more than a couple of decades, the Lamello joining system was developed more than 50 years ago. The machine's inventor, Hermann Steiner, founded Lamello in 1944. The company, based in Bubendorf, Switzerland, has produced many different models of biscuit machines, all of watch-like quality. One of its most popular models, the Lamello Top 10, was first imported to the U.S. in the 1980s.

THE LAMELLO TOP 10 shown here outfitted with an accessory top handle, which many users prefer to the original loop handle.

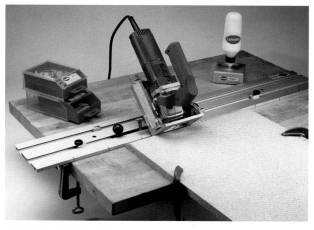

LAMELLO ACCESSORIES include the precision Assista positioning system and special glue bottle with a nozzle designed to spread glue in biscuit slots.

Those who purchased the tool were treated to a handsome wooden carrying case that came as standard equipment; a pleasant surprise for woodworkers more accustomed to receiving new tools in cardboard boxes. Opening the case revealed the Top 10's precisely machined aluminum surfaces and attractive hammered-finish green paint, visual indications of the tool's careful construction and manufacture.

LAMELLO TOP 20

If you'd rather do your biscuit joinery with the machine and work flat on the benchtop but would like to change the position of the slot on an edge, check out the Lamello Top 20's Step Memory system. A top-mounted dial moves the entire cutter assembly up and down relative to the baseplate. You have a range of more than 4mm (about 3/16 in.) in which to set the position of the slot. That means you can center a slot in stock that's between 5/8 in. and 1 in. thick with just the turn of a dial. The dial has a click stop every 0.1mm, to assure precise settings that are easily repeatable.

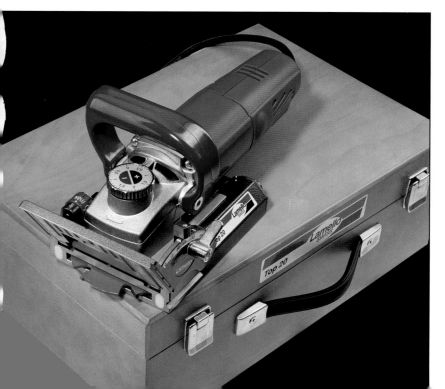

LAMELLO TOP 20 atop its handsome wooden case.

ADJUSTABLE AND TILTING FENCES

By using the joiner's fence against the top of the workpiece, you position the slot on the thickness of the work by adjusting the fence up or down. Economy models have a one-piece fence that simply clamps to the face of the machine. Deluxe models have a mechanism that moves the fence in precise increments. The Porter-Cable model 557 has a thumbwheel at the top that turns and lifts or drops the fence, while the Makita 3901 uses a rack-and-pinion adjustment mechanism. A built-in scale and cursor on the side or edge of plate joiners, like the one on the DeWalt DW682K, helps you set the fence height accurately.

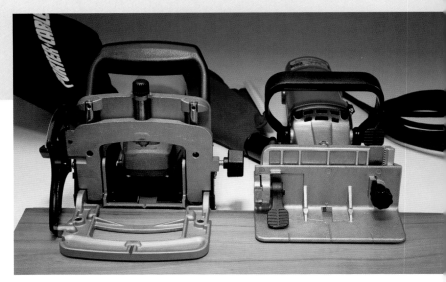

ADJUSTABLE FENCES on the Porter-Cable 557 and the Makita 3901.

JOINING MITERS AND BEVELED WORK

The front fences on most joiners tilt forward so plate slots can be cut on a beveled edge. A slotted metal compass and scale on the side of the DeWalt DW682K show the fence's precise angle. The compass on the Porter-Cable 557 has two sections: The lower compass sets the fence between vertical and 90°. By using the upper scale, you can set the fence all the way down to 135°, for slotting sharply beveled edges.

FENCE-HEIGHT adjustment scale on the DeWalt DW682K.

THE FENCES on the Porter-Cable 557 and the DeWalt DW682K angle up, for beveled work.

BISCUIT SIZE AND SLOT DEPTH ADJUSTMENT

To accommodate workpieces of different thicknesses, plate joinery biscuits come in several different sizes, the most common being #0, #10, and #20. All biscuit machines adjust to work with these different-size biscuits. What is in reality a depth stop controlling the plunge depth of the blade, the knob on the Lamello Top 20 or the turret stop on the Porter-Cable 557 sets the size of the slot.

Although not as commonly used, there are two more sizes that many plate joiners can handle: smaller #H9 and giant #S6 biscuits. But any machine with a standard-size blade and its depth dial set to "Max" (maximum depth) can cut slots for the leviathan #S6s, which are more than $1^3/_{16}$ in. wide and $3^5/_{16}$ in. long.

IN ADDITION TO standard biscuit-slot settings, the depth knobs on most joiners have S and D settings, designed to cut recesses for an entire line of specialized cabinet hardware.

ANTISLIP FRONT ENDS

Once the face of a plate joiner bears against the edge in which it's going to cut a slot, any movement can compromise the accuracy of the slot. Therefore, all plate joiners have some sort of antislip treatment on the face around the blade. The Porter-Cable 557 has a nonslip, coated abrasive strip, similar to the kind you see on the edges of stair treads; the face of the Makita 3901 bears a strip of ribbed rubber; the DeWalt DW682K sports a pair of retractable metal cleats, which bite into the edge of the stock like new soccer shoes grip a grass field.

ANTISLIP SOLUTIONS: a nonslip abrasive strip, ribbed rubber, and retractable metal cleats.

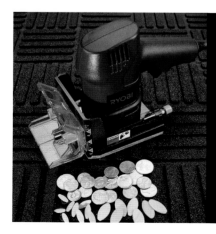

MINI BISCUITS

The Ryobi DBJ50 Detail biscuit joiner includes biscuits so small that you might need a magnifying glass to see them. Deemed the R1, R2, and R3, the smallest size—the R1—is only $7/_{32}$ in. by $5/_8$ in., small enough to join parts that are less than $1/_4$ in. thick. The DBJ50 also cuts mortises for tiny hinges, just right for mounting the front door on your grandchild's dollhouse.

Power Planes

A HANDPLANE WITH ATTITUDE

If you've never had the pleasure of running a power plane down the length of a long fir or pine beam and watching the plume of full, wispy shavings fly up like a rooster tail from a power-boat, you're missing something fun. A power plane is a cross between a handplane and mini jointer. It has a long sole, like a handplane, but the cutting's

done with a fast-spinning cutterhead, like the one found in a jointer. The cutterhead is fanged with a pair of replaceable knives and driven by a lightweight electric motor. Changing the depth of cut is similar to the way it's done on a jointer: The infeed table (or front shoe, as it's called) is moved up or down, exposing

CLOCKWISE FROM RIGHT: Freud FE82, Porter-Cable 9125, Makita 1050DWA.

MAKITA 1050DWA and Makita 1806B power planes.

FREDERICK STANLEY'S ELECTRIC LEGACY

The Stanley Works, which produces some of the finest handplanes ever made in America, also manufactured the first electrically powered plane. The model H had an 18½-in. sole, longer than most modern powered portables, but a smaller cutterhead, which was only 2⅜ in. wide. The cutterhead was powered directly by the arbor of its routerlike motor. Unfortunately, the motor stuck out so far from the side of the tool that its offset balance took some getting used to. While its front grip doubled as a depth-of-cut adjuster (much like on modern power planes), its rear handle, which resembled a checkered wooden plane grip, was a real throwback to the early days of handplaning.

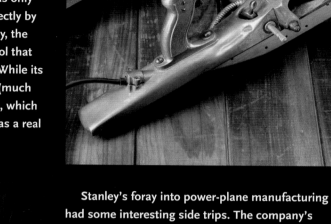

Stanley's foray into power-plane manufacturing had some interesting side trips. The company's affordable and popular Handyman Series power tools included a dome-topped router. One of the clever accessories was the model A planer attachment. After the router was removed from its base, its cylindrical body slipped easily into the side of the attachment. With a 1¾-in.-long cutter chucked in the router's collet, the tool was ready for action. The fit and finish of both router and attachment were high quality, but it was designed for only light-duty work. After all, that long router bit had only a ¼-in. shank, severely limiting the depth of cut you could take on a single pass.

more or less of the cutterhead for a deeper or shallower cut.

Depending on the kind work you want to do, you have a wide range of power planes from which to choose; they come in all shapes and sizes. The length of most machines is roughly equivalent to a jack plane, with cutterheads 3¼ in. wide. These are everyday tools that can accomplish all-around duties in the workshop or on the job site. If you're building a barn and have a stack of really big planks and beams that

need a shave, Makita makes the tool for you: The gargantuan model 1806B has a 6⅜-in.-wide cutterhead powered by a brawny 10.9-amp motor. On the other hand, if a freewheeling, light-duty model is more to your fancy, Makita also makes the cordless model 1050DWA power plane. This 12-volt portable has a smaller, 2-in.-wide cutterhead but is capable of doing some serious shaving—for a tool that weighs only 4.6 lb.

POWER PLANE FEATURES

To assure that a planer trims an edge square and true, all models come with a side fence, including the Freud model FE82. Mounted to the tool's front shoe, the fence guides the plane and stabilizes it against the side of the work. The rabbet guide is another useful accessory. You can set the size of the rabbet by first adjusting the side fence to limit the width of the cut, then setting the rabbet guide so that the planer bottoms out on it when the desired depth is reached.

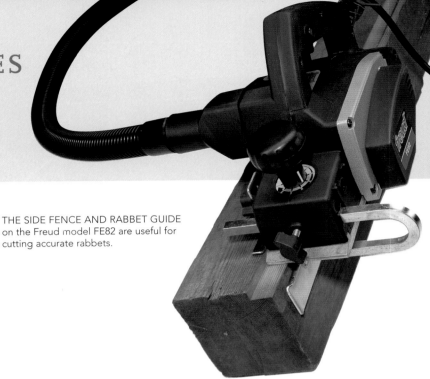

THE SIDE FENCE AND RABBET GUIDE on the Freud model FE82 are useful for cutting accurate rabbets.

DEPTH-OF-CUT ADJUSTMENT

While you set the depth of cut on most portable planers by turning the front knob, each model has a slightly different way of showing you what the current setting is. An easy-to-read scale on the Festo HL 850 E-Plus indicates depth of cut precise to 0.1mm. Metabo's model 0882 electric plane has a shiny metal semicircular scale that wraps around the base of the front grip. The stamped numerals are easy to see, even when the chips are flying. The Porter-Cable 9125 has a spiral depth-of-cut legend on the top of its planer's grip, but you must remember how many times you've rotated the grip in order to know which depth indication is correct.

DEPTH-OF-CUT adjustment knobs (clockwise from left): Metabo 0882, Festo HL 850 E-Plus, Porter-Cable 9125.

SAFETY FOOT

Setting a portable plane down before it's savage cutter has stopped spinning can spell disaster (what's the number for 911?). That's why most plug-in planes have a small but vital safety feature: a small foot that hangs down to keep the cutter from contacting the bench or the work. When you're ready to take a pass, the safety foot simply hinges back up and out of the way.

THE DEWALT DW678K safety foot.

CUTTERHEADS

Flip a portable planer upside down, and what you see looks remarkably like a mini jointer: infeed and outfeed tables with a gap spanned by a rotary cutterhead. The single blade of the Festo HL 850 E-Plus is spiral shaped to take a shearing cut for cleaner surfaces and quieter operation. Remove the standard cutterhead, and the Festo accepts a special concave cutter (sitting on the tool) with a curved knife that scoops away wood much like a scrub plane.

The cutterhead in the Porter-Cable 9125 holds a pair of straight carbide-blade inserts, which are quick-changing and reversible.

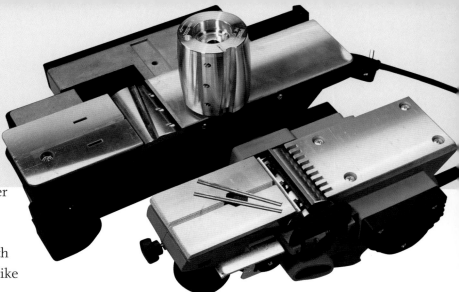

ONE END OF THE FESTO CUTTERHEAD (rear) is flush with the side of the tool, allowing rabbet cuts of unlimited depth (shown with the optional concave cutterhead for rough work). The Porter-Cable 9125 cutterhead (front) uses quick-change blades.

A MINI JOINTER

A stand inverts a power plane and holds it securely, effectively turning the portable tool into a small benchtop machine. The Festo stand shown below includes a large fence that's adjustable for beveled cutting. Its inventive design includes a special plastic clip (seen on the end of a short chain at the lower front of the photo) that holds the trigger in the on position (for safety reasons, the Festo doesn't have a button that locks the switch on). The stand also includes an auxiliary depth dial, which slips over the tool's front grip, making the depth-of-cut scale read right side up while the tool is upside down.

AN OPTIONAL STAND with an adjustable fence can turn the Festo HL 850 E-Plus into an effective mini jointer, which can shave a square edge or make bevel cuts.

VIRUTEX CURVED-SOLE PLANER

The Spanish company Virutex brought the compass plane to the power-tool generation when it produced its CE96H curved-sole electric plane. Like its traditional counterpart, the adaptable Virutex has a sole made from flexible metal, supported at either end by adjustable brackets. The brackets let you bow the sole in either direction, depending on whether you're planing hills or valleys.

Rotary Tools

A COMPACT JACK-OF-ALL-TRADES

I once met a retired gentleman who offered to tell me about his woodcarving hobby. "I do it on a really small scale," he said, as he opened a drawer in his study and pulled out what he referred to as his "woodshop in a shoebox." Inside was a well-used Dremel rotary tool, a bag full of burrs and bits, and a couple of the most handsome fine-relief carvings I had ever seen. After seeing the kind of serious work it was capable of, I decided to buy my own rotary tool.

I've used my rotary tool to cut recesses for delicate inlays, to drill tiny holes, to sand hard-to-reach places, to polish brass hardware, to carve my initials into the back of my work, to cut off bent nails and stripped screws (using a thin, abrasive cutting wheel), and lots more. I'd have to say that, pound for pound, it's one of the most versatile and useful tools in my shop—which is considerably bigger than a shoebox.

BITS, BURRS, AND WHEELS

Part of what makes a rotary so versatile is the wide range of accessories that are made for it, including jigs for sharpening chainsaw teeth or for using the tool as a small router or a drywall cutout tool. But it's the endless array of bits, burrs, and wheels that helps transform this jack-of-all-tools into a specialist ready to carry out any particular task at hand.

CORDED OR CORDLESS, rotary tools are terrifically versatile. Top to bottom: Ryobi HT20VSP variable-speed Multi-Tool with cutout base attachment, Ryobi HTC18 cordless Power Pen, Dremel Professional high-speed rotary tool with digital readout.

CLOCKWISE, around the outer ring, starting from the rear: bonded abrasive cutoff wheels, drum sander, rubberized abrasive wheel, grinding wheels and shapes, diamond-coated burr. In the center, in front: fine grinding points, wire and fiber-filament wheels, cotton and felt buffing wheels and bullet. In the center, in the rear: diamond-abrasive-coated grinding/cutting wheels. In front: dental-type burrs.

CORDLESS ROTARY TOOLS

Rotary tools are already pretty compact and easy to handle. Those qualities are further amplified when you remove the power cord. The Ryobi HTC18 Power Pen is sleek enough to hold comfortably, yet its 4.8-volt battery-powered motor has plenty of oomph for most jobs. A small button near the chuck keeps bits spinning as long as you hold it down (that way, you can't forget and leave it on, draining the batteries). The cordless Ryobi comes with a charging base, which serves as a stand and storage for several bits. Leaving the tool in the base keeps the batteries topped and ready for use.

THE 4.8-VOLT RYOBI HTC18 Power Pen.

DIE GRINDERS

Just think of a die grinder as a pumped-up, World Wrestling Federation–version of a rotary tool. While your typical rotary has an $\frac{1}{8}$-in. collet and a motor that draws an amp or two, die grinders have hefty $\frac{1}{4}$-in. collets that handle large burrs, cutting wheels, and other accessories. And die-grinder motors are powerful enough to push those big bits as hard as you're willing to go. For example, the Metabo GSE 7145 has a generous 6.4-amp motor and comes with an auxiliary handle, which clamps to the tool's long arbor housing to give you better control.

In addition to metal workers, woodcarvers love the power and versatility of die grinders. Fitted with a rotary rasp or a structured tungsten-carbide burr, a die grinder makes short work of roughing out a carved figure or bas relief. Woodturners use die grinders fitted with small sanding disks to clean up torn wood grain as the work spins on the lathe (a feat that requires slow lathe rpm and practiced skill to perform safely).

DIE GRINDERS: the Metabo GSE 7145 and Makita GE0600.

A BUTTERFLY-WEIGHT ROUTER

Just when you thought you didn't have room in your life for another router, here come some nifty accessories that will metamorphose a fat caterpillar of a rotary tool into a butterfly-weight mini router. You can use regular burrs or buy a set of midget router bits with ⅛-in. shanks that fit the rotary tool's collet.

Ryobi's rotary-tool router base has a small clamping collar that holds the tool in a small base, holding it vertically like a fixed-base router. A screw adjustment lets you raise or lower the tool, to change the depth of cut. Channels in the Ryobi's translucent plastic base direct chips to a small dust-collection hose at the rear of the base.

Another possibility for mini routing is to clamp a rotary tool into an elfin router table. Dremel's 231 router-table accessory clamps to the edge of a benchtop or work table. A small knurled screw conveniently raises and lowers the bit. The little table comes complete with an adjustable fence and swiveling top guard.

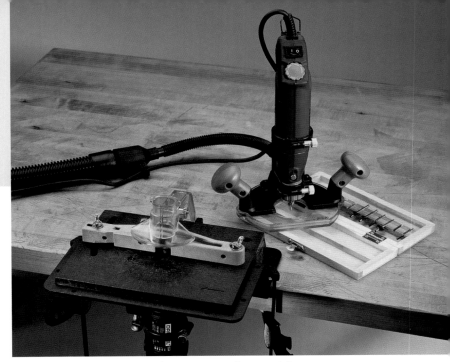

THERE ARE TWO WAYS to transform a rotary tool into a mini router: Mount it in a diminutive router table (with a fence and guard) or slip it into a special router-base accessory, for freehand use.

RYOBI'S ROTARY-TOOL ROUTER BASE and a selection of ⅛-in.-shank mini router bits.

DIMINUTIVE PLUNGE ROUTER

If you're a modeler or luthier with a penchant for precise inlay work, you'll appreciate the accuracy and convenience of using a plunge base with your rotary tool.

Machined and assembled from aluminum, the Bishop Cochran plunge-router base is a beautifully made precision tool. The heavy-duty base accepts either a Dremel or Ryobi rotary tool, securing it firmly into a thick aluminum collar. The tool rides in a carriage that slides up and down on hard-steel guide posts, and final plunge depth can be preset, just like on a full-sized plunge router. For routing grooves parallel to an edge, the Cochran base has a microadjusting edge guide, which also doubles as a circle guide.

BISHOP COCHRAN plunge-router base will hold either a Dremel or Ryobi rotary tool.

DRILL-PRESS ACCESSORY

Little holes can be a big hassle. The smallest bit most drill-press chucks hold is ¹/₁₆ in. An effective way to drill diminutive holes in small parts is to use a rotary tool in a Dremel 212 drill-press fixture. Once the tool is secured by a pair of clamping bands and fitted with a tiny four-jaw chuck, it operates just like a miniature drill press. A spring-loaded arm presses the tool down when boring, and a threaded depth-stop rod limits the boring depth. The head that holds the tool clamps to a tubular column and can be set higher or lower to accommodate work of different thicknesses. The head also has a second mounting hole, which fits on the column horizontally, positioning the rotary tool to work like a stationary arbor.

DREMEL 212 DRILL-PRESS FIXTURE.

FLEXIBLE SHAFT

Although rotary tools are compact and light enough to hold for most work, really fine work benefits from the use of a flexible shaft attachment. The shaft, which looks like a mechanical snake, attaches to the rotary tool via a special collar and chuck. Power is transmitted to the handpiece (a slender handle with threads on the end for a standard collet) through a flexible plastic-clad metal sleeve with a rotating core inside.

A FLEXIBLE SHAFT is an accessory in Dremel's 3956 Super Kit.

The light handpiece is noticeably more comfortable to hold than the rotary tool itself and is easier to control. It allows you to do all the things you'd normally do with a rotary tool but with greater dexterity and delicacy. If you're into fine carving, jewelry making, model building, or inlay work (or would like to be), a flexible shaft is a purchase you won't regret.

Angle Grinders

A SANDER AND MORE

Although they are primarily associated with metal shops and auto body–repair garages, angle grinders are potentially useful to many woodworkers and do-it-yourself enthusiasts. Fitted with a standard abrasive disk made of Carborundum grit pressed into a fiber-reinforced wheel, an angle grinder makes short work of cleaning up pitted or heavily rusted metal surfaces. If welding is your bag, an abrasive disk quickly removes splatter and slag around a weld or smooths out irregularities in welded seams. Equipped with a cutoff wheel (a thin abrasive disk), an angle grinder can cut off frozen bolts or nip the shank off an old padlock you've lost the key to.

ANGLE GRINDERS like the Hitachi G18SE2 excel at metal finishing.

But abrasive disks are only the beginning: There are lots of different grinding and polishing accessories made specifically for angle grinders. A wire wheel or cup brush (left center in the photo at right) scrubs rust from iron or steel parts or creates a pleasant brushed luster on nonferrous parts and hardware. Although designed for metalwork, a coarse abrasive flap wheel (front) cuts through wood like a hot knife through butter, to shape a sculpture or remove tool marks from a scooped chair seat.

THE MAKITA 9060L with one of its vintage cousins.

WOODCARVING ACCESSORIES

If you really want to get serious about carving with an angle grinder, no accessory makes more sense than a carving wheel, such as the Arbortech wheel. Mounted on a 4½-in. or 5-in. angle grinder, the Arbortech includes a special clear plastic guard unit that not only protects you from the wheel's sharp carbide teeth but adjusts to expose more or less of the wheel to help control the rate and depth of cut. The unique carbide teeth are round and meant to be rotated when one section of the tooth is worn.

THE ARBORTECH CARVING accessory with mini grinder extension (foreground).

With a little practice, the Arbortech will deftly carve a seat or other furniture part or plow a channel across a stud wall to run a pipe or electrical conduit. I use it to add tool marks to lumberyard-bought joists used for an open-beam ceiling to make them look hand-hewn.

Another interesting accessory for a small angle grinder is the Mini Grinder Extension, also made by Arbortech. At the end of a 5-in.-long extension arm, the Mini's 1⅞-in.-dia. wheel is crowned by six chainsaw-like teeth. To mount the attachment, a pulley is fastened to the angle grinder's arbor, which drives the wheel with a short V-belt. Extending the small wheel beyond the edge of the angle grinder lets you carve deep hollows or work in recesses without the head of the angle grinder getting in the way.

THE AMAZING CORDLESS CHAINSAW

Admit it. Deep down, your secret ambition is to carve a bear out of a section of old telephone pole. Those guys at the roadside stands make it look easy, don't they? When it comes to heavy sculptural carving, nothing beats the speed and voracious efficiency of a chainsaw.

By running on battery power, the Makita UC120DWA cordless chainsaw lets you work away from outlets, unrestrained by a power cord. Equipped with a 6-in.-long chain bar, the Makita will quickly cut through branches or beams up to 4½ in. thick. The saw's 12-volt battery packs enough juice to scream through a lot of timber; just don't try to cut down any redwood trees with it.

PART TWO

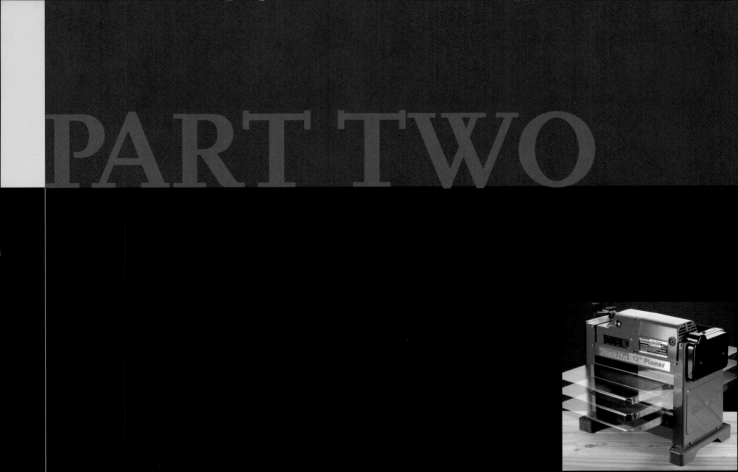

•BENCHTOP & STATIONARY MACHINES

TABLE

If there is a single piece of machinery that many crafts-men would say they couldn't do without, it would have to be the table saw. This woodshop workhorse is a master of multiple functions. Fitted with standard equipment and the right blade, a table saw makes short work of a great variety of cuts, including rips, bevels, crosscuts, miters, compound-angle cuts, rabbets, and dadoes and grooves. By employing special jigs and fixtures, this talented saw's repertoire expands exponentially to include cutting tenons and box joints, raising panels, and shaping coves and moldings.

Fit a saw with a powerful motor; a cast-iron or aluminum-alloy table with slots for a miter gauge; an accurate, adjustable rip fence; and a precision carbide-tipped sawblade and you have a machine that's ready for some serious work. But one model does not fit all needs. Therefore, table saws come in several styles—cabinet, contractor's, and portable—each of which best suits the work style of a different breed of user.

SAWS

The Classic

THE DELTA UNISAW

Even in 1939 dollars, $166.85 for a brand new Unisaw—complete with a 1-hp motor, extension wings, and its characteristic goose egg–shaped cast-iron motor cover—was a bargain. While the historically minded argue over whether the first Unisaw was born in 1939 or 1937, the rest of us admire—and still covet—this impressive table saw, which generations of woodworkers have made the centerpiece of their workshops.

The Unisaw was built by a company that began business in a one-car garage in 1919 as The Delta Specialty Co. The first tools built were the American Boy scrollsaw and the American Girl sewing machine. Delta spent decades building light-industrial and home-shop machinery, including the Unisaw—the first saw of its size available with a tilting arbor. Delta was purchased by Rockwell in 1945, and the factory was moved to Bellefontaine, Ohio, in 1952 and later to Tupelo, Mississippi—where all American-made tools are manufactured today. In 1973, the Delta name was dropped, and all machines were branded Rockwell. When Pentair bought Rockwell's machine-tool division in 1984, it was renamed the Delta International Machinery Corp.

Although the cast-iron base and goose-egg motor cover have been replaced by sheet metal, a modern Unisaw still has many of the characteristics of a vintage model. The saw is still built in the United States, with a heavy trunnion and blade arbor assembly that's more than ample for the 10-in. blade—or for a stack of dado cutters or a molding head. The current Unisaw comes with either a 3-hp or 5-hp motor (single- or three-phase) and three V-belts, which transmit power from the motor to a beefy saw arbor that rides on lubricated-for-life ball bearings. There are currently Unisaw models with right-tilting and left-tilting blades, and the saws are available with either a basic fence, Delta's unique Unifence, or the Biesemeyer T-Square commercial saw-fence system.

DELTA UNISAW 10-IN. CABINET SAW

MOTOR POWER: 3 hp or 5 hp (depending on model)

ARBOR/BLADE SIZE: ⅝ in./10 in.

BLADE SPEED: 4,000 rpm

CAST-IRON TABLE DIMENSIONS (WITH EXTENSION WINGS): 36 in. wide by 27 in. deep

CUTTING DEPTH (MAX.): 3⅛ in. (2⅛ in. at 45° tilt)

RIP CAPACITY (WITH EXTENSION TABLE) (MAX.): 50 in. or 52 in. (depending on which rip-fence model is installed)

WEIGHT: 400 lb. to 500 lb. (depending on motor/rip-fence options)

Table Saw World

CABINET SAWS

While you can build amazing furniture and cabinets with a portable circular saw fastened to the underside of an old desk (yes, I've seen it done), if you earn your living or live for making sawdust, it doesn't hurt to own a high-quality cabinet saw, such as the Powermatic model 66.

The "cabinet" in cabinet saw refers to the saw's boxy base, which totally encloses the saw's inner workings and provides a sturdy foundation for the heavy machine. In the early days when massive weight meant high quality, cabinets were made from cast iron or, later, heavy-gauge sheet metal with a cast-iron base surrounding the bottom. Today's cabinet saws have sheet-metal bases that are sturdy but light and a lot easier to move around.

The cabinet has to be rigid because it supports the key mechanical workings of the saw, including the trunnions that hold the arbor assembly. (In a contractor's saw, the trunnions support everything including the motor.) The cabinet-saw arrangement is stable and easy to adjust for

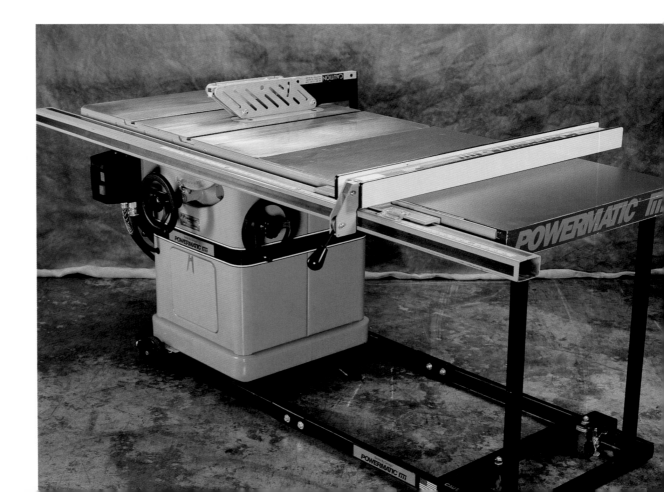

A POWERMATIC classic: model 66 cabinet saw.

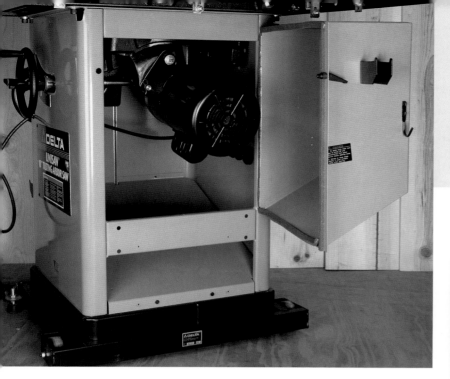

THE INTERIOR OF A DELTA UNISAW, showing the trunnion and motor assembly typical of a cabinet saw.

squareness to the blade: just loosen the table bolts and tap the table into position. Not only is it easier to get everything in alignment and keep it there, but the sheer mass of the machine helps keep down vibration.

Open the motor cover on the side of the saw, and you'll see a large trunnion and motor assembly designed to stabilize the saw arbor and keep the sawblade—or dado stack or molding head—running rock solid during the most grueling cutting sessions. Most 10-in.-bladed models come with a 2-hp or 3-hp motor (up to 5 hp, single- or three-phase) controlled by a magnetic-motor starter switch. Multiple V-belts transmit power from the motor to the blade, enabling the saw to rip or resaw thick hardwoods without the slightest stutter.

Some saw models come with a large extension table to the right of the cast-iron saw table, with rails that allow you to rip wide panels—up to 52 in. wide, depending on the table/rip-fence options you choose. Fitted with an outfeed table, a cabinet saw can easily cut 4x8 sheet goods down to size.

CHOOSE YOUR TILT

In the past, the majority of table saws tilted their blades to the right, in the direction of the rip fence, as used by right-handed people. The exception was the Powermatic model 66, which tilted its blade to the left to help prevent stock from binding and kicking back during bevel cuts. On miter cuts with the blade left-tilted (using a miter gauge in the right-hand slot), the advantage is that marked cut lines are on top, where you can see them. Also any tearout is on the inside edge of the mitered end—not at the tip where it shows on the assembled frame or carcase.

While many woodworkers still prefer a right-tilt saw, left-tilting saws have become so popular that the Delta Unisaw, long a right-tilt model, is now also available in a southpaw version. Jet's Xacta cabinet saw also comes in right- and left-hand models. Even contractor's saws like the Sears 10-in. stationary saw are made as left-tilters, as are the majority of portable table saws.

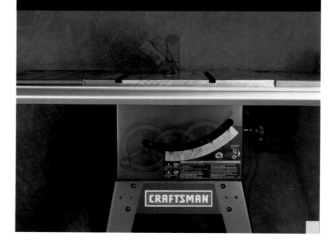

CONTRACTOR'S SAWS

The mainstay of many serious home workshops is a contractor's saw, so-named because it was invented as a job-site machine. Compared to their bigger cabinet-saw brothers, contractor's saws are indeed more portable, but they're not featherweights—so be prepared for some heavy lifting.

Contractor's saws are heavy-duty, professional-grade tools meant for hard use. They pack about three-quarters of the features of cabinet saws into a lighter and more affordable package. Most contractor's saws have large and sturdy cast-iron tables and typically feature extension tables and fence rails long enough for ripcuts 24 in. wide or more.

How can you spot a contractor's saw? The motor and belt cover hanging off the back side of the saw are a sure sign. Aside from a few direct-drive models with universal-type motors, contractor's saws feature induction motors of $1\frac{1}{2}$ hp to 3 hp. That's enough power to rip wet construction lumber or saw hardwood parts. The saw's open-legged stand is a sheet-metal affair that's light and sturdier than it looks—that is, if all the small bolts and screws are still in place and haven't rattled loose over the years.

SEARS CRAFTSMAN contractor's saw.

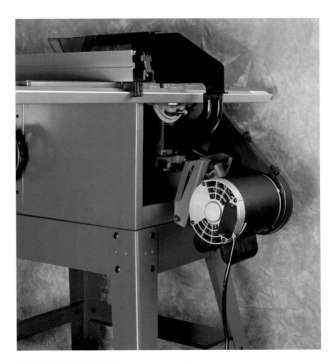

THE MOTOR MOUNT on a contractor's saw.

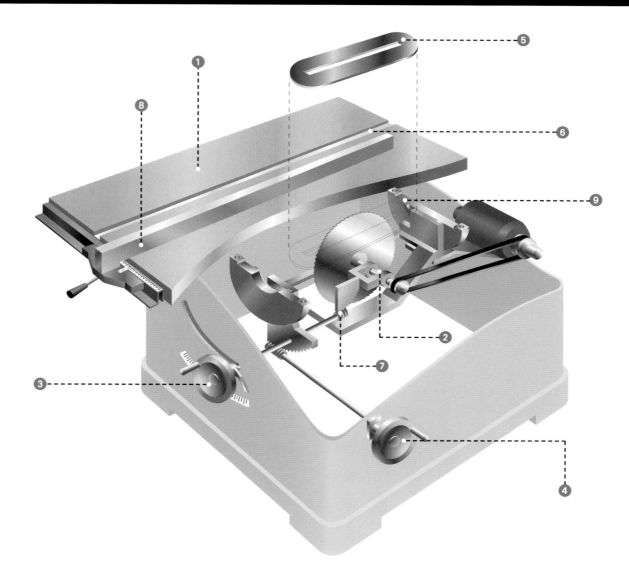

1 Cast-iron table supports the workpiece.

2 Blade arbor is a shaft on heavy bearings that allows blade to run true.

3 Blade-elevation wheel raises and drops the blade to change the depth of cut.

4 Blade-tilt wheel sets angle of blade for bevel cuts.

5 Throat plate supports stock around the blade.

6 Table slots allow miter gauge and other jigs to slide past blade.

7 Worm gear and rack raises and lowers sawblade.

8 Rip fence for safe, accurate, repeatable ripcuts.

9 Trunnions support the entire blade arbor assembly and allow it to tilt relative to saw table.

BENCHTOP TABLE SAWS

The question asked by most craftsmen is "Are benchtop table saws serious machines?" The pint-sized saws of yesteryear may have been more toy than tool, but contemporary consumers can choose from about a dozen portables that are all remarkably powerful and full featured. Most models use a standard 10-in. sawblade and have the same depth-of-cut capacity (3⅛ in. at 90°) as full-sized saws (Ryobi manages to squeeze a 3⁹/₁₆-in. cutting depth out of its BT3000SX saw). That's no small feat, considering that such performance is packed into a tool most folks can easily toss into the back of a pickup truck.

DESIGN INNOVATIONS

To get a portable's weight down to between 40 lb. and 65 lb., there are a few design hoops to jump through. Heavy cast-iron parts are replaced by strong-but-light aluminum-alloy castings. Induction motors with a lot of weight and torque are also eliminated, replaced by the same kinds of universal motors found at the heart of portable power tools. A universal doesn't pack the punch of an induction motor but is far lighter and more compact. Unfortunately, universal-motored table saws are quite noisy, a shortcoming of most benchtop machines. To save weight without sacrificing function, the motor, trunnion, and blade arbor assembly is built as a single unit. The assembly is attached to the underside of the saw table, which is mounted atop a light but strong plastic or sheet-metal base. To keep accessories handy, most portable saws have on-board storage for the rip fence, miter gauge, and extra sawblades and tools.

BENCHTOP SAWS ARE MEANT TO BE PORTABLE. Here the DeWalt DW744 waits for a ride in a pickup truck.

A LOOK UNDER A BENCHTOP SAW reveals the universal motor (right) and the space-saving single-unit runnion and blade arbor assembly.

UNIQUE BENCHTOP FEATURES

While you won't find big extension tables and 50-in.-wide ripping capacity on a portable, you will find some features that don't come on big saws. Thanks to some electronic wizardry, saws including the Makita 2702 and Hitachi C10RA2 feature a built-in electric-blade brake that stops cutting action in a hurry when you hit the off switch. The motor of the Bosch 4000 portable has both soft start, for safer operation, and electronic feedback, which works to maintain blade speed under load for better cutting performance.

HANDY ON-BOARD
accessory storage
on the Bosch 4000.

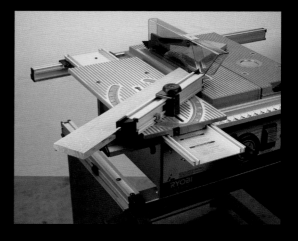

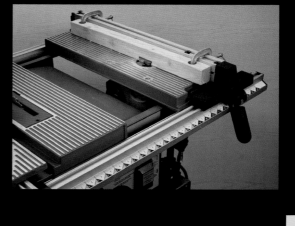

RYOBI'S TABLE-SAW SYSTEM

Ryobi's BT3000SX table saw has a unique rail-mounted table system. The front and back rails, which guide the rip fence, slide side to side on the table and accept a pair of nifty extension tables, including a small sliding table with an adjustable positioning fence for crosscutting and mitering lumber and small panels. The saw's other extension wing is designed to double as a router table.

Features

RIP FENCE

Ripping is probably the single most indispensable thing that a table saw can do. But without a rip fence to keep a board or panel moving in parallel fashion past the blade, ripping would be more dangerous than hand-feeding sharks. That's because anytime the workpiece goes awry and binds in the kerf, the sawblade has a tendency to grab the piece, kicking it back in your direction with great velocity, faster than you can say "emergency room."

To maintain the fence parallel with the blade, the front rail that supports and guides the rip fence must be arrow-straight and precisely perpendicular to the line of cut. Also, the head of the fence must lock the bar parallel to the blade regardless of where the fence is positioned along the rail.

Fence designs vary widely. Some models lock the bar to both front and back rails; some, including the popular T-Square fence system developed by Biesemeyer, have a wide head that squares up and locks only on the front rail. Here's an important hint: Even the highest-quality fence must be adjusted properly and tweaked from time to time to assure the cutting quality and safety of the table saw.

TAKING QUICK MEASURE

Another feature that makes a modern saw fence fast and pleasurable to use is an accurate scale and cursor. The scale, often a sticky-back measuring tape, is mounted to the top of the front rail.

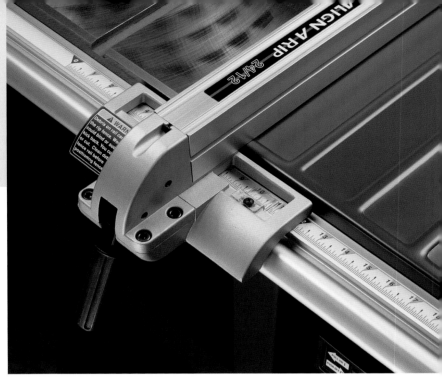

MEASURING SCALE AND CURSOR on Sears 315.228310's rip fence.

THE BIESEMEYER FENCE uses a cam system to lock it to the front rail.

The cursor resides in the head of the fence itself and may be a simple arrow pointer or a clear plastic lens with an inscribed hairline, such as the fence on the Sears 315.228310 stationary saw. Either type of cursor must be fine tuned so the reading on the scale accurately reflects the width of the rip-cut part.

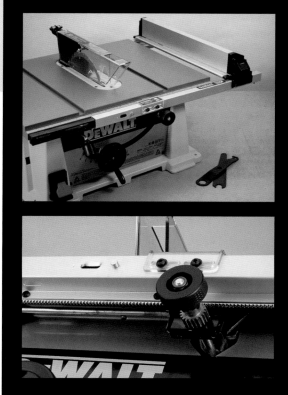

DEWALT'S TELESCOPING RIP FENCE

On a typical table saw, the length of the fence rails limits the width of parts that can be ripped. On portable saws, the problem is that long rails make transportation and storage awkward. DeWalt's ingenious solution was to give their DW744 portable saw telescoping fence rails. With the fence bar secured to both front and back rails, the rails themselves move side to side, allowing ripcuts up to 24½ in. wide. Because there's no extension table, a flip-down stock support keeps wide stock from snagging below the edge of the fence bar. When transporting, the rails reel in nearly flush with the edges of the saw table. A small knob drives a rack-and-pinion mechanism under the front lip of the saw to move the rails precisely. The rail itself carries a cursor that reads a scale attached to the front of the saw table.

REPLACEMENT RIP FENCES

Flip through the pages of a good mail-order woodworking-supply catalog, and you'll be amazed at how many different kinds of after-market rip fences are available. All it takes is a few basic tools and couple of hours to upgrade what is indisputably your table saw's most important component.

Expanding the ripping capacity of the saw is one reason to switch to an aftermarket fence. Beyond that, some fences offer additional useful features. For example, Excalibur's fence system has T-slots that run along the top of the bar, which accept a number of accessories, including hold-down wheels and a sliding push bar for ripping narrow strips more safely.

THE EXCALIBUR RIP-FENCE SYSTEM.

MITER GAUGE

Although crosscutting is not its forte, a table saw can hold its own if cuts are taken using good technique and a properly adjusted miter gauge. Most table saws, including the Delta Unisaw, come with a stock miter gauge that has three stops: at 90° and at 45° in both directions.

The industry-standard miter gauge slides in either of two ¾-in.-wide and ⅜-in.-deep grooves in the saw top, one on each side of the blade. The Makita 2702 and 2703 portables have undersized slots, while the sliding table–equipped Ryobi BT3000SX has no table slots at all. Most cabinet saws and some contractor's models have T-slots, sized as standard slots but with small side grooves. A washer attached to one or both ends of the miter gauge (or other miter-slot accessory) locks into the T-slot, preventing the gauge or accessory from lifting out when crosscutting parts wide enough to overhang the front and back of the saw table.

THE STANDARD DELTA MITER GAUGE.

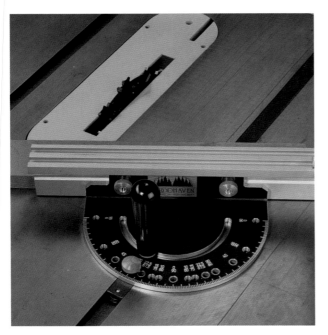

WOODHAVEN DELUXE MITER GAUGE.

REPLACEMENT MITER GAUGES

Even when it's in good shape, a standard miter gauge isn't great for crosscutting parts much longer than a foot or two. The gauge's short face just isn't long enough to stabilize longer work. There's also the matter of setting the gauge to the exact angle.

Aftermarket gauges, such as the Woodhaven Deluxe Miter Gauge, increase both the accuracy and capacity of crosscuts on a table saw. The gauge has positive locking stops at most common angles. To keep the gauge running true in the table slot, the Woodhaven's bar has graphite-impregnated inserts, which adjust so that the bar fits snugly in the slot yet slides smoothly. A fence mounted to the head has an aluminum track that accepts flip stops, allowing a gang of parts all to be crosscut to the same length.

BLADE ELEVATION AND TILT ADJUSTMENTS

Controlling the height and tilt angle of a table-saw blade are the duties of two control handwheels found on the front of the table saw's base. On most full-size saws, the blade-elevation wheel sticks out of the curved slot where the tilt gauge is (see the DeWalt DW746X in the photo at right). The wheel that controls the blade tilt is on the side of the saw, mounted to the left on right-tilt saws and to the right on left-tilt saws (see the sidebar on p. 161). A large compass scale and cursor indicate the degree of tilt. Adjustable stops on the trunnion limit the blade angle at 90° and 45°, the most commonly used settings. Locking knobs, found in the center of wheels on better saws, secure the settings.

Things are done a little differently on portable table saws. To make their mechanicals simpler and more compact, both elevation and tilt adjustments are handled from the front of the saw.

BLADE ELEVATION AND TILT MECHANISM on the DeWalt DW746X.

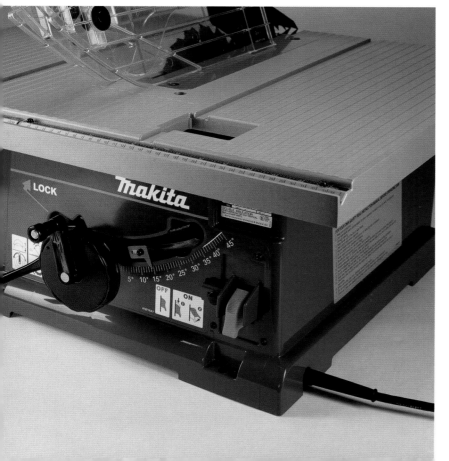

Most models have a small handwheel for blade elevation, with a lever behind it to lock and unlock the trunnion for tilt adjustments. To set the blade angle, grab the wheel, manually tilt the trunnion to the desired position, and lock the lever. The Makita 2702 uses a second wheel, mounted behind a blade-elevation crank, to tilt the trunnion in a more controlled manner.

BLADE TILT on the Makita 2702.

SAFETY FEATURES

The table saw, approached with skill and respect, offers years of great cutting performance without incident. To prevent unfortunate moments when conditions may conspire against us, manufacturers have created some important safety features to protect us from serious injury.

BLADE GUARDS

One of the single most important pieces of equipment that comes with a table saw—a standard blade guard—may take some getting used to, but it provides a crucial degree of protection during everyday use. Besides the clear plastic or cast-metal hood that surrounds the blade, which prevents hand or finger contact, a good guard has two other essential features: a splitter and antikickback fingers.

The splitter (sometimes called a riving knife) is the thin steel vein right behind the blade. On some designs, it's also the bracket that attaches the guard to the saw. A splitter keeps the saw kerf from closing up (due to misalignment or warped stock) and binding at the back of the sawblade. This keeps the motor from stalling and prevents the work from being thrown back at the user.

Mounted on either side of the splitter, a pair of spring-loaded, antikickback fingers have serrated points that scrape against the top of the passing work, acting as one-way devices that block kickback.

REPLACEMENT GUARDS

Unfortunately, stock blade guards are usually fussy to set up and *must be removed* for operations when the blade doesn't penetrate the top of the workpiece, such as dadoing. Besides making and using shopmade guards during these special operations, one solution is to retrofit the saw with an over-arm guard. Designed primarily for large cabinet saws, an over-arm guard has a long

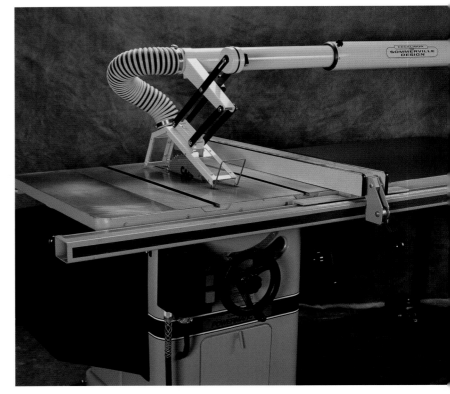

THE STANDARD GUARD on the Sears 315.228310 stationary saw showing splitter and antikickback fingers.

THE EXCALIBUR OVER-ARM GUARD also provides dust pickup above the blade, sucking chips and dust through a flexible hose and hollow arm, which connects to a dust-collection system.

support arm that attaches to the edge of the extension table, out of the way of the rip fence. Suspended above the saw table, most guards are counterbalanced, clear plastic boxes that keep the entire blade area covered. Some of these guards also capture sawdust thrown up by the blade, whisking chips away to a central collection system.

QUICK ON/OFF SWITCHES

If there's one thing in a woodshop that shouldn't require thoughtfulness or accuracy, it's turning off a power tool. If something goes wrong and the thick plank you're resawing kicks back, you want to stop the blade as quickly as possible. The *last thing* you want is to have to fumble for the off switch.

Fortunately, most shop machines built in recent years, including table saws, feature power switches with oversized buttons. For example, DeWalt's newest Woodworker's Saw (see p. 174) and its DW744 portable saw have large, easy-to-find paddle-like on/off switches. All it takes is a quick slap of the knee or fist to shut these machines off in a heartbeat.

A LARGE, easy-to-reach on/off switch, like this one on the DeWalt DW744, is an important safety feature.

DUST COLLECTION

Table saws are among the worst machines from which to collect sawdust. The open backs and bottoms on contractor's models allow the sawdust to fly around like mad. Cabinet saws contain sawdust in their enclosed bases, but there's usually only a single, inefficient dust port at the bottom. The only real champs in the area of dust collection are portable table saws. Practically all models have blade enclosures that feed a dust port protruding from the rear of the saw. These 2½-in. ports make it easy to connect the saw to a shop vacuum or, with a size adapter, to a central collection system. The Bosch 4000 even comes with a long dust bag for rudimentary collection without a vacuum.

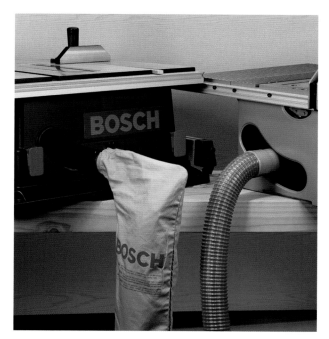

DUST COLLECTION WORKS BEST in benchtop table saws that have dedicated dust ports.

Accessories

SAWBLADES

In the name of saving money, you can stick with the inexpensive steel sawblade that came with your new table saw until its teeth wear off. But if you do, you'll get mediocre results at best, and you'll miss out on a lot of the useful things of which your saw is capable. Just by fitting your saw with a good carbide-tipped, general-purpose sawblade, such as the Forrest Woodworker II, you can coax impressive everyday performance from your saw, whether you cut solid wood or sheet goods. A Teflon-coated blade, such as Freud's LU84R, is easier to clean than a steel-bodied blade, plus the coating reduces friction and heat buildup during heavy cuts.

Ripping requires a blade with an entirely different tooth configuration. A special-purpose ripping blade has few teeth, typically only 24 teeth on a 10-in.-dia. blade. Each tooth has a flat grind and a high hook angle—so it acts like a small chisel, slicing through hardwood or softwood fibers along the length of a board. What you get are edges that are clean and ready for glue-up right from the table saw. A thin-kerf ripping blade, such as the Freud LU87R, requires less power to run because it removes less material. Therefore, your table saw has more effective power for cutting thicker stock more quickly.

A SELECTION OF TABLE-SAW BLADES (clockwise from left): Forrest Woodworker II, general-purpose blade; a dado set (black); and two red Teflon-coated blades: the top is a rip blade and the bottom is a combination blade for both ripping and crosscutting.

TWO DADO STYLES: a wobble dado blade (top) and stacking dado set (bottom).

DADO SET

The biggest trick outside a table saw's standard repertoire of rips and crosscuts is dadoing. Dadoes (wide grooves cut into solid stock or plywood for joinery or decoration) are made with a special dado blade. There are two kinds of dado blades, very different from one another. A wobble-style adjustable dado head features one or two sawblades mounted on an eccentric hub. After loosening the saw's arbor nut, you can turn the hub to change the width of the groove without removing the blade. In contrast, a stacking dado set sandwiches individual chipper blades between a pair of outer sawblades. You change the width of the dado by using more or fewer chipper blades (use shims to fine-tune groove width). Dado stacks take more time to set up but generally produce cleaner, flatter-bottomed grooves than most adjustables do.

TENON JIG

With its vertical blade and large depth capacity, the table saw is the perfect power tool with which to cut tenons. The trick is how to keep a frame member, chair leg, or stretcher aligned vertically while you pass it over the top of the blade. A cast-iron tenon jig, like the Powermatic jig shown at right, has the heft and capacity to handle big tenons. Designed to fit any table saw with a standard $3/8$-in. by $3/4$-in. miter slot, the jig has large grip handles, for better control and safety, and the convenience of a built-in stock clamp that holds large or long members securely. The jig tilts up to 45° for making angled tenons that are difficult to handsaw accurately. A fine-adjustment knob sets the side-to-side position of the jig precisely, and an adjustable stop can be used for repeating settings.

The Cutting Edge

DEWALT DW746x WOODWORKER'S TABLE SAW

It's not quite as big or heavy as a full-size cabinet saw but has more features than a contractor's model. And, at over 250 lb., it's definitely *not* a portable table saw. The DW746X, a machine DeWalt refers to as a Woodworker's Table Saw, is an unusual hybrid, combining some of the best features of all three types of saws in an impressive Big Bird yellow package.

Standing on four sturdy legs, which run from the floor to its saw table, the left-tilting DW746X has a large cast-iron top and a compact drive layout, with the 1 ³/₄-hp induction motor hanging from a hinged platform below the trunnion assembly. A tensioning spring keeps power transmission efficient, from the motor to the saw's 10-in. blade. A shroud that encloses the blade connects to a dust port for efficient chip collection.

DeWalt's T-square fence locks to the front rail with a wide head, which assures that the bar stays consistently parallel to the blade. An ingenious sliding face on the fence bar lets you position the face at the back edge of the blade, minimizing kerf binding when ripping.

The saw's optional sliding table is made of heavy cast iron but moves easily and accurately on its full-extension, double-action slides. The table's modified miter gauge, which has a wide aluminum fence face and a hold-down clamp, works well either in the table slots or fastened to the sliding table.

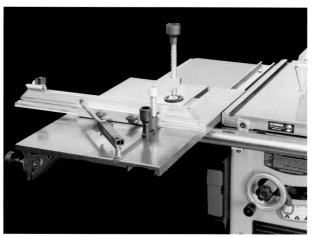

THE CLEVER AND COMPACT SLIDING-TABLE MECHANISM is like an oversized, superheavy-duty, ball-bearing drawer slide.

THE SOLIDLY BUILT T-SQUARE RIP FENCE features an easy-to-read cursor and a sliding face.

DEWALT DW746 WOODWORKER'S TABLE SAW

MOTOR POWER: 1¾ hp

BLADE SIZE (NO LOAD): 10 in. dia.; 3,000 rpm

MAXIMUM CUTTING DEPTH:
90°: 3⅛ in.
45°: 2⅛ in.

MAXIMUM RIP CAPACITY (RIGHT OF BLADE WITH STOCK RIP FENCE): 30 in.

WEIGHT: 254 lb.

OPTIONAL ATTACHMENTS: 52-in. rip-fence rails; sliding table; mobile base, outfeed table; cast-iron extension wings

If you're like me, your first means of crosscutting lumber was a handsaw and a simple wooden miter box. Fast-forward a few decades: The only reason I'd drag out my old miter box is to burn it if the firewood ran low. Now when I need to crosscut a board for a bookcase shelf, miter a frame member for a dormer I'm adding to my house, or compound-cut a piece of molding, I use a power cutoff saw—a tool that makes a handsaw seem as primitive as a sharpened rock.

Power miter saws, compound miter saws, and sliding compound miter saws are powerful, practical, and portable cutting machines.

They don't have the capacity of radial-arm saws or table saws, but these saws perform most crosscutting chores. Power cutoff saws accurately trim frame members to length, square up narrow plywood panels, or miter decorative moldings. Light enough to carry, they work equally well as built-in saws, temporary benchtop tools, or mobile portables at a job site.

SAWS

The Classic

HITACHI C8FB2 SLIDING COMPOUND MITER SAW

While some old-timers would argue that radial-arm saws are the classic cutoff saws, it was a crosscutting saw of another kind that wowed woodworking baby boomers. When introduced to the American tool market in 1988, the Hitachi C8FB2 sliding compound miter saw was a new type of cutoff saw. It combined the pivoting chop action and turntable base of a miter saw with a sliding carriage that allowed wider cuts. Professional contractors and house builders were the first to embrace this 8½-in.-bladed machine. Soon, it replaced many power miter saws and radial-arm saws as the tool of choice for framing and finish-carpentry work.

In the dozen years since its introduction, most portable power-tool manufacturers have created their own versions of the sliding compound miter saw. Many of these saws have a greater cutting capacity and a greater range of features. Even Hitachi now makes a larger, more sophisticated saw: the model C10FS, a 10-in. sliding dual-compound miter saw with a head that tilts both ways for easier compound mitering. Hitachi has also made some improvements on the original C8FB2, including a better self-retracting blade guard, which should make it popular with a whole new generation.

HITACHI C8FB2 SLIDING COMPOUND MITER SAW

MOTOR POWER: 9.5 amps

BLADE SIZE: 8½ in.

SPEED (NO LOAD): 4,900 rpm

SQUARE CUTTING CAPACITY: $2\frac{9}{16}$ in. thick by 12 in. wide

COMPOUND CUT
(45° MITER, 45° BEVEL):
$1\frac{25}{32}$ in. thick by $8\frac{21}{32}$ in. wide

WEIGHT: 38.6 lb.

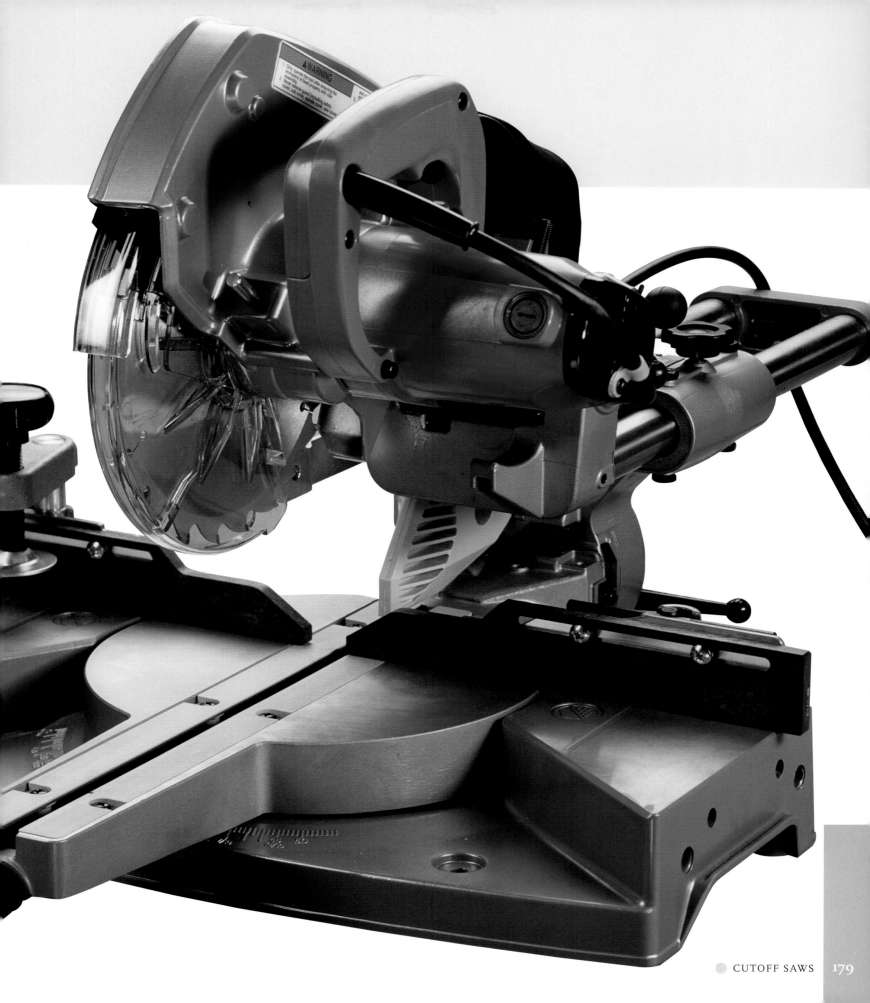

Miter Saw World

POWER MITER SAWS

Known in carpentry vernacular as chopsaws, power miter saws were one of the first portable machines to come along as an alternative for a handsaw and traditional miter box. A relatively simple machine, a power miter saw has a universal-motor-driven blade attached to a turntable, which pivots beneath a fence to allow either square or miter cuts.

Although they're not capable of beveled or compound-angle cuts, chopsaws are great for basic crosscuts in construction lumber and trim. Even a 10-in.-bladed model, like the Ryobi TS254, will take a square crosscut across nominal 4x4 or 2x6 lumber. Move up to a model with a really big blade, like the 15-in. Hitachi C15FB, and you have the capacity to square-cut a 4x8 in one pass or put a 45° miter on a 4x6. This is a blessing if you're building a new house or remodeling your old one.

Although they aren't as versatile as compound or sliding compound miter saws, chopsaws are simpler, so they're less likely to break down under heavy use. They are also less expensive. After all, even woodworkers who build complicated projects take more square and 45° cuts than any others. For them, a chopsaw might be a good choice for a second crosscut saw to keep on hand.

RYOBI TS254.

COMPOUND MITER SAWS

Take a chopsaw and add a tilt mechanism to its pivoting head and you have a compound miter saw. You set miters by rotating the tool's turntable—just like with a miter saw—and tilt the head for bevel cuts. Combine both settings and you're ready for compound cuts, useful when framing a roof or installing crown moldings. Most compound miter saws tilt their blades only to the left, making life more complicated when you're cutting both right- and left-hand compound-angled pieces. One model, the Hitachi C10FCD, is a dual-compound saw that tilts in both directions.

Although they can't match the width-cutting capacity of sliding compound miter saws, the majority of compound miter saws, like the DeWalt DW705, possess big 12-in. blades capable of mitering or beveling 2x8 lumber. Compact and affordable, they are a good choice if you usually work with moldings and trim.

DEWALT DW705.

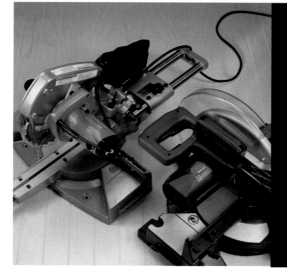

GOT A GRIP?

When it comes to cutoff saws, the handle can make an otherwise beautifully made machine a pain to use. Some users prefer vertically oriented handles on saws like the Hitachi C8FB2 for control, while others prefer the flat-wrist position on a horizontally handled saw such as the Bosch 3912. Hand and wrist comfort is important because the handle also houses the saw's on/off trigger. Most saw handles have wide triggers with room for two or three fingers. Some triggers have a safety catch that you must depress before it will work—a safety feature that prevents you from inadvertently firing up the saw. A second, top-mounted handle makes the saw easy to carry.

DEWALT DW708 and
Porter-Cable 3807.

SLIDING COMPOUND MITER SAWS

No cutoff saw is higher up the totem pole than the sliding compound miter saw (SCM). An SCM takes the miter-setting turntable and pivoting head of a chopsaw and the tilt-ability of a compound miter saw and combines it with the in-and-out sliding carriage of a radial-arm saw. The result is a machine of great sophistication that can handle practically any kind of cut across wood's grain.

The secret to the performance of an SCM saw is its motor carriage, which is designed to pivot downward for narrow cuts, combined with the fact that it slides on one or two guide rails to cut wider panels. Although their width-cutting capacity is limited to stock approximately 12 in. wide or less (much less when mitering), SCM saws come with blades that range from 8½ in. to 12 in. The arbors on these saws are too short to handle a dado blade.

When it comes to head tilting, there's some variation in models. Regular SCM saws, like the classic Hitachi C8FB2 and Porter-Cable 3807, tilt the blade only to the left. Sliding dual-compound saws, like the Makita LS1013 and DeWalt DW708, tilt both left and right. If you plan to install crown moldings or other complex trim, this is definitely the way to go.

Variations in rail design, motor configuration, and handle style make a big difference in how various models are set up and how they feel in use. This is one power tool that's good to try out before buying. Amps and cutting-capacity charts don't tell the whole story, so you're more likely to be satisfied with a purchase if you try several saws before deciding on the one to buy.

A funny thing happened to the radial-arm saw on the way to the 21st century. Once the staple of every contractor and home-shop craftsman, these versatile but temperamental saws have been gradually phased out. DeWalt (the company that launched radial-arm saws) hasn't manufactured them in decades, and Sears recently announced a major safety recall. Radial-arm saws have gradually been replaced by the portable and easier to use (and often more accurate) cutoff saws.

The radial-arm saws—as well as the contemporary cutoff saws that have followed them—are built based on the same basic idea: that the work remain stationary while the sawblade moves over and through it. It's an idea for cutting wood that predates even the radial-arm saw. Early crosscutting saws, with names like the Vertical Column-Bracket Cutting-Off Saw and the Over-Hung Traversing Gainer and Cut-Off Saw (I'm not making these up!), were cast-iron monsters with huge, unprotected circular sawblades that cut well, but the saws were expensive to build and *very* dangerous to use.

Raymond DeWalt is popularly credited with the invention of the radial-arm saw (woodshop veterans often call their radials "DeWalts"). His machine suspended a bladed motor carriage on a yoke, which slid along a long horizontal arm. The yoke allowed the head to tilt for bevel cuts and to swivel for ripcuts. Mounting the arm to a pivoting column allowed miter cuts, and raising and lowering the column changed the blade's depth of cut. He built his first production model, the Universal Woodworker, in 1924, the year he established the DeWalt Products Co.

The basic DeWalt design has changed little over the years, as evidenced by the classic model GA 12-in. saw, shown here. But don't think that radial-arm saws are extinct. This example—and thousands of others—are still in daily use in garage shops, professional cabinet shops, and industrial factories all over the world.

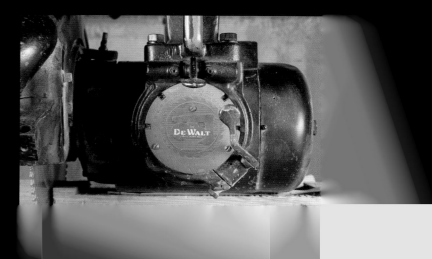

Features

ROTATING TURNTABLE

One of the interesting features shared by both sliding compound miter and compound miter saws is the way their heads pivot on a turntable set into the base. By releasing a locking lever and/or knob, the turntable smoothly rotates around, reorienting the line of cut relative to the fence for miter cuts up to at least 45° in either direction. Many saws miter 52° or more to the right (or in both directions), so you can cut 52°/38° crown moldings.

Each turntable base has a large compass scale marked in degrees, as seen on the Makita LS1013 and Porter-Cable 3807. Click stops (detents) at 0°, 15°, 22.5°, 30°, 45°, and square help you find these commonly used angles quickly and accurately (see the DeWalt DW705 compound miter saw in the photo in the sidebar on the facing page). A separate handle or lever locks the setting firmly and accurately. Some saws have additional detents at 31.6° and 35.3°—standard settings for crown-molding work. A scale pointer helps you find and set undetented angles. For greater precision in setting odd angles accurately, the DeWalt has a vernier scale on its cursor. This is particularly handy when doing remodeling work since older buildings rarely have square walls and ceilings, making off-angle cuts the norm.

TURNTABLE BASES: Makita LS1013 and Porter-Cable 3807.

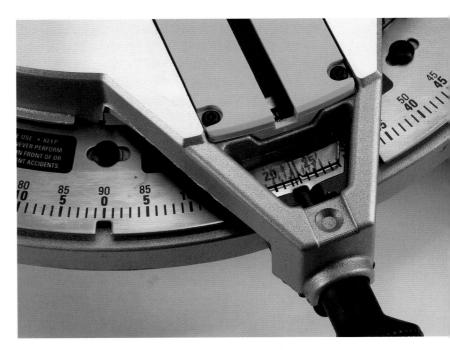

VERNIER SCALE for setting odd angles on the DeWalt DW705.

BLADE TILT

Tilting the head of a compound or sliding compound miter saw lets you bevel cut parts: Tilt the saw and rotate the turntable, and you're ready for compound miter cuts. Most saws tilt only to the left, which requires you to flip and cut some parts upside down. However, dual-compound miter saws and sliding dual-compound miter saws tilt both left and right, a real convenience and a time-saver when making lots of complex cuts. It's a feature you'll appreciate if you ever miter all the skirt boards for a spiral stairway.

Before a saw's head will tilt, you must unlock a lever or handle at the back of the saw. The DeWalt DW708 SCM saw tilts its entire guide rail and head assembly, while saws with retractable rails, such as the Makita and Porter-Cable, only tilt their heads for bevel cuts.

DEWALT DW708.

SETTING STOPS

To make setting the most-often-used 45° and square cuts easier, there are positive stops at these bevel angles. Dual-compound saws have stops at 45° in both directions. The stops are adjustable, just in case they're jarred out of alignment. A cursor and angle scale let you set odd angles fairly accurately; however, it's best to take a test cut on a scrap to check the bevel angle before cutting into good stock.

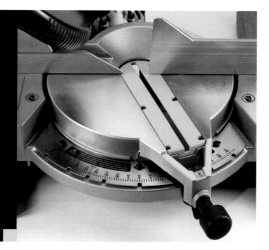

WORK CLAMP

One of the most useful accessories on a cutoff saw is the work clamp. Resembling a threaded handscrew, a work clamp presses the work against the saw's base or turntable to keep it from moving or lifting during a cut. Mounted on the end of a short post, these removable clamps lock into sockets on either side of the base. The quick-action work clamp that comes with the Porter-Cable 3807 has an eccentric-cam lever to make securing the stock even more expedient.

A horizontally mounted work clamp is often used on chopsaws, including the Hitachi C15FB. Attached to either side of the base, the clamp presses the stock directly against the fence. This clamp's wide face holds flat lumber or round stock—wooden dowels or metal tubing and pipe—securely.

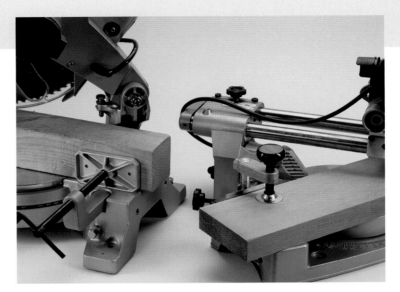

HITACHI C15FB and C8FB2 work clamps.

THE PORTER-CABLE 3807 quick-action work clamp features an eccentric-cam lever.

FENCES

To align the workpiece to the blade, a cutoff saw has a fence on either side of the turntable, supporting the work for right- or left-hand cuts. Although they're fairly short in length to keep the saws compact and portable, these fences are long enough to accurately align most work. For large or long stock, extension rails and aftermarket fence/stop systems are available.

To keep the gap between the two halves of the saw's fence small but still allow enough clearance for bevel cuts, the Makita LS1013 has a pivoting section on its left-hand fence; flip it clockwise for small work and counterclockwise for bevels. The 12-in.-bladed Bosch 3912's right fence has a sliding top section, which supports tall stock close to the fence yet unlocks and slides to the left to provide tilting clearance for bevel cuts.

FENCES: Bosch 3912 and Makita LS1013.

GUIDE RAILS

The feature that distinguishes a sliding compound miter saw from all other crosscut machines is its guide rails, which enable the motor and blade carriage to slide through the cut. Most SCMs have two rails, and use linear ball bearings to keep the blade alignment precise and the sliding friction low. The location and orientation of the rails and the manner in which the head slides are different on practically every brand. The DeWalt DW708 has a pair of rails set one above the other with the motor carriage attached to the front end. The rails slide in and out of a stanchion behind the turntable base. The Porter-Cable 3807 mounts its motor carriage to the end of a pair of side-by-side rails that slide in and out of the base. The Freud TR215's motor carriage is mounted to the front of a pair of side-by-side rails, which slide on a stanchion behind the fence.

Which design is better? Each design is precise and durable and has its own "feel" of use. The advantage of the Porter-Cable's retract-into-base rail system (shared by several Makita models) is that the saw is more compact when not in use. DeWalt's high rails provide great cutting stability and allow the head to tilt in both directions. Freud's twin rails are housed beneath a protective shroud, which keeps off sawdust and, thus, helps keep the rails sliding smoothly.

GUIDE RAILS on the Porter-Cable 3807 and DeWalt DW708.

FREUD TR215.

SAFETY FEATURES

There's nothing like having a big 10-in. or 12-in. sawblade whirring just inches from your bare hands to make you a carbide-tooth-fearing fellow. But you'll have less to fear if you're using a cutoff saw equipped with a blade brake and self-retracting guard.

Designed to retract and expose only enough of the blade to take the cut, a clear plastic guard lets you keep an eye on the stock as the cut progresses. A small wheel on the leading edge of the guard keeps the guard from hanging up on the work.

The second half of a cutoff saw's safety one-two punch is a blade brake. The brake, triggered electronically when the saw's universal motor is switched off, causes the motor and blade to stop in a nanosecond.

A SELF-RETRACTING GUARD combines convenience and safety.

DUAL DUST COLLECTION in the Freud TR215.

DUAL DUST COLLECTION

The canvas dust bags hanging off the back of a cutoff saw are reassuring; a single saw plowing through a pile of 2x4s can produce an impressive pile of sawdust. Usually fed from the saw's blade enclosure, the bag catches only a lion's-cub-size share of the chips and fine dust thrown by the blade; the force of the blade hurls much of it behind the workpiece. Freud deals with the problem by adding a second dust pickup to its TR215 sliding compound miter saw. Located directly behind the fence and blade, the pickup connects to a vacuum hose.

Accessories

SPECIAL CUTOFF SAWBLADES

Because a cutoff saw cuts across wood grain, it stands to reason that any sawblade specifically designed for crosscutting will yield a nice clean cut. But, you'll get the best—and safest—performance if you fit your chopsaw, compound miter saw, or sliding compound miter saw with a blade specifically designed for it. Besides shearing wood fibers cleanly, a crosscutting blade must also resist the tendency to self-feed into the wood. This happens when the teeth grab the wood fibers aggressively, and the rotation of the blade pulls them farther into the stock. At best, self-feeding can ruin wood; at worst, it can sever limbs. Specially designed cutoff sawblades, like the CMT and Freud blades shown in the photo above right, have lots of teeth set at either a low hook angle or a negative angle, which makes them less grabby yet still keeps them cutting cleanly.

CLOCKWISE from bottom: CMT 210 melamine and fine cut-off blade; Freud LU85R Ultimate Cutoff Blade; and Freud TK606 sliding compound miter blade. Underneath: CMT 219 compound miter and radial blade.

ABRASIVE CUTOFF WHEELS

Although woodworking cutoff saws aren't designed for metal-shop duty, you can fit the saw with an abrasive blade (that's like a thin grinding wheel) and cut mild-steel bars, pipes, and angles to length. Just work in a clean area so that sparks from the blade won't touch off a fire.

AN ABRASIVE WHEEL cuts ferrous metals quickly, creating a shower of sparks.

SUPPORT RAILS AND FENCE EXTENSIONS

To stay compact and easily transportable, cutoff saws don't have long fences or huge bases. You can get away with medium-length stock, as long as it isn't too heavy to hold in place either by hand or with the tool's work clamp. For longer stock, you need more support. Made from durable metal rods, table extensions are an optional accessory available for most saw models. These simple wings slip into holes on either side of the tool's base. Some extensions come with a pivoting end stop, as seen on the Hitachi C15FB compound miter saw. Although limited by the length of the extension, an end stop is handy for cutting multiple workpieces to the same length.

AUXILIARY CUTOFF FENCE

Any miter, compound miter, or sliding compound miter saw bolted to a counter or benchtop can do a great job as a shop's main crosscut saw. They're so handy, that cabinet, furniture, and picture-framing shops often mount two or more saws on the same bench, each set to a different cutting angle—for example, one square and the

FASTTRAK MITER SAW SYSTEM.

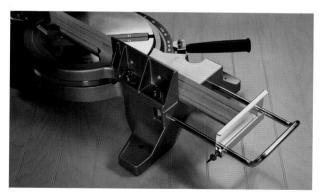

SUPPORT RAILS AND PIVOTING END STOP on the Hitachi C15FB compound miter saw.

other at a 45° miter, or both set at 45° in different directions for right- and left-hand miters. By adding a long auxiliary fence and fitting it with a glued-on tape measure and sliding stop block, you can cut parts to accurate lengths and repeat cuts easily without measuring and marking each board separately. If you'd rather not build the fence yourself, a number of ready-made systems are available, including the FasTTraK Miter Saw System. This extruded-aluminum track mounts to your saw's existing fence so the tool can remain portable. Large yellow "banana stops" lock anywhere along the fence and conveniently flip out of the way when not in use.

The Cutting Edge

CAUTION: WHEN PERFORMING SLIDE CUT,
FIRST PULL CARRIAGE FULLY AND PRESS
DOWN HANDLE, THEN PUSH CARRIAGE
TOWARD THE GUIDE FENCE.
810635-7

MAKITA LS711DWBEK

When you think of battery-powered portable tools, you usually imagine a drill or a saw—something small enough to hold in your hand. But cordless-tool technology has brought us to the point where even benchtop-size machines will run on batteries. The 18-volt Makita LS711DWBEK is the world's first cordless sliding compound miter saw. Although petite compared to full-size corded models, the 7½-in.-bladed Makita is still capable of handling full-size lumber, taking square crosscuts in lumber up to 2 in. thick and 7⅛ in. wide.

As far as power is concerned, the LS711DWBEK uses the same rechargeable battery packs used in Makita's other 18-volt cordless power tools. These nickel-metal-hydride (NiMH) battery packs have a longer running time than standard nickel-cadmium (NiCad) batteries common in other cordless tools.

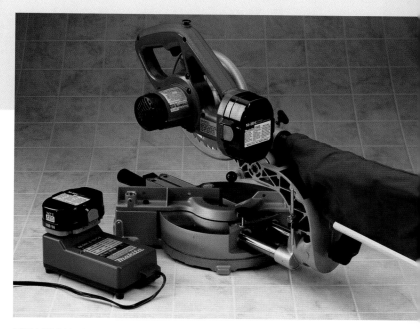

THE MAKITA LS711DWBEK uses the same battery pack that powers other Makita 18-volt cordless tools.

Makita packs its cutting-edge saw in an interesting case. The saw's molded-plastic carrying chest opens at both the top and the front, to make removing and replacing the 23-lb. saw easier. Besides providing a protective home for the saw, the chest has molded compartments for an electric drill and accessories, making it a handy tool kit for cordless jobs away from home and shop.

THE INGENIOUSLY designed case does more than protect the LS711DWBEK. There are molded compartments for a cordless drill and accessories.

MAKITA LS711DWBEK

BATTERY VOLTAGE/CAPACITY:
18 volts; 2.2 amp hr.

BLADE DIAMETER: 7½ in.

BLADE SPEED (NO LOAD): 2,000 rpm

MAXIMUM CUTTING CAPACITIES:
Square cuts: 2 in. by 7⅛ in.

45° compound cuts: 1⅜ in. by 5 in.

OVERALL DIMENSIONS: 21⅝ in. long, 17 in. wide, 17⅞ in. high

WEIGHT: 23.1 lb.

BANDSA
SCR

When you think of sawing wood, it's usually cutting it straight: crosscuts, ripcuts, joinery. But curves add interest and detail to any wood project. The champions of curve-cutting machines are the bandsaw and the scrollsaw. Of the two, bandsaws are more versatile curve cutters: stationary machines that can handle large blades and cut thick stock or resaw it (cut it thickness wise). Scrollsaws are more delicate players: benchtop-size machines with fine blades that cut tight curves in thinner stock.

To suit various kinds of curve cutting, each saw is built differently. A bandsaw's blade is a continuous loop, with lots of teeth for deep cuts or sawing dense materials, such as exotic hardwoods. Scrollsaw blades are short but easy to replace (and inexpensive). They won't cut thick stock, but you can insert them through a hole drilled through the stock to do inside cuts, something bandsaw blades can't easily do.

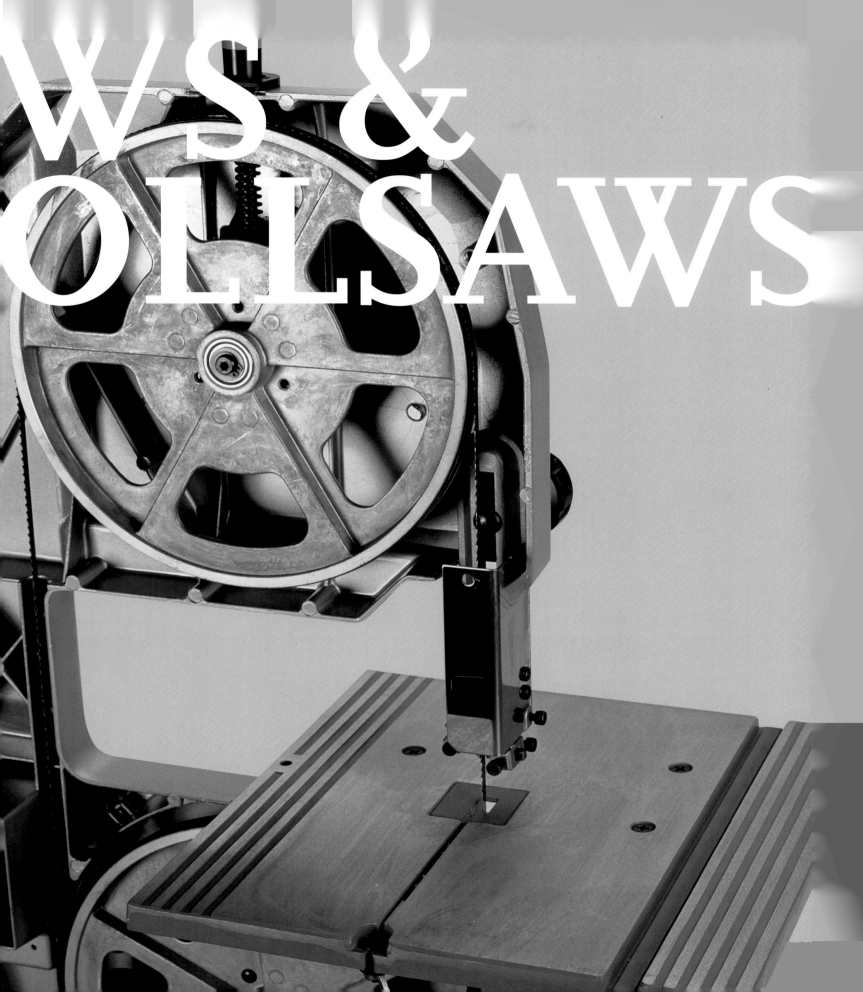

The Classics

DELTA 14-IN. BANDSAW

Big enough for heavy cuts or resawing yet compact enough to fit into the most cramped shop, this light-industrial workhorse has a simple construction that's functional as well as versatile. Delta's basic 14-in. saw comes in several versions, including the ivory-colored Platinum Edition model 28-263 and the enclosed-base model 28-280, shown here. Both versions have a sturdy cast-iron frame, a large tilting table, balanced 14-in. aluminum wheels, and a resilient motor mount that reduces noise and vibration. And these Delta bandsaws can grow with your needs: Unbolting the saw's two-piece cast frame and installing the 28-984 riser attachment extends the saw's cutting depth to a whopping $12\frac{1}{4}$ in.

DELTA 28-280 BANDSAW

WHEEL SIZE: 14 in.

MOTOR POWER/VOLTAGE: 1 hp; 115/230 volts

BLADE SPEED: 3,000 sfpm

BLADE LENGTH: $93\frac{1}{2}$ in. (105 in. with height attachment)

CUTTING CAPACITIES: $13\frac{3}{4}$ in. wide, $6\frac{1}{4}$ in. tall ($12\frac{1}{4}$ in. with optional height attachment)

TABLE TILT: 45° right, 10° left

HEIGHT: $65\frac{1}{2}$ in.

WEIGHT: 224 lb.

ACCESSORIES: riser block kit; rip fence (with either 25-in. or 37-in. rails); Cool Blocks guide blocks; 5-in. dust port

HEGNER 18V SCROLLSAW

The first Hegner scrollsaws, introduced in the early 1970s, were built in Germany, a country know for its high-quality manufacturing (think Porsche and BMW). The precision-manufactured Hegner quickly set a standard for curve-cutting excellence. Almost three decades later, Hegner scrollsaws are still revered for their silky smooth operation and European luxury-car quality. Hegner's most popular current model, the Multimax 18V has an 18-in.-deep throat. The "V" in 18V stands for variable speed, and this Hegner has an electronic motor that allows continuous adjustment of blade speed from 400 strokes per minute to 1,700 strokes per minute.

The saw's block-style blade clamps or optional Quick Clamps make rapid blade changes a breeze—a blessing when sawing fancy fretwork, where the blade must be clamped and unclamped repeatedly. For greater versatility, the Hegner's stroke length is adjustable: The long (19mm) stroke is good for most work, but when cutting fine veneers or sheet brass, the shorter (12mm) stroke increases control and reduces vibration.

HEGNER 18V SCROLLSAW

MOTOR POWER/VOLTAGE:
2.8 amps; 110 volts

MOTOR SPEED (STROKES PER MIN.):
400–1,700 variable speed

CUTTING CAPACITIES: 18-in. width
(throat depth), 2¼-in. depth

TABLE TILT: 45° left, 10° right

WEIGHT (WITHOUT STAND): 38 lb.

ACCESSORIES: metal stand; foot switch;
quick blade clamp; overlay table

Bandsaw World

FLOOR-STANDING BANDSAWS

With their heavy cast-iron or welded-steel frames, motors powerful enough to handle thick stock, and throats deep enough for wide panels, floor-standing models are the bandsaws of choice for woodshops of all sizes. Whether mounted on an open stand or enclosed base, floor-standing saws are a seminal machine in many fields of woodworking, including boatbuilding, chairmaking, and lutherie. Woodturners also use bandsaws regularly for cutting out turning blanks. And cabinetmakers and architectural woodworkers use bandsaws to resaw planks into veneers for matched grain patterns on wall paneling, doors and drawer fronts, and cabinet sides.

There's a stationary bandsaw size to suit any scale of work or amount of shop space: Saws with wheels 12 in. dia. or less are for hobby use, while a 14-in. to 16-in. wheeled saw powered by a ³/₄- or 1-hp motor is a great all-around setup that's tops in any small shop. For production work or heavy resawing, you'll be thankful if you spend the extra money on an 18-in. to 24-in. bandsaw with a motor that pumps out at least 1¹/₂ hp, such as the Epic BS-24, 24-in. bandsaw. Although you need a forklift to move the really big guns (with wheels 36 in. or larger), big stationary saws are terrific if you need to saw a plank for the yacht you're building or to cut a new wing spar for a Sopwith Camel you're restoring (we can dream, can't we?).

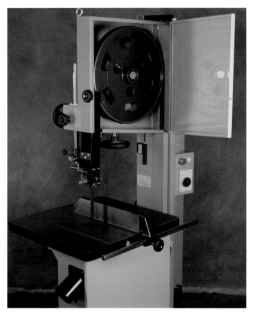

THE EPIC BS-24.

TABLE SAW OR BANDSAW?

There's a long-standing controversy among experienced woodworkers as to which machine is the cornerstone of a well-equipped woodshop. In one camp are sawdust jockeys who deem the table saw numero uno; in the other are proponents who claim the bandsaw is just the ticket. Although I currently reside in the table-saw camp, the versatility of the bandsaw is indisputable. From narrow ripping to re-sawing planks into veneers to cutting out a cabriole leg to shaping dovetails to scroll cutting intricate patterns, a well-tuned bandsaw can do it all. On top of that, a bandsaw is quieter, generally less expensive, and takes up less space than a table saw (hey, maybe I should switch camps!).

BENCHTOP BANDSAWS

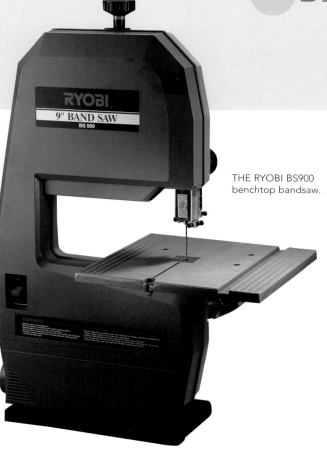

THE RYOBI BS900 benchtop bandsaw.

If benchtop machines have the right combination of compactness and storability for your small shop, chances are you either already own a small bandsaw, such as the Ryobi BS900, or it's on your short list of future acquisitions. With wheels sized between 8 in. and 12 in., benchtop bandsaws are smaller, lighter, and less powerful than floor models but are also *a lot* less expensive. As compact, self-contained units, bantam bandsaws come ready to bolt to a worktable or stand (or the floor, if you're acrophobic). Most models have a universal motor that drives the lower wheel with a toothed belt. This arrangement is adequate for light cutting tasks, such as cutting small parts out of wood or plastic. Benchtop bandsaws rarely accept blades wider than $1/2$ in. but can handle blades smaller than many floor models can—down to $1/16$ in. They're capable of very sensitive scrollwork, zooming around tight curves, or making delicate cuts in veneer or thin stock. Just don't expect these saws to do much resawing or to cut thick hardwoods.

THREE-WHEEL BANDSAWS

Question: How do you build a bandsaw with only 11-in.-dia. wheels that can cut a 40-in.-wide panel in half? Answer: Use three wheels instead of two! Threading the blade around a trio of wheels increases throat capacity significantly, without making the saw much larger than a benchtop model. Although cleverly designed, three-wheelers do have their characteristic quirks: The small-diameter wheels make blade tracking more difficult and they flex the blade considerably more than larger-diameter wheels do, resulting in more frequent blade breakage. Also, most threes don't have the depth capacity for resawing wide stock.

THE EUROPEAN INCA 710 BANDSAW has a 20-in.-deep throat, thanks to its three-wheel design and frame made from reinforced aircraft-quality aluminum-alloy castings.

If sawing small logs into lumber or ripping planks edgewise (namely, resawing) is a big part of your profession—or passion—you'll do it much more efficiently with a dedicated resaw. Resembling a short, stocky bandsaw, a resaw such as the Hitachi CB75F differs from a regular bandsaw in some important ways. First, in order to handle hefty logs and lumber, resaws have a large cutting depth relative to their throat depth (the Hitachi cuts more than $11^{3}/_{4}$ in. deep). Second, the saw's wheels and wide guide blocks are designed to handle extrawide blades (up to 3 in. wide), which resist bowing and deflection and handle heat better than narrow blades. To guide the stock, the CB75F is fitted with a short, sturdy rip fence, which adjusts with a rack-and-pinion mechanism that accurately sets cutting thickness. Larger commercial resaws are fitted with power feeds that utilize a pair of motorized rotating rollers, one on either side of the blade.

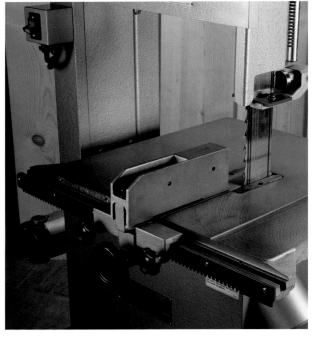

THE RESAW FENCE adjusts for precise cutting thickness using a rack-and-pinion mechanism.

THE HITACHI CB75F RESAW.

In a bandsaw, a pulley powers the lower wheel. The tension of the blade against the tires drives the upper wheel. The rotation of the blade around the wheels provides the cutting action.

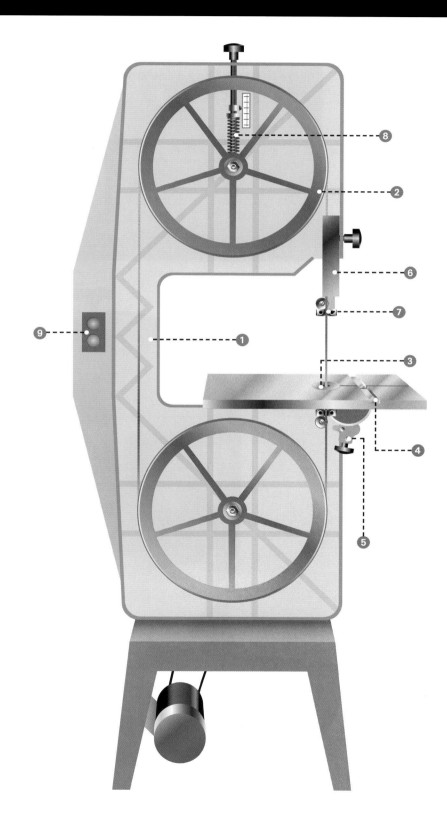

1. The cast or welded frame supports and aligns the wheels and table.

2. Wheels with rubber tires keep the blade running quietly and tracking smoothly.

3. Throat plate supports stock close to blade.

4. The tilting table has a miter-gauge slot.

5. Trunnions attach the table to the frame and allow tilting for beveled cuts.

6. The guide post slides down from the upper frame.

7. The guide assembly stabilizes and supports the blade close to the workpiece.

8. A spring assembly raises upper wheel to properly tension the blade.

9. The switch activates an electric motor in the base. Pulleys turn the lower wheel.

Bandsaw Features

FRAME CONSTRUCTION

The frame is the backbone of a bandsaw, the single component that supports the wheels, table, guide assemblies, and most other important parts of the saw. It takes a strong, rigid frame to support and align its wheels so that the blade maintains tension and tracks properly.

C-FRAME

Practically all vintage bandsaws have massive C-shaped frames. A very early design, often seen in giant cast-iron saws with 36-in. wheels, the C-frame supports the bandsaw's wheels and table. Wheel housings and blade guards fasten to the frame. C-frames are used on many contemporary saws, including the Delta 28-180.

BOX FRAME

Another saw design is based on a box-type frame, a one- or two-piece casting that provides both the main framework for the bandsaw and a cover for the back of the wheels. Internally ribbed for maximum strength, one-piece box frames of cast iron are used on heavy-duty saws, such as the Powermatic model 141 and the General model 490 15-in. saw.

Because of their light weight and ease of manufacture, cast-alloy box frames are common on small benchtop bandsaws like the Ryobi BS900, three-wheel bandsaws, and light-duty floor models, which are often constructed from separate upper and lower castings bolted together.

THE GENERAL MODEL 490 has box-frame construction.

THE DELTA 28-180's wheels and table mount to a cast-iron C-frame.

WELDED FRAME

A third type of frame, used in many large, industrial bandsaws such as the Epic BS-24, is the welded-steel frame. Welded frames provide the rigidity these big saws need without the weight or expense of cast iron.

TILTING TABLE

By tilting its table, a bandsaw can do all kinds of beveled and angled cuts. Most tables tilt up to 45° to the right to cut cone-shaped parts or curved, beveled bases for sculpture and other items. By also tilting up to 10° or 15° left, some models can cut pins for dovetail joints, which require both right-angled and left-angled cutting. On a good-quality bandsaw, the table is supported by a pair of semicircular trunnions, which fit into brackets attached to the frame.

It's worth noting that there's one breed of bandsaw out there that lacks a tilting table. The Sears 12-in. tilt-head bandsaw accomplishes bevel cuts by angling its entire cast-aluminum frame and wheel assembly relative to its large table, which remains level. A larger version of this saw, known as a bevel bandsaw or boatbuilder's bandsaw, is a huge cast-iron machine with a stationary table and tilting frame. These precision machines are designed for making the complex angled cuts needed for the planks and ribs used to build the hull of a large wooden ship.

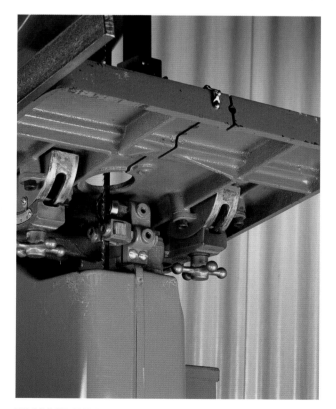

TRUNNION AND TILT MECHANISM on the General model 490 bandsaw.

BLADE GUIDES

While it's the alignment of a bandsaw's wheels that keeps the blade tracking evenly, the guides are responsible for supporting and aligning the blade directly above and below the workpiece. Each guide assembly in a typical set of guides, as found on the 15-in. General, has two components: (1) a pair of adjustable guide blocks, one on either side of the blade, provides side support that keeps the blade from twisting, and (2) a thrust bearing behind the rear edge of the blade keeps it from being pushed off the wheels by the force of the work being fed into the blade. Both guide blocks and thrust bearing adjust in and out to accommodate blades of different width and thickness.

REPLACEMENT GUIDES

Traditional metal guide blocks create heat and friction that can fatigue a bandsaw blade and cause premature tooth dulling and breakage. The most inexpensive yet effective improvement is to simply the replace the stock metal guides with Cool Blocks. Made from a phenolic plastic impregnated with a dry graphite lubricant, Cool Blocks can be set closer to the blade than metal guides for better support and longer blade life with less performance-robbing friction (these guides are stock on some Delta bandsaws).

Another solution to the bandsaw guide-block-friction blues is to replace both guide assemblies with ball-bearing guides. Available as retrofits for many different brands of saws, Carter Guide Conversion Kits include both upper and lower guide assemblies, each with three sealed ball bearings: one thrust bearing behind the blade and two set directly against the sides of the blade.

BLADE GUIDE ASSEMBLY on the General model 490.

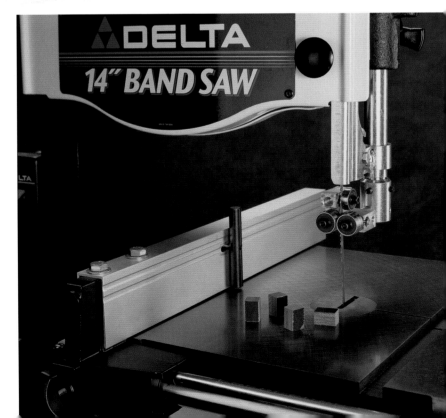

REPLACING STOCK METAL BLADE GUIDES with Cool Blocks reduces blade wear. Carter guides support and align the blade with ball bearings.

BLADE BRAKE

It's a principle of physics that once a body is in motion, it wants to stay in motion. Therefore, big, heavy bandsaw wheels act like flywheels and continue to spin a long time after you shut the power off. But most big (20-in. plus) bandsaws, like the Epic BS-24, let you stop the wheel quicker than nature allows with a simple foot brake. This not only stops the action pronto if there's an emergency, but it lets you make safe adjustments to the saw after a cut without the wait.

The Epic BS-24 bandsaw also features a built-in wheel brush to whisk away dust, which could coat the wheels and throw off the tracking.

A BLADE BRAKE can stop motion in a heartbeat. The Epic BS-24 has a brush to reduce dust buildup on the tires.

RIP OR RESAW FENCE

THE FASTTRAK BANDSAW FENCE with optional resawing attachment.

Because they're so popular for freehand curve cutting, many bandsaws don't come with a rip fence. But there are at least two good reasons to cut stock lengthwise on a bandsaw. First, even small bandsaws can cut stock thicker than what a table saw can handle. Second, the thin kerf of a bandsaw blade wastes less stock than even the thinnest thin-kerf table-saw blade. When sawing veneers, that means you get more slices per board and less waste.

Most manufacturers offer optional rip fences for their saws, but these are often fairly primitive, much like table-saw rip fences from 25 years ago. A more modern, full-featured alternative is to buy an aftermarket fence, such as the FasTTraK bandsaw fence, shown on a Delta 14-in. saw. This extruded-aluminum fence mounts to any saw table and has T-slot channels for smooth adjustment and for mounting accessories, like the optional resawing attachment shown in the photo at left.

Scrollsaws

THE MASTER OF TIGHT CURVES

Those skinny, fine-tooth scrollsaw blades can turn on a dime and cut out intricate patterns with edges smooth enough to pass without sanding. And because it's held at both ends, a scrollsaw blade can fit through a starter hole in the center of a part to make an inside cut.

What makes a good scrollsaw? Some qualities are universal, like smooth cutting with little vibration (try the penny test: put a coin on its edge on the saw's table and see if it falls over as the saw runs). Other qualities depend on the

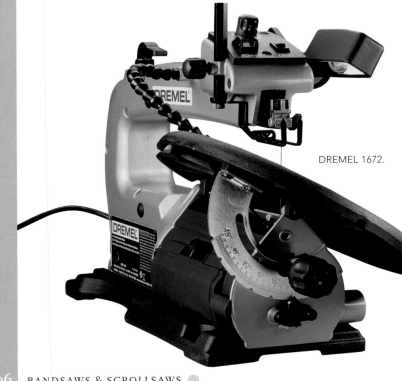

DEWALT DW788.

DREMEL 1672.

kind of work you want to do. If you cut lots of fretwork, quick blade changes are paramount and require a saw with easy-to-operate blade clamps. Big throat capacity and an ample-size saw table are essential if you work with large panels. Scrollsaws are sized by their throat capacity, which ranges from 14 in. to 30 in. deep. Most scrollsaw tables tilt, but if you often tackle beveled cuts, a large trunnion with stops for commonly used angles (0°, 15°, 30°, 45°), as featured on the Dremel 1672, will speed setup.

Variable-speed models are more expensive but add versatility. Slower speeds are better when cutting delicate materials with thin blades. Medium speeds are best for thick work or plastics, while high speed is reserved for fast or rough work.

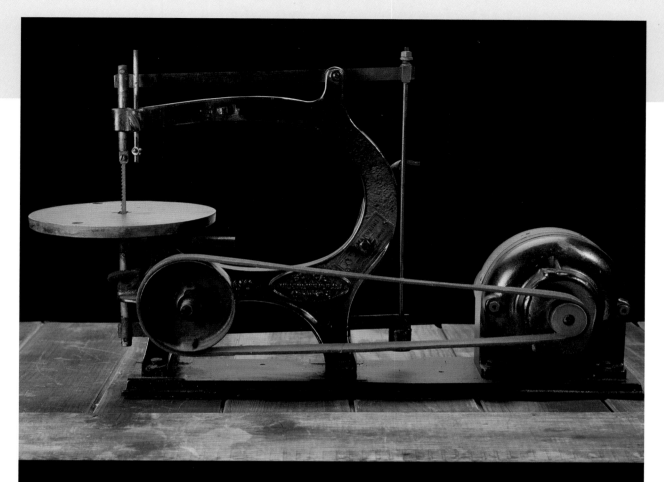

BOICE-CRANE MODEL 600

Harold Crane and the Boice brothers made some really great machinery in the early 20th century. Many of the Comet brand radial-arm saws they manufactured are still in use today in lumberyards and on construction sites. One of their smaller tools was the model 600 scrollsaw manufactured in the 1930s.

Although this saw has a relatively shallow, 10-in.-deep throat and has only enough capacity to cut 1¼-in.-thick stock, it's massively built—with a beefy C-frame, 8-in. round table, and base, all made from thick cast iron. The frame supports a parallel-arm

drive system that powers the blade, held in an interesting sliding rod assembly above the table. An on/off switch, conveniently mounted in the C-frame within easy reach, controls a ¼-hp-rated Robbings and Meyers motor, probably added by the dealer (a common practice at the time).

A 1¼-in. leather belt and wide pulleys (reminiscent of the old line-shaft driven tools of the time) transfer power to an eccentric wheel, which drives the saw's arms. A thin rod at the back of the C-frame links the arms and adjusts the blade tension.

Scrollsaw Features

ARM DESIGN AND CUTTING ACTION

The exact manner in which a scrollsaw moves its arms up and down has a lot to do with the way a saw performs. Modern scrollsaws use one of three arm designs: parallel arm, double parallel-link, and C-arm.

Parallel arms are most common. They link pivoting top and bottom arms with a tension rod at the back. The arms pivot on separate axles, both of which are mounted to the same frame. This design keeps the blade in a nearly vertical position during its entire up-and-down travel, re-sulting in great precision when using extrafine blades or when gang-cutting a stack of parts.

The double parallel-link arm design is found on saws made by Excalibur and on the DeWalt DW788. Two sets of small pivoting arms that hold the blade are connected by rods that pass through the saw's stationary top arm and base. The rods are driven back and forth by a pivoting link that connects them. This in-and-out action drives each arm in an up-and-down motion, keeping the blade more or less vertical during its stroke.

The C-arm design, used by saws such as the Delta Q3, holds the blade taut between the ends of a single C-shaped arm that rocks back and forth on a pivot at the rear. The rocking motion causes the blade to swing up and down in a slight arc, so it cuts more aggressively than other types of scrollsaws do, but it can take some getting used to when making delicate cuts with fine blades.

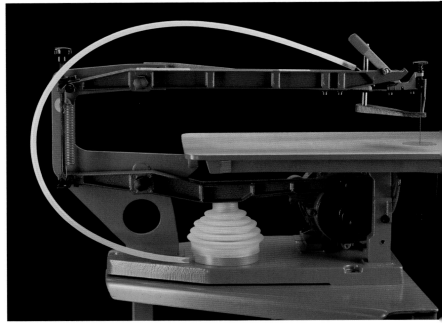

HEGNER MULTIMAX 18V features parallel-arm blade action.

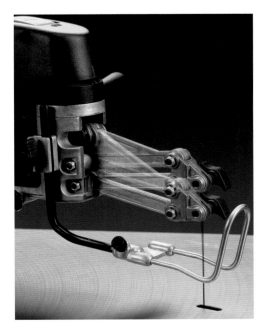

DOUBLE PARALLEL-link arms move the DeWalt DW788 blade up and down.

BLADE CLAMPS AND TENSIONING

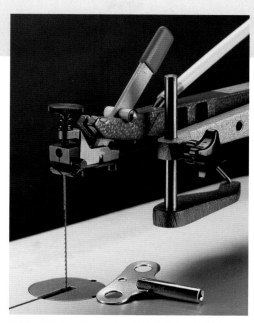

Scrollsaw blades are fairly delicate and tend to break, so blade clamps can be a scrollsaw's Achilles' heel. Contemporary saws use plain-end blades that fasten tightly into a pair of blade clamps, one at each end. Many saws, including Hegner's, use removable block-type blade clamps. One advantage of this system is that you can buy extra blade clamps and set them up with fresh blades. When a blade breaks, you clip in the already-clamped blade and you're in business.

Delta scrollsaws feature nonremovable Quick-set II blade clamps mounted to the ends of their arms. A flip of the locking lever on each clamp releases the blade or secures it in a flash.

TO TIGHTEN THE CLAMP BLOCKS that hold the blade on a Hegner scrollsaw, you use a cute windup-toy-like key.

TENSION ADJUSTMENT

Correct blade tension is critical in scrollsawing: too loose and the blade wanders and follows the grain of the wood; too tight and it breaks prematurely. Older parallel-arm saws have their tensioning rods at the rear of the saw, a long reach to a knob that requires many turns every time you change the blade. Most modern parallel-arm designs have a tension quick-release lever near the front of the upper arm, so that once the tension rod at the back is set, only a slight tweaking is necessary after blade changes. Civilized saws, such as the DeWalt DW788 and Delta Q3, have their tension adjusters up front, where they're easier to reach. The DW788 tension lever turns one way to release tension and the other way to add tension slowly and predictably.

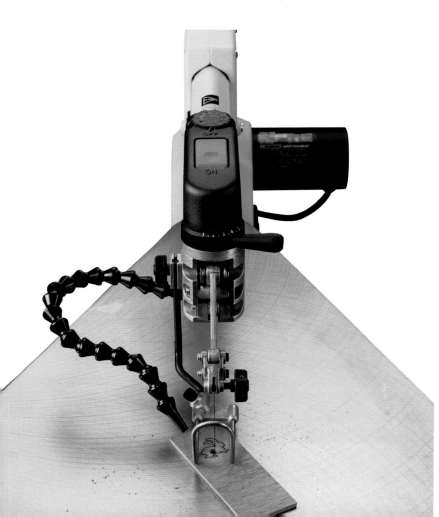

THE DEWALT DW788 BLADE-TENSION LEVER has a numbered scale so you can apply the same degree of tension each time.

The Business End

A BASIC BANDSAW blade kit includes a ¼-in. blade for basic cutting, a ½-in. blade for resawing and heavy cutting, and an ⅛-in. blade for scrolling and tight curves. A narrow sanding belt turns a bandsaw into an effective strip sander.

BANDSAW BLADES

Choosing a bandsaw blade from a well-stocked tool store or machine-supply catalog can make you as crazy as trying to pick only one scoop at a fancy ice-cream parlor with a hundreds of flavors on hand. Fortunately, just a small handful of blades will handle the majority of bandsaw cuts the average woodworker is apt to make (you're on your own with the ice cream).

A BASIC BLADE KIT

A ¼-in.-wide blade handles a wide variety of different cuts. Able to saw curves down to ⅝-in. radius, it's a great general-purpose blade you can leave on the saw. Choose a ¼-in. 4-tpi (tooth per inch) skip-tooth blade, for quick curved cuts in hardwoods up to 1½ in. thick, or a 6-tpi blade, for less speed but smoother cut edges.

For long, straight cuts, including rips and re-sawing, the ½-in. hook-tooth blade is a favorite.

Its 5° or 10° raked (angled) teeth produce a cut that's coarse, but they chew through thick wood quickly. While a 3-tpi blade is great for thick stock and resawing, a 4-tpi or 5-tpi blade yields smoother edges on medium-thick (6/4 or 8/4) stock and dense hardwoods.

If tight scroll cuts or joinery are the order of the day, then try an ⅛-in. 14-tpi blade on your bandsaw.

BANDSAW STRIP SANDER

Try using your bandsaw as a strip sander by fitting it with a loop sanding belt. It tracks like a wide blade, and most floor-model bandsaws can run a sanding belt—just back the guards off and increase the size of the slot in the throat plate.

SCROLLSAW BLADES

Unlike an all-purpose blade you can mount on a table saw and then forget about, scrollsaws need just the right kind of blade for the job if they're to perform at their best. First of all, that means you need to use a blade that's the right size for the thickness of the stock. Larger-numbered blades (12, 10, 7) are thicker and have fewer coarse teeth, so they're best for thick stock. Smaller-numbered blades (2, 00, 0000) have more fine teeth and are thinner, to suit cutting thinner materials.

SCROLLSAW BLADES come in many different types and sizes, each suited to a different task and thickness of material.

A SCROLLSAW BLADE PRIMER

A blade's tooth style is another choice you have to make when selecting the right blade—and it's a hot topic among scrollers. Here's a quick primer on some popular blade styles:

PTG stands for precision-ground teeth. These accurately ground teeth slice through wood fibers (as well as other materials) quickly and cleanly. A good choice for all-around scrollwork.

Double-tooth blades have pairs of teeth followed by a flat gullet for better chip removal. These blades are fast cutting and leave cleaner edges in wood, plastic, and soft metals, like aluminum and brass. They also cut thin materials very cleanly.

Reverse-tooth blades have 5–9 reverse teeth per blade to reduce tearout on the underside of the cut and keep the kerf smooth with no feathering. They do cut a bit slower than blades of the same size that lack reversed teeth.

Crown tooth blades have bidirectional teeth that cut on both the up and the down stroke. These blades have the advantage of running either end up. They cut relatively smoothly but can burn dense hardwoods or chip delicate materials. Their rate of cut is also slow compared to reverse-tooth blades.

Spiral blades look like regular blades that have been twisted so their teeth can cut in any direction. They are good for intricate fretwork, especially with large workpieces, because you don't have to turn the work to negotiate changes in cutting direction. On the down side, they leave a rougher kerf than standard blades do, so some sanding is in order.

Skip regular- and reverse-tooth blades have a space between each tooth for better chip clearance. These are great blades for fast cuts in thick woods when the smoothness of the cut edge isn't crucial. Skip reverse-tooth blades have 5–9 teeth reversed at the bottom end for less splintering on the underside of the work.

The Cutting Edge

PORTER-CABLE
725 PORTA-BAND

Even the most hard-core sawdust jockey needs to work with metal now and then. Whether building a table-saw extension table from angle iron or a grinder stand out of tubular square stock, cutting steel and iron is tough work. But these cuts are a lot easier if you use a tool that I consider the ultimate hacksaw: a portable bandsaw. A longtime staple of plumbers and metalworkers, the portable bandsaw isn't some new technological marvel, but it is a remarkably handy tool that performs cuts well beyond the capabilities of a regular bandsaw.

THE METAL-MUNCHING CHAMP

Made primarily for cutoff work, the Porter-Cable model 725 Porta-Band cuts pipe, angles, bars, rounds, or rectangular tubing up to $3\frac{3}{8}$ in. wide and $4\frac{1}{8}$ in. deep. Unlike stationary bandsaws, the Porta-Band isn't for curves; it uses a bimetal blade to straight-cut mild steel, aluminum, brass, bronze, cast iron, stainless steel, and even fiberglass and plastic stock. At 17 lb., the saw isn't much heavier than a big router, so you can carry it into the deepest recesses of a basement or crawl space to cut a sewer pipe or work at the top of a ladder to shorten a steel stanchion.

THE INTERIOR of the Porter-Cable model 725 shows how closely it resembles its two-wheel big brothers.

PORTER-CABLE 725 PORTA-BAND

MOTOR POWER/SPEED: 4.5 amps/ 195 sfpm; 6.5 amps/245 sfpm

BLADE LENGTH: $44\frac{7}{8}$ in.

CUTTING CAPACITIES: $3\frac{3}{8}$-in. round stock; $3\frac{3}{8}$-in. by $4\frac{1}{8}$-in. rectangular stock

LENGTH OF TOOL: $19\frac{1}{2}$ in.

WEIGHT: 17 lb.

ACCESSORIES: portable vise; stationary stand

A MINI TWO-WHEELER

A portable bandsaw looks something like a stationary two-wheel model but has big differences. Instead of having flat rims, the wheels have beveled rims, so the blade runs at an angle. This provides clearance so the saw isn't limited by its throat depth and can cut material of any length. Instead of a table, the Porta-Band has an alignment foot, which positions the blade squarely to the work. Precision ball-bearing guides stabilize the blade, which travels at either 245 surface feet per minute (sfpm)—for nonferrous metals, mild steel, and cast iron—or 195 sfpm, necessary for tough-to-cut materials like chrome or tungsten steel.

If lumber came from trees all square and straight, we wouldn't need jointers and planers. Even boards sawn arrow-straight usually twist, bow, crook, and cup and need to be dressed flat, straight, and true. For those of us that don't have time to true every edge and surface with a handplane, jointers and thickness planers are miraculous time-savers.

A jointer's sharp cutterhead quickly cleans up rough-sawn, irregular, or warped edges, bringing them to perfect square. It also flattens a board's face, preparing it for phase two of the milling process: thickness planing. A few passes under a planer's cutterhead produces flat lumber at the required thickness.

Once only available as expensive industrial machines that took enormous effort to move, jointers and planers now come in many sizes and capacities. Compact benchtop jointers and portable planers are affordable enough for hobbyists, while stationary planers and jointers suit the requirements of professional shops.

DELTA
WOODWORKING MACHINERY

12 1/2" PORTABLE PLANER

DELTA
6" VARIABLE SPEED
BENCH JOINTER

PLANERS

The Classics

POWERMATIC MODEL 50 JOINTER

Featuring king-size tables, heavy iron castings, and a stable enclosed base, the 6-in. Powermatic model 50 has long been a classic heavy-duty performer. The 56¼-in.-long table makes the model 50 a long-bed jointer, capable of truing up planks lengthy enough to build a clipper ship. Both infeed and outfeed tables are mounted on sturdy dovetailed ways to keep them aligned. Depth of cut is set at the infeed table via a rapid-adjustment lever. The cutterhead's three M2 tool-steel knives are easy to set to the same cutting arc, thanks to jackscrews that elevate them precisely (see the photo on p. 225). The Powermatic's cast-iron fence is the model of what a good jointer fence should be: large, solid, and dead-on accurate.

Unfortunately, the model 50 is no longer in production. The Powermatic Co., now owned by Jet, has replaced it with the Taiwanese-made Artisan series model 54, a 6-in. jointer for the home-shop woodworker. The model 50's big brother, the 8-in. model 60, is still produced for the professional market.

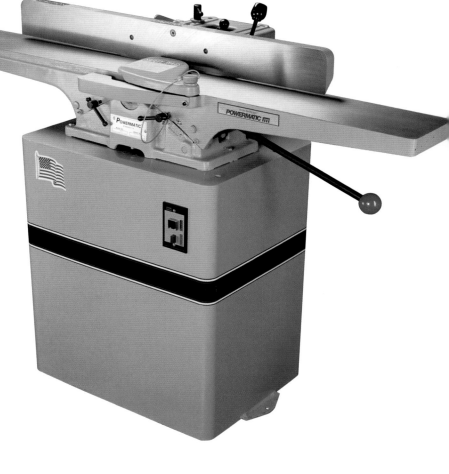

POWERMATIC MODEL 50
6-IN. LONG-BED JOINTER

TABLE SIZE: 56¼ in. long, 6¼ in. wide

TABLE OPERATION: infeed: lever; outfeed: crank

FENCE SIZE: 36 in. long, 4 in. high

MOTOR TYPE/SIZE: induction; ¾ hp

CUTTERHEAD SPEED/CUTS PER MIN.: 7,000 rpm/ 21,000 cuts per min.

CUTTING CAPACITY: 6 in. wide by ½ in. deep

WEIGHT: 265 lb. (with stand)

RYOBI AP-10
PORTABLE PLANER

In 1985, Ryobi revolutionized home-shop wood-working by developing and marketing the first portable planer. Unlike expensive cast-iron giants, the AP-10 was an affordable machine compact enough to stow under a benchtop when not in use. The lightweight machine was also easily portable, a feature that allowed contractors and carpenters to surface lumber right at their job sites. Although its capacity was limited (10-in.-wide boards up to 5 in. thick) and its universal motor could only shave off $3/32$ in. in a single pass, the AP-10 fulfilled the thicknessing needs of a great many small-shop woodworkers, evidenced by its resounding popularity: Ryobi sold over 50,000 machines in the first four years (it was also sold under the Sears brand, as model 351.23372). By the time the model was retired in 1993, a year after its larger-capacity replacement (the 12-in. AP-12) was introduced, Ryobi had sold almost 100,000 AP-10 planers!

RYOBI AP-10 PORTABLE THICKNESS PLANER

MOTOR TYPE/SIZE: universal; 13 amps

CUTTING CAPACITIES: 10⅛ in. wide, between ⅛ in. and 5 in. thick

MAX. CUT PER PASS: ³⁄₃₂ in.

CUTTERHEAD SPEED: 8,000 rpm

FEED RATE/CUTS PER IN.: 26.2 ft. per min./51 cuts per in.

WEIGHT: 57.2 lb.

OPTIONAL ACCESSORIES: dust hood; rollers; carbide knives

Tools of the Past

THE INDOMITABLE PARKS PLANER

Founded in 1884, the Parks Woodworking Machine Co. established an early reputation building interesting combination machines with names like the Carpenter Shop Special, Cabinet Shop Special, and Wagon Shop. Although Parks later built bandsaws and other machines, its greatest success (in the nearly 100 years it remained in business) was its 12-in. No. 95 planer.

THE MANY GUISES OF PARKS 12-IN. PLANER

Clumsy compared to its streamlined 20-in. model, the popular No. 95 with its odd side-mounted gearbox and 1930s' industrial styling was small and affordable enough for amateurs but beefy enough for many commercial shops. Parks sold its cast-iron 12-in. planers in a variety of configurations, all built around the No. 95, which was the basic machine without stand or motor. The Parks No. 97 shown at right included a stand, pulley guard, motor, and motor control.

Parks planers were sold direct and also through Sears stores, relabeled under the Sears brand. The 12-in. planer appeared in the Sears 1939 catalog selling for $185 without stand or motor. Available today only on the used-machinery market, Parks planers remain popular, and replacement parts are still available for them.

THE PARKS NO. 97 was so popular and sturdy that many of these planers are still in use today.

THE CLASSIC DAVIS & WELLS JOINTER

In the 1930s, a fellow named Davis had just bought a house in Los Angeles and needed some woodworking equipment to build furniture. A patternmaker by trade, he decided to build his own machinery and make it as durable and simple in design as possible. (Legend has it that he ran the plans for each machine he designed by his grandmother. If it was too complicated for her to understand, he simplified it further.)

Davis's machinery business got off to a successful start, and he soon formed a partnership with an investor named Wells. Davis & Wells produced many simple, precisely built machines, which are still highly prized, including bandsaws, tilting-arbor table saws, spindle shapers, and sin-

gle and double horizontal boring machines. In recent decades, the company was bought and sold half a dozen times (manufacturing rights were once sold to mainland China). The last Davis & Wells machinery was manufactured in 1982, after which the company was liquidated.

Although it has only a 6-in.-long cutterhead, the Davis & Wells jointer shown above has a generous $8\frac{1}{4}$-in.-wide by $44\frac{1}{2}$-in.-long table (the company also made a 62-in. long-bed model). The tables show Davis's penchant for elegant design solutions: Both infeed and outfeed tables are made from the same casting—just reversed on the tool's ways. The jointer's extralarge ($2\frac{3}{8}$-in.-wide) rabbet ledge not only makes rabbeting easier but provides a mounting ledge for the fence on the outfeed table side. A pair of knobs raises and lowers the tables for depth-of-cut adjustments.

UNIQUE FENCE DESIGN

The Davis & Wells unique 29-in.-long cast-iron fence sits on a base with two long slots in it. Loosen a pair of levers and the fence not only moves back and forth but can be set skewed. By running stock at a slight angle, the knives take a shearing cut that leaves curly wood grain cleaner than straight cutting can. Positive stops lock the fence square or allow tilting 45° in either direction.

THE DAVIS & WELLS JOINTER FENCE allows it to be skewed, which reduces tearout when jointing highly figured or wild-grain stock.

Jointer World

STATIONARY JOINTERS

Like boats, jointers come in all shapes and sizes, from little dinghy-size short-bed models, just right for light cuts and occasional use, to aircraft-carrier size long beds that will stand up to daily abuse in a factory that makes log-cabin kits. Jointers are sized by the length of their knives, which limits the widest board you can surface in a single pass. The most popular jointers are 6 in. long, as 4-in. jointers are too small and 8-in. models are too big for most small shops.

Less expensive models are mounted on open stands, while enclosed cabinet models (costing slightly more but well worth it) are more stable and heavier, to dampen vibration. If you saw and dry lumber yourself or buy rough stock to save money, get the widest- and longest-table jointer you can afford. Besides squaring up crooked edges, your jointer will flatten cupped, bowed, and/or twisted boards on one surface so they're ready to run through a thickness planer.

MODERN MODELS ARE SAFER

While many a vintage jointer works as well today as it did 50 years ago, woodworkers often prefer the modern safety and convenience features that newer models afford. For example, the Delta model 37-195 Professional 6-in. jointer has a cylindrical cutterhead (far safer than the square cutterheads found on older models). The knives are adjusted with jackscrews, for quicker and easier changes. The Delta's on/off switch is mounted on a stalk above the infeed table where it's easy to reach. And to make operation a cleaner proposition, there's also a 4-in. dust port built into the tool's enclosed base.

DELTA MODEL 37-195
Professional 6-in.
stationary jointer.

A Look Inside

A pair of parallel tables joined to a base, a jointer guides wood over a cutter-head, which trims an edge or surface straight and smooth.

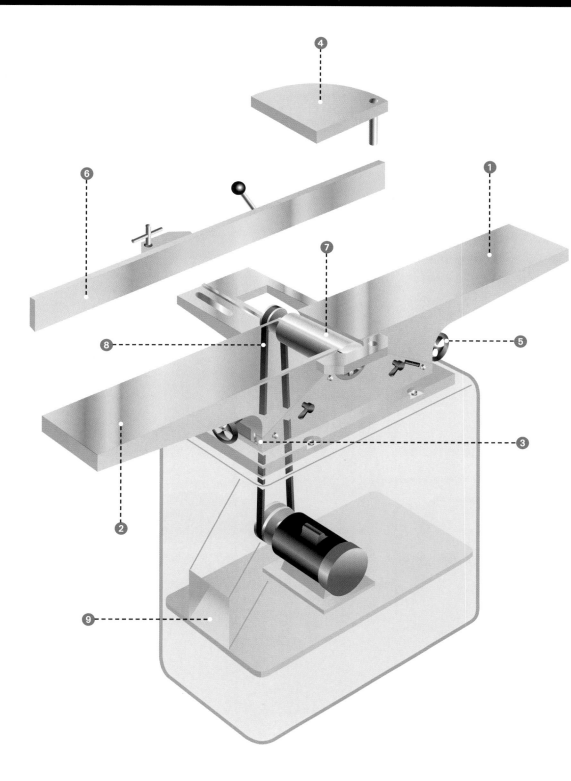

1. The infeed table raises and lowers to set the depth of cut.

2. The outfeed table supports the stock after the cut.

3. The ways allows tables to slide on the base and adjust up and down.

4. The knife guard is spring retracted; it protects the user from the cutterhead.

5. The handwheel adjusts the infeed table height.

6. The adjustable fence holds the work square or at an angle to the table.

7. The cutterhead holds two or three knives.

8. The belt drive from a large motor pulley spins the cutterhead at high rpm.

9. The chip chute or dust port ejects shavings to the floor or dust-collection system.

BENCHTOP JOINTERS

Professional woodworkers need the power and capacity of a stationary jointer. But part-time wood craftsmen often don't have the budget or shop space to devote to a full-size machine. A benchtop jointer is a good choice for space-challenged individuals, as well as model makers, luthiers, and hobbyists who routinely joint short parts and rarely handle long stock. Made from lightweight alloys rather than heavy cast iron, benchtop jointers are portable and easy to store.

Unfortunately, if a benchtop jointer is right for you, your choices are quite limited. Since Ryobi discontinued their pint-sized JP155, Delta's 6-in. 37-070 is one of the only benchtop models currently on the market. Nevertheless, this Delta is a sophisticated machine with a variable-speed universal motor, which lets you change cutterhead speed to suit the material you're jointing: slow

for plastics, medium for softwoods, and fast for hardwoods. Other innovative features on the 37-070 include a pivoting depth-of-cut pointer, with a large easy-to-read scale, and a flip-up cutterhead lock, which helps make knife changes safer and easier.

DELTA'S 6-IN. 37-070 BENCHTOP JOINTER.

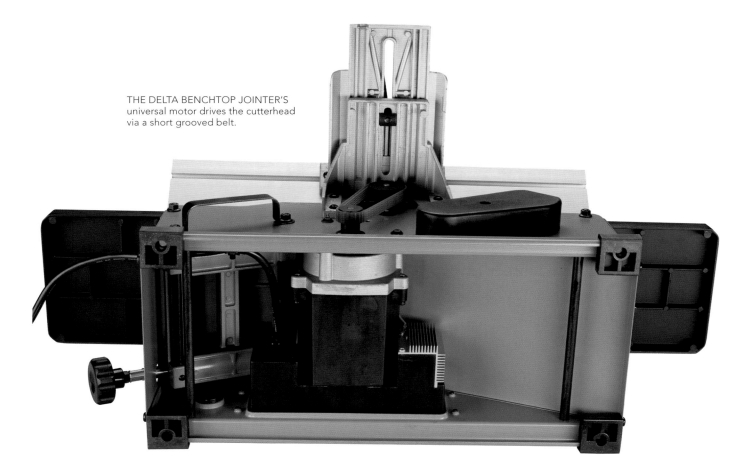

THE DELTA BENCHTOP JOINTER'S universal motor drives the cutterhead via a short grooved belt.

COMBINATION JOINTER/PLANERS

Serious woodworkers regard the jointer and planer as a performance team, like Astaire and Rogers (only for dressing and dimensioning lumber, not dancing). What would be more natural, then, than to combine the abilities of these two machines into a single unit?

INCA MODEL 570 combination jointer and planer.

If you have a small shop or work rough stock only on occasion, the advantages of a combination jointer/planer are many. A dual-purpose machine takes up only one spot in a crowded garage or basement shop. With over/under combo units (with top tables for jointing and a planer bed underneath), such as the Inca model 570, the same cutterhead is used for both jointing and planing, so there's only one set of knives to have to keep sharpened (side-by-side models, like the Hitachi P12RA, have separate cutterheads driven by a single motor). And over/under machines have the same width capacity for jointing as for planing—$10\frac{1}{4}$ in. for the Inca 570.

But just as Astaire and Rogers didn't always prance in perfect harmony, combo jointer/planers have some drawbacks. On the over/under Inca, you can't jump from one operation to the other without taking the time to switch the machine over. Before planing is possible, you must remove the jointer's outfeed table, fit a depth-adjustment wheel, and pivot the dust hood up over the cutterhead.

SWITCHING FROM THE JOINTING FUNCTION to planing requires some setup.

Jointer Features

DEPTH ADJUSTMENT AND FENCE

The majority of jointers have a pair of tables, infeed and outfeed, that move independently on a dovetailed ways machined into a heavy cast base. The infeed table raises or lowers relative to the cutterhead, to set the depth of cut. The outfeed table is set level with the top of the cutterhead's cutting arc.

Most jointers use either adjustment levers or handwheels. Levers are fast to use, especially when you want to make a big change quickly—say, to take a chamfer or rabbet cut. Although they're not as quick, handwheels for setting depth allow for finer adjustments.

FENCE STYLES

A jointer's fence supports the stock on the bed when edge jointing. Changing its position across the table exposes more or less of the cutterhead, for wider or narrower stock. A good fence is long enough to keep long work steady and tall enough to stabilize wide workpieces.

The majority of fences, including the Delta jointer's, attach to a center-mounted sliding bracket. General and Woodtek jointers feature an end-mounted fence, with a lever that locks both lateral motion and fence tilt.

Although they're set square 99 percent of the time, all jointer fences tilt up to 45° for bevel work, with positive stops at 45°, 90°, and 135°.

THE DELTA PROFESSIONAL 6-IN. JOINTER has an ingenious locking mechanism mounted to the end of its lever that prevents inadvertent depth changes.

THE FENCE ON THE DELTA PROFESSIONAL 6-IN. JOINTER is center mounted on a tubular arm and bracket, which adjusts with a rack-and-pinion mechanism. Turning a large knob easily moves the fence in or out.

A KNIFE GUARD IS AN essential safety feature. Most spring-loaded guards, such as on this vintage Rockwell 8-in. jointer, adjust themselves automatically if the position of the fence changes.

GOOD CUTTERHEAD

Regardless of how pricey a jointer is, its knives eventually dull and need removal and resharpening. You can forestall the process by fitting long-lasting carbide knives, but these are quite expensive. Getting knives out is a breeze; the chore is remounting them so that each knife is raised to the same cutting arc and is flush and parallel with the outfeed table.

Predictably, some cutterheads make knife adjustments easier than others. Modern portables feature reversible and/or disposable insert knives (see p. 233). In stationary planers, three knife-

(see p. 233)

adjusting systems are commonly used. The most basic has only gibs and setscrews to secure each knife, making adjustments painstaking. The most commonly used system, featured in Delta and Powermatic cutterheads, employs special lifters called jackscrews in each knife slot. These let you raise or lower a knife by turning Allen screws. The third system, featured on many Taiwanese-made jointers, features a special knife-setting jig that works in conjunction with springs in the cutterhead's knife slots.

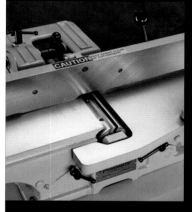

RABBETING LEDGE

On a table saw or with a router, yes. But cutting a rabbet on a jointer? That's what the small ledge that extends beyond the leading edge of the infeed table is for, as seen on the Powermatic 6-in. jointer. The larger and longer the ledge, the easier it is to support a wider or thicker board during the cut. Cutting depth sets the rabbet's depth, though rabbets that are much deeper than $1/8$ in. are best done in several passes.

THE CUTTERHEAD ON THE DELTA 37-070 BENCHTOP JOINTER (for clarity, shown with the gib and knife removed) has a pair of jackscrews that engage slots in each knife to allow easy height adjustments during replacement.

Planer World

STATIONARY PLANERS

Stationary planers are distinguished by heavy bases and powerful induction motors controlled by magnetic on/off switches, which provide over-load protection and safety. The switch turns off automatically if there's a blown breaker or power failure. With cutterheads that range from 12 in. to 18 in., 24 in., 36 in., and wider, midsize 15-in. stationaries are most popular in smaller shops.

A light-industrial planer, such as the 15-in. Delta DC-380, is a cast-iron, four-post machine with a three-knife cutterhead. Stationary-planer design hasn't changed much over the years. The Delta and other imported planers are very similar in design to the Rock-well 13-in. planer made in the 1970s.

Although they're a lot more expensive than portables, stationary planers give you your money's worth if you surface lots of rough lum-ber or often level glued-up panels. The heavy, vibration-damping construction of these solid machines not only produces good results in fig-ured woods (see the sidebar on p. 230) but lets you take fairly deep cuts—$1/8$ in. or more in a single pass. That's just the ticket when you need to reduce rough 8/4 stock down to $1\,3/8$ in. in a hurry. Just remember, even the best machines leave tool marks, so surfaces require some sand-ing or scraping after a run under the cutterhead.

THE DELTA DC-380 15-in. stationary planer.

A planer uses powered rollers to feed lumber under a whirring cutterhead. The distance between the planer bed and cutterhead determines the depth of cut and final thickness of the planed board.

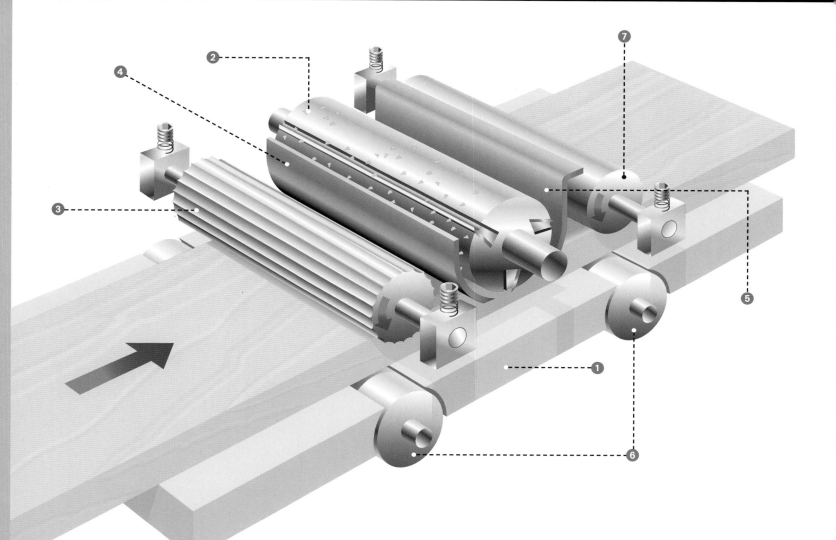

1. The bed supports the stock as it passes under the cutterhead.

2. The cutterhead contains two or three knives.

3. The infeed roller, which feeds the stock into the cutterhead, is often serrated for a better grip on the board.

4. The chipbreaker deflects the chips, which are forced out of the planer by the action of the cutterhead.

5. The pressure bar keeps the stock firmly on the bed to prevent sniping (gouges in the surface).

6. The bed rollers (on some models) reduce friction to make stock feeding easier.

7. The outfeed roller is smooth to avoid marring the freshly surfaced board.

PORTABLE PLANERS

If you wanted to change the thickness of the boards you bought at the lumberyard, there was a time when your only choices were to work up a sweat with a handplane or buy an expensive stationary planer. All that changed when Ryobi introduced the first affordable portable planer in the 1980s. Ryobi's small-size AP-10 opened the floodgates on a slew of portable machines, which have made thicknessing lumber possible for a whole generation of small-shop woodworkers.

While they aren't build to handle the day-in, day-out rigors of a cabinet shop or furniture-production plant, portable planers do a great job of smoothing and reducing lumber to a desired thickness. Unlike large planers, portables are light enough to carry to wherever you need them. You want to chainsaw some planks out in the yard? Why not run an extension cord and surface them right where they've been cut? Portables let you dimension lumber on the job site, making them popular with carpenters and home remodelers. And despite their lighter construction and smaller cutting capacities, portables are full-featured machines capable of doing quality work.

Planer Features

FEED ROLLERS

Take a peek up above a planer's bed and you'll see that there's a lot going on up there. Astride the cutterhead is a pair of spring-loaded, chain- or gear-driven rollers whose job it is to propel the stock through the planer while keeping it flat against the bed. Infeed rollers are rubber or serrated metal to grab stock and feed it steadily with less slippage. Segmented infeed rollers on heavy-duty planers, like the Delta DC-380 15-in. stationary model, are great when two or more boards of slightly different thicknesses are fed through at the same time.

THE SEGMENTED INFEED ROLLER on the Delta DC-380 15-in. planer.

OUTFEED AND BED ROLLERS

Outfeed rollers are either smooth metal, rubber, or plastic. Softer rubber rollers are great if you use a planer without dust collection (it is hoped only outdoors or at a job site) because hard rollers tends to emboss chips into smoothly planed surfaces. Stationary machines also have bed rollers, located directly below the infeed and outfeed rollers. These reduce friction so that rough-sawn or sappy green lumber sail through the machine without hanging up on the bed.

Stationary planers usually have two feed-rate speeds (15 or 16 feet per minute and 20 to 30 feet per minute), controlled by a lever on the feed-roller gearbox. Slower rates are better for getting a clean final surface on hardwoods, whereas faster rates provide a quick way to smooth rough softwoods.

THE DELTA DC-380 has two feed rates, which are switched on and off from the gearbox at the center.

PUTTING THE WORK TO BED

Every planer has some kind of table or bed that supports and guides the stock that's being thicknessed. The distance between the cutterhead and the bed determines the thickness of the planed work. Although each planer has a mechanism for changing this distance, not all work the same way. Most portables and light-industrial stationary models have compact motor-feed roller-cutterhead heads, which raise and lower to change cutting depth. Some heavy-duty stationary models change table height instead, thus leaving their heavy-duty cutterhead and feed mechanisms in place (one portable, the Makita 2012 also has a moving bed). Stationary models have the advantage of heavier cast-iron beds and more powerful induction motors, but their movable bed arrangement requires you to readjust the height of infeed and outfeed roller stands or auxiliary supports every time you change the planing thickness.

WHILE MANY PORTABLE PLANERS adjust for thickness by changing the cutterhead position relative to the bed, the Makita 2012 moves the bed relative to the cutterhead.

KEEPING THE PRESSURE ON

Something that most stationary planers have (and most portable planer owners *wish* their machines had) is a chipbreaker and a pressure bar. Located in-between the infeed roller and the cutterhead, a planer's chipbreaker works as it does on a handplane: to prevent wood grain from lifting and tearing out ahead of the cutter. The pressure bar is just behind the cutterhead and keeps warped, thin, or long boards flat on the planer bed as they pass under the cutterhead, thus preventing planer snipe (gouges in the stock due to the board lifting up off the bed and into the cutterhead).

DEPTH SETTING

How thick is a board going to be when it comes out the end of a thickness planer? That's what the machine's scale and cursor tell you. Mounted on top or on the infeed side of the machine, most scales are calibrated in inches, in millimeters and centimeters, or both. But even if you know how thick you want your surfaced lumber to be, how do you know how much the planer is going to remove during a given pass? That's what a cut indicator is for. Unfortunately only found on a handful of planers, a cut indicator is a small spring-loaded device that presses down on the top of the stock just as it's entering the planer. The indicator's needle reads a scale that shows you the thickness of cut, such as on the DeWalt DW733. The indicator helps prevent you from accidentally taking too big a cut on a single pass, which can result in a jammed board or some nasty grain tearout.

DEPTH SCALE AND CUT INDICATOR on the DeWalt DW733.

DEPTH-STOP PRESETS

Setting the cut on a planer to an exact thickness setting can take careful cranking and a little hand/eye coordination. But clever portable planer designers have added a smart innovation: adjustable depth-stop presets that make common cutting thicknesses—$\frac{1}{4}$ in., $\frac{1}{2}$ in., etc.—easier to set accurately. The DeWalt DW733 portable planer, shown at bottom left, uses a turret-style depth stop, just like the kind you'd find on a plunge router. Once the turret is set to the desired preset, it stops the motor/cutterhead carriage as it is cranked down. The Ridgid TP1300 features a depth stop that's not a turret but a sliding gauge with eight different preset thicknesses.

THE DEPTH STOP TURRET on the DeWalt DW733 is similar to that used on a plunge router.

SPECIAL FEATURES

A thickness planer's powered feed rollers send boards through in one direction as they're surfaced, but there's no reverse setting to bring them back after the pass. A seemingly small feature built into some planers, a stock transfer roller lets you glide heavy boards across the top of the unit from the outfeed side back to the infeed side, so you can take lots of passes without passing out from exhaustion. By working with a helper on the other side of the planer, you can scoot through a pile of rough lumber in no time. On portable models like the Delta 22-560, the foam rubber–covered roller doubles as a comfortable carrying handle.

THE FOAM RUBBER–COVERED stock transfer roller on the Delta 22-560 doubles as a carrying handle.

ON THE DELTA 22-560, the cutterhead is locked by means of a lever on the side of the planer.

THE DEWALT DW733 uses a bar to set the cutterhead lock.

PUTTING YOUR PLANER IN A HEAD LOCK

The heads or integrated motor/cutterhead carriages found on many newer portable planers help keep them light and easy to use. Unfortunately, any slop in the mechanism that raises and lowers the head can cause snipe and upset surfacing quality. To combat this problem, portables like the 12½-in. Delta 22-560 and the DeWalt DW733 have built-in head locks. Operated by a lever, the lock clamps the head carriage to the planer's support columns, so it remains rock steady during thicknessing. The lock must be released before cutting-depth changes are possible. Therefore, to save the time involved in repeatedly releasing and resetting the head lock, most people only use it during the final planing pass when surface quality is most crucial.

THE NARROW BLADES
of the Makita 2012
planer are secured by a
locking bar.

REVERSIBLE KNIVES

To make knife changes less tedious, many portable planers have cutterheads that use dual-edged, disposable knives, which are easy to reverse and inexpensive to replace (the Esta disposable-knife system is an available option on Bridgewood stationary planers). For accurate positioning, these cutterheads have positioning pins or ledges that engage holes or notches in each knife. A special magnetic knife tool, included with portables like the Delta 22-560 and the Ridgid TP1300, lets you remove and replace sharp knives without touching them.

A slightly different cutterhead design in planers like the Makita 2012 uses narrow insert blades, which are aligned and secured by a locking bar that engages a slot running the length of the blade.

DUST HOOD

Despite a planer's natural ability to shower a shop with impressive quantities of shavings, many units come equipped only with a chip deflector, which doesn't provide a connection to a shop vacuum or dust-control system. A dust hood is a highly recommended option for practically any model, unless you like to wade through knee-deep sawdust piles. Hoods on stationary models often draw chips directly upward, while portables, such as the Makita 2012, have hoods with side-exhausting dust ports. Although a portable's ports are typically sized for a standard $2\frac{1}{2}$-in.-dia. vacuum hose, even a small planer's output can quickly fill up the average shop vacuum.

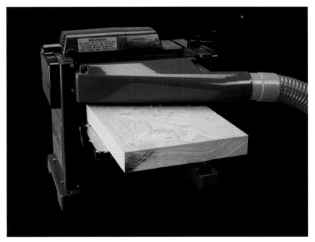

OPTIONAL DUST HOOD for the Makita
2012 portable planer.

The Cutting Edge

RIDGID TP1300 PORTABLE PLANER

The newest, easiest-to-use machines in the wood-shop aren't always the largest and most powerful ones. While various portable planers have lots of great individual features, Ridgid's TP1300 seems to have them all—and then some. Its basic design is much like other portables, with a consolidated motor/cutterhead, which travels on four steel posts, and a locking lever that secures the carriage for silky-smooth surfacing. Its universal 15-amp motor has thermal overload protection and is controlled by an oversized on/off switch that's easy to shut off in a hurry. With a bed big enough to handle stock up to 13 in. wide and 6 in. thick, the TP1300 has a pair of extralarge fold-down extension tables to support long stock.

Some features that make the Ridgid easier to operate include a depth-of-cut indicator and a sliding depth stop with eight different presets. Another innovative touch on the TP1300 is the small storage compartment on the side, which holds wrenches and a special magnetic holder used for changing its double-edged, reversible knives. Inside the lid, there are even printed instructions (in three languages) for changing knives, in case the instruction manual isn't handy when you need it.

THE RIDGID TP1300 has both a depth-of-cut indicator and preset depth stops.

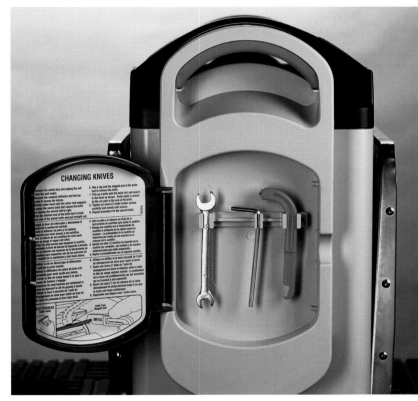

THE CLEVER, ON-BOARD TOOL-STORAGE COMPARTMENT holds a wrench, an Allen key, and a magnetic tool for knife changes.

RIDGID TP1300 THICKNESS PLANER

MOTOR POWER: 15 amps

CUTTERHEAD SPEED/CUTS PER MIN.: 9,500; 19,000

STOCK FEED RATE: 26 fpm (feet per minute)

CUTTING CAPACITY (WIDTH; DEPTH): 13 in.; 6 in.

MAX. CUT ON A SINGLE PASS: ⅛ in.

WEIGHT: 84 lb.

SPECIAL FEATURES: 14-in.-long infeed/outfeed tables; Ind-I-Cut depth presets; Sure-Cut carriage lock; toolkit and extra set of knives included

Originally designed for boring holes in metal, the first drill presses were essentially heavy arbor presses fitted with rotating shafts that held a bit.

Contemporary drill presses have come a long way since then. They offer powerful electric motors, multiple speeds, keyless chucks, and adjustable tables that make them versatile machines for boring a variety of materials, including wood. Compared to drilling freehand with a portable electric drill, a drill press has at least three advantages: alignment accuracy, improved control, and enhanced feed pressure.

A good drill press bores holes exactly where you want them and keeps them square to the work surface or, with the table tilted, at an exact angle. Driving a large-diameter bit deep into rock-hard wood or composite materials requires lots of pressure. That's something a drill press offers loads of, so you can drill dozens of big holes without working up a sweat.

Drill Press World

FLOOR-STANDING DRILL PRESSES

Standing between 5 ft. and 6 ft. tall, a floor-standing drill press has its cast-iron base firmly planted on the ground. Many woodworkers choose a floor model because of its generous capacity yet small footprint, which doesn't take up much shop space. By pivoting the worktable out of the way, extra tall or long workpieces fit between the chuck and the base, useful when boring a hole in the end of a frame member or into the top of a cabinet or chest that's already been assembled. Floor-standing drill presses also have a long quill travel, typically between $3\frac{1}{4}$ in. and $4\frac{1}{2}$ in., so they can bore deep holes.

Like all drill presses, floor models are sized by their swing, which equates to the biggest-diameter disk (or widest board or panel) you could drill a hole in the center of. The swing distance then is actually half the distance between the column and the centerline of a bit in the chuck. The swing of floor-model presses ranges from the smallish 12 in., of affordably priced home-shop models, to the larger 22 in., in heavy-duty industrial models like the Powermatic 2000. Drill presses with a mid-sized swing, such as the $16\frac{1}{2}$-in. Jet JDP-17MF are about right for most small shops. Unless you're planning to drill monster holes in titanium, power usually isn't an issue: The stock $\frac{1}{2}$- or $\frac{3}{4}$-hp motor is just right for a midsize machine.

JET JDP-17MF floor-standing drill press.

A Look Inside

The "press" part of a drill press puts a bit-holding chuck at the end of a mechanism that allows motor power to be transmitted while the bit is fed down into the stock.

1. The head, usually a single casting that contains the quill assembly and motor, is mounted to the top of the column.

2. The head cover protects the user from accidental contact with the pulleys and V-belt.

3. The quill and spindle allow the chuck to rotate and move up and down.

4. The chuck secures drill bits or the shafts of accessories.

5. Stepped pulleys on the motor arbor and spindle allow the V-belt position to be changed for speed changes.

6. Belt-tension lever loosens the V-belt for speed changes.

7. The feed lever or quill handle raises or lowers the chuck and bit.

8. The depth gauge indicates and limits the drilling depth.

9. The column, mounted on a base, supports the head and table.

10. The table moves up and down and also tilts for angled boring.

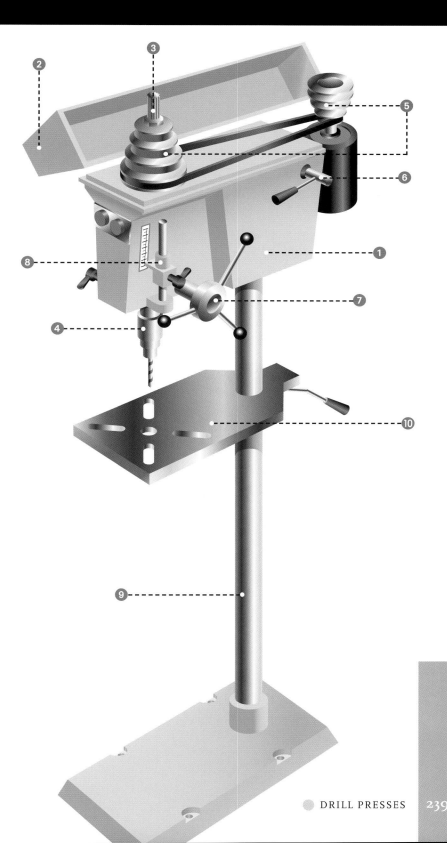

BENCHTOP DRILL PRESSES

If a drill press is too short to use without being mounted on a stand or table, it's a benchtop model. However, not all of these height-challenged drilling machines are the same breed. Some manufacturers simply mount the same head, table, and base on long or short columns and sell them as floor and benchtop models. Other small drill presses are built more economically, intended for light-duty work, such as the 8-in. Sears Craftsman 21908. These have shorter quill travel, smaller motors ($\frac{1}{4}$ hp to $\frac{1}{2}$ hp), and less swing (between 8 in. and 12 in.) than their taller cousins do. Although they lack the drilling capacity of heavy-duty models, they're more compact and affordable yet are still capable of satisfying many small shops' needs. (Here's a handy trick: To drill tall parts, rotate a benchtop's head around on its column and drill with the part sitting on the floor).

SEARS CRAFTSMAN 8-in. benchtop drill press.

RADIAL-HEAD DRILL PRESSES

A versatile yet strange-looking beast, a radial-head drill press, like the Delta 11-090, angles the drill head instead of the table (as a regular drill press does) so that the work stays flat and level, making it much easier to bore large or heavy stock. Radial presses pack a very large swing capacity—32 in.—in a compact benchtop machine. By having its head and motor at opposite ends of a horizontal column that slides in and out of a sleeve atop its vertical column, throat depth can be reduced or increased as need dictates (maximum throat depth is great when boring holes for Euro-style hardware in wide cabinet sides). For angled boring, a radial press's entire head assembly tilts. Most radials tilt up to 90° in at least one direction, allowing horizontal boring operations.

DELTA 11-090 RADIAL-HEAD DRILL PRESS.

A CAST-IRON CLASSIC

Most tool junkies remember their first power tool at least as well as their first car or their first kiss. The first machine I purchased was a drill press, an old Sears Craftsman bench model I discovered in the back room of a dusty used-machinery shop. When I questioned the dealer about the quality of the Sears brand, he quickly retorted, "That's vintage-quality cast iron, son! I wish I had a dozen like 'em."

Probably made in the late 1940s, my drill press was manufactured by King Seely, a company that built many of the woodworking machines sold under the Sears Craftsman brand label. (King Seely switched gears and made Thermos vacuum bottles in the 1960s.) With a short, 32-in.-tall column and heavy cast-iron head, base, and table, this classic drill press has some handsome touches, like

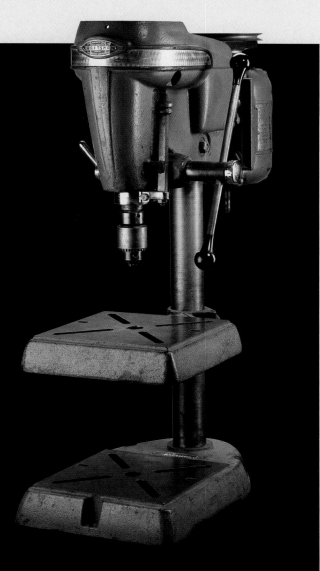

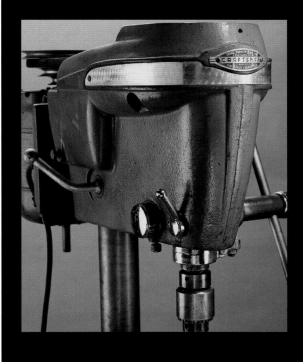

shapely Bakelite knobs on the ends of its single-lever feed handle and an engine-turned band around the top, which bears the Craftsman logo (note that the original top pulley cover is missing in the photo at left). The original ½-hp Craftsman motor and alloyed four-step pulleys power the quill via a standard V-belt. After more than 25 years of use (and occasional abuse), my old Sears drill press still runs as well as the day I bought it.

VARIABLE-SPEED DRILL PRESSES

All modern drill presses are multispeed machines, regardless of type or size. But the majority change speed with a stepped pulley and V-belt. The exceptions are continuous variable-speed models, like the Delta 15-341. This useful feature lets you change speeds as easily as rotating a lever, which is mounted on the front of the head (it's probably the only adjustment on a machine of any kind that *must* be made while the machine is running). The lever actuates a variable-diameter pulley atop the quill, which expands and contracts (along with the motor pulley) to change the speed of the spindle. The speed of the 15-in. Delta drill press shown at right can be set anywhere between 450 rpm and 4,700 rpm.

DELTA 15-341 variable-speed drill press.

BENCHTOP MORTISING MACHINES

If you build most of your wood projects with mortise-and-tenon joinery, then a benchtop mortising machine, such as the Jet JBM-5, might be just right for you. Built like a small, squat drill press, a mortising machine is specially designed to use a hollow chisel and auger bit to make accurate, square-shouldered mortises. The bit drills out the center while the chisel presses in and cleans up the corners. Multiple square holes in a row form mortises of any length. By fitting different-size bits and chisels, you can create mortises of different widths (¼ in., ⅜ in., ½ in., etc.).

The Jet's ½-hp induction motor directly drives the chuck that holds the auger bit. An extralong lever feed handle and rack-and-pinion drive move the head up and down on the column, providing all the mechanical advantage needed to drive the chisel into the work.

JET JBM-5 benchtop mortising machine.

THE CHUCK IS ACCESSED through doors in the head.

Features

SPEED-CHANGE PULLEYS

Unless you're fortunate enough to own a variable-speed drill press, you'll need to get involved with your drill press's V-belt and pulleys any time you want to change the bit's rotation speed. The simplest speed-change arrangement is a pair of stepped pulleys, one on the motor and one on the quill sleeve.

Moving the V-belt to a smaller-diameter step on the motor pulley and a larger one on the quill pulley gives you a slower speed, while the reverse arrangement yields a higher speed. To increase the number of speed choices, many drill presses

have a jackshaft and center pulley, as shown on the Jet JDP-17MF. By switching the belt position on either or both sets of pulleys, a total of 16 speeds can be set. A lever on the side of the head sets the tension of the V-belt, which must be slackened before making speed changes.

SPEED-CHANGE PULLEYS
on the Jet JDP-17MF.

WHY CHANGE SPEEDS?

Getting clean, straight holes requires that you choose the right speed and feed rate (how fast you advance the bit into the work). Running a large-diameter multispur bit at the same speed and fast feed rate as a hay straw–thin twist drill is not only unsafe but generates enough heat to burn the wood and overheat—and likely ruin—the big bit. Conversely, spin a thin bit too slowly or feed it sluggishly and it won't cut cleanly and may wander, resulting in a crooked or uneven hole.

DEPTH GAUGES AND STOPS

All contemporary drill presses have a depth gauge and stop, which help you determine and limit the depth of holes you bore. The gauge is usually a simple threaded rod connected to the bottom of the quill sleeve. A scale on the rod shows the depth of the bit, or a pointer on the rod indicates depth on a scale mounted on the head. Threaded nuts on the rod adjust to limit the motion of the quill and thus the drilling depth. Most drill presses also have a locking lever to secure the quill in a down position, useful when using the tool to spin a sanding drum or other accessory.

Another kind of depth gauge, often found on drill presses made in Asia, features a circular dial at the base of the feed lever. An inch scale that runs around the circumference of the dial shows the quill's length of travel; the dial can be locked to limit drilling depth.

CIRCULAR-DIAL DEPTH GAUGE AND STOP SYSTEM.

SCALE AND THREADED-ROD DEPTH GAUGE.

CRANK-OPERATED WORK TABLE

Moving a drill press's table up and down on the column changes the distance between a bit and the workpiece (an exception: the Ryobi's WDP1850 raises and lowers its head instead of the table). The small, light tables on benchtop drill presses are easy to elevate with a little muscle power. But moving the heavy cast-iron tables found on floor-standing presses is enough to strain anyone's back. Thank goodness for the rack-and-pinion cranking mechanisms featured on models such as the Jet JDP-17MF. For really tall or thick work, just pivot the drill-press table out of the way (the rack is loosely held to the column to allow the table to move sideways).

A STANDARD CAST-IRON TABLE and rack-and-pinion raising-and-lowering mechanism.

Accessories

BITS, DRUMS, AND CUTTERS FOR EVERY TASK

One of the pleasures of using a drill press is that you can run big bits and accessories easily and safely. For example, large-diameter twist drills, Forstner bits, and hole saws produce the cleanest-edged, straightest-sided holes when chucked in a drill press. Adjustable circle-cutting bits, useful for cutting out large holes in sheet metals and plastics or for cutting disks from thin plywood or hardboard, should *only* be used in a drill press.

When working with any large bit, choose an appropriately slow speed and always clamp the workpiece firmly to the table; a slow-spinning big bit generates a lot of torque, which can grab the workpiece from your hands and ruin it—or you.

Beyond mere bits, a drill press's adjustable chuck can power any number of different accessories specifically designed to be used in a drill press.

On the short list of useful goodies are: rotary rasps, for shaping parts and rounding edges; flap sanders, for smoothing carved or irregular parts; rotary planers, for thicknessing and/or surfacing parts too small to run through a planer; and sanding drums, for smoothing curved edges.

SOME OF THE ACCESSORIES that can be chucked in a drill press (clockwise from left): circle cutter, hole saw, sanding drum, Forstner bits (for large flat-bottom holes), and beefy twist bits.

A pattern sander (a sanding drum with a pilot bearing on the end) is another handy accessory (the Robo Sander is shown mounted in the drill press in the photo above). The bearing follows a pattern temporarily fastened to the bottom of the workpiece, thus sanding the edges smoothly and to a precise size.

HOLDING TIGHT AND GETTING THE RIGHT ANGLE

A big drill bit can grab a small part with stunning speed and enough force to fling it off the drill-press table. One solution is to outfit your drill press with an auxiliary table, such as the Woodhaven table. Besides providing an adjustable fence and large surface area to support large or long parts, the table has two aluminum T-tracks with sliding hold-downs that can be positioned wherever they're needed to clamp the stock. If you'd rather have a hold-down that works with your drill press's regular cast-iron table, try a quick-action clamp, as shown in the bottom photo at right. Secured in one of the table's slots by a big wing nut, the clamp adjusts for different-thickness workpieces and uses the same kind of tightening mechanism as found on locking pliers, to bite down on the work with alligator-jawlike force.

WOODHAVEN'S AUXILIARY DRILL-PRESS TABLE and Bridge City Tool's MP-8 machine protractor, which can also be used on band-saw tilting tables, stationary sanders, jointer fences, and jigs.

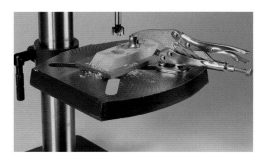

IF YOU'D RATHER have a hold-down that works with your drill press's regular cast-iron table, try a quick-action clamp. Like a pair of locking pliers, this clamp adjusts to suit a wide range of stock thicknesses.

MORTISING ATTACHMENT

A hollow-chisel mortising attachment enables you to get clean, crisp square mortises from a standard drill press. Mortising attachments are great for woodworkers who occasionally build cabinets or furniture with traditional mortise-and-tenon joinery but who don't want to chop them by hand or invest in a dedicated mortising machine. A fence clamped to the drill-press table squares the workpiece to the chisel while a hold-down (included with the attachment) keeps the workpiece from lifting during mortising.

MORTISING ATTACHMENT, showing fence, hold-downs, and hollow-chisel mortising bit chucked.

The Cutting Edge

RYOBI WDP1850

While most drill presses are really metalworking machines that woodworkers use and adapt for their own purposes, the Ryobi WDP1850 benchtop model is a bit different. Ryobi calls it a "wood-drilling system" because the company designed the benchtop tool specifically for woodworkers. A unique feature is the VersaTable, an MDF-topped, large-capacity table with a sliding fence and a cursor-and-scale stop system designed to position the work accurately. The tabletop tilts for angled work (detents are set at 0° and 45° in either direction), and a single eccentric clamping handle locks the VersaTable to the base so that it can be removed or repositioned in a flash. Since the Ryobi's table doesn't change elevation, the head cranks up and down to set the distance between the bit and the work. The head also boasts some clever features, including a stock hold-down clamp, which descends from the head, and variable speed, a feature usually found on much more expensive drill presses. Kudos to Ryobi for putting the WDP1850's work light at the front of the head; other drill presses with work lights mount them behind the chuck, so the area you want to see is usually in shadow.

RYOBI WDP1850

MOTOR POWER: 6 amps, ⅓-hp induction motor

SWING: 18½ in.

CHUCK CAPACITY: ½ in.

QUILL TRAVEL: 3⅓ in.

SPEED: 500–3,000 rpm, variable

TABLE SIZE: 25¼ in. by 12¾ in.

WEIGHT: 120 lb.

ACCESSORIES: metal work stand; mortising attachment

THE VERSATABLE features a sliding fence, cursor-and-scale stop system, and clamp for accurate and precise drilling.

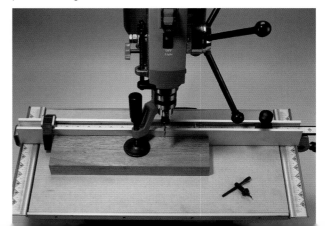

Sure, you've got great tools in your shop, but it probably won't feel complete until most of the floor space is taken up by handsome machinery. And why not? There are so many great iron (or steel or alloy) machines out there, many of which provide the only practical way of performing certain operations.

Regardless of how remarkable your table saw or planer is, you'll need a lathe to turn stretcher spindles for that set of chairs you're building. A belt sander can smooth a panel, but you'll get faster and flatter results with a stationary wide-belt sander or drum sander. A router table is capable of creating lots of intricate shaped edges and parts, but even those big ½-in.-shank router bits are no match for a spindle shaper's capacity and the speed with which it slices through thick hardwood. Oscillating-belt sanders and random-orbit bench sanders can take the tedium out of smoothing project parts and can make sanding easier and, perhaps, even fun.

KLEIN DESIGN INC.
17910 SE 110TH STREET
RENTON, WA 98059
425-226-5937
9 8 5 1 4 5

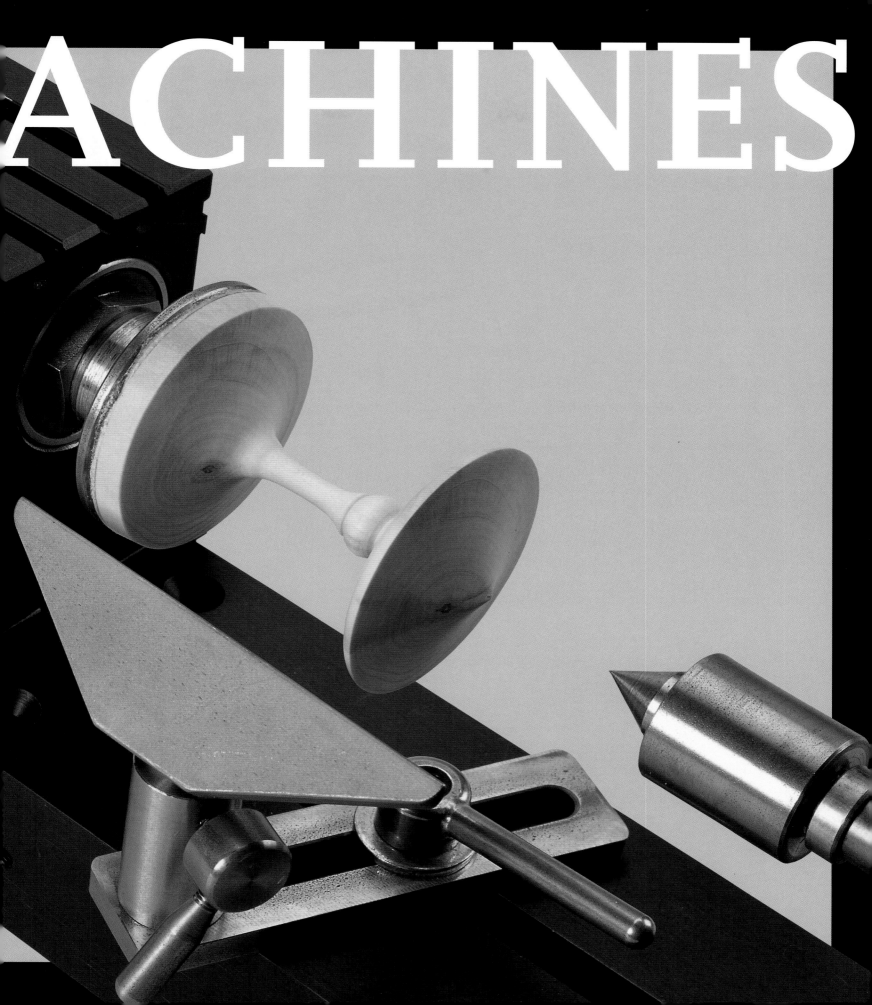

ACHINES

Lathes

THE TURNING MACHINE

The parts of a lathe—one of the simplest and oldest kinds of woodworking machines ever devised—are few: A headstock secures and drives the turning blank, a tailstock supports long turnings, and a bed joins the two ends together and provides a mount for the tool rest. Lathes range in size from tiny desktop models, useful for turning pens and small parts, to superheavy-duty lathes professionals use to turn giant bowls and lamppost-size spindles.

A BASIC LATHE

If you're just getting started, an affordable benchtop or stand-mounted model, like the Jet JWL-1236 lathe, has enough capacity and features to let you undertake a wide variety of turnings, including spindles and bowls. A lathe's "between centers" capacity indicates the length of the longest stock that you can mount between the headstock and tailstock. A stand-mounted lathe with 36 in. to 40 in. between centers is large enough for turning stairway balusters and most spindles used for chairs and other furniture.

A lathe's "swing over bed" indicates the diameter of the largest piece you can turn, either between centers or on a faceplate. To give them even greater faceplate capacity, lathes like the

JET JWL-1236 LATHE.

Delta 46-701 and the Jet JWL-1236 have a pivoting headstock. Unbolting the headstock allows it to rotate 90°, providing clearance for turnings larger than you could do over the bed. An extension arm mounted on the bed repositions the tool rest for turning in this position.

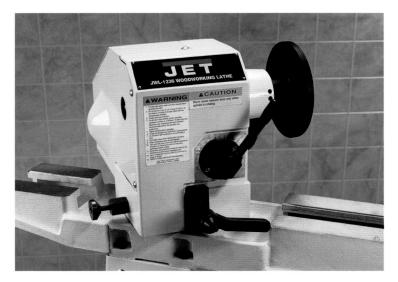

PIVOTING HEADSTOCK of the Jet JWL-1236.

PRODUCTION LATHES

If you're serious enough about lathe work to get into production turning or you want to create vessels large enough in which to bathe children, you won't regret buying the biggest, heaviest lathe you can afford. What does a big lathe, like the General 160-1, have that smaller lathes don't? First and foremost: vibration-dampening mass. With its cast-iron bed, headstock, and tailstock, a big lathe can weigh several hundred pounds (models with cast-iron bases are even heavier!). All that weight and the lathe's heavy-duty bearings and thick spindle keeps big, heavy chunks of green wood or off-balance turning blanks spinning smoothly. Plus, the lathe's beefy ways and tool rest provide a stable platform that prevents chattering during heavy cuts.

To expand their swing-over capacity, large lathes sometimes feature a space between the end of the bed and the headstock. A gap-bed lathe, like the General 160-1, has enough clearance for turning large (up to 15 in. dia.) narrow projects, such as platters and shallow bowls. For even bigger and/or deeper turnings, use a big lathe's second spindle on the left side of the headstock, which is intended for outboard turnings using a separate tool rest.

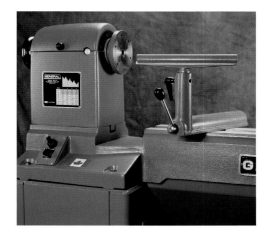

GENERAL 160-1 headstock with gap bed—good for large, shallow faceplate turnings.

GENERAL 160-1 production woodturning lathe.

MINIATURE LATHES

Not every woodturner dreams of owning a giant lathe capable of handling tree trunk–size turnings. In fact, novice turners often start at the other end of the spectrum and turn small objects, like spinning tops, round boxes, and wood pens. It takes a special lathe and tools to handle such miniature wonders, such as the Klein lathe and small-scale turning tools shown in the top photo at right. Created by renowned woodturner and instructor Bonnie Klein, the precision pint-sized lathe is made primarily from aluminum extrusions. By replacing the lathe's tailstock with an optional threading accessory, the Klein lathe can create screw-top boxes and other threaded vessels.

HARDLY LONGER THAN a standard full-size turning tool, the Klein lathe is designed for precision turning of small projects, including spinning tops.

HOW MUCH WOOD COULD A GOOD CHUCK CHUCK?

Even a great lathe isn't much use if it doesn't have a strong chuck to hold the turning blank firmly when it's spinning at high rpm. The New Zealand–made Nova chuck system (and the SuperNova chuck that has superceded it) can put a viselike grip on either round or square stock. Using a pair of locking handles, the chuck's four jaws can be closed down around the blank or expanded to grip a hollow or recess in the base of the turning. You can mount different sets of jaws on the chuck for different-size turnings. The Cole jaws, seen at the rear in the bottom photo at right, are designed for reverse mounting a bowl so that its foot can be finished. The Nova also accepts a screw center (front center in the bottom photo), handy for turning small boxes and goblets.

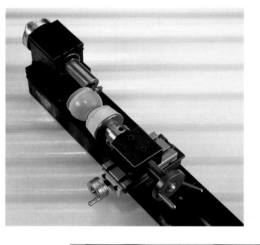

TURNING THREADS on the lip and lid of a wooden screw-top box requires that the lathe be fitted with a special attachment. The lathe's headstock spins the cutter while the box is rotated slowly on the attachment.

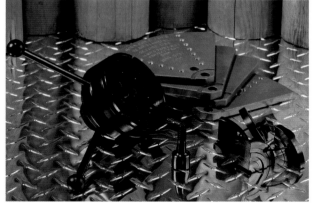

THE NOVA LATHE CHUCK SYSTEM.

TREADLE LATHES

When you think of power tools, you usually think of the electric kind. But the precursors to many modern electrically powered machines were run by muscles, not megawatts. Turned by a treadle plate and flywheel mechanism virtually identical to the ones used on old-fashioned sewing machines, treadle-powered lathes ranged from the simple to the amazing. The basic treadle lathe—an example from the American Precision Museum in Windsor, Vermont, shown in the photo at right—was a small, simple machine sold to hobbyists looking to turn small spindles and bowls for recreation. Treadle-lathe technology reached its zenith with the beauti-

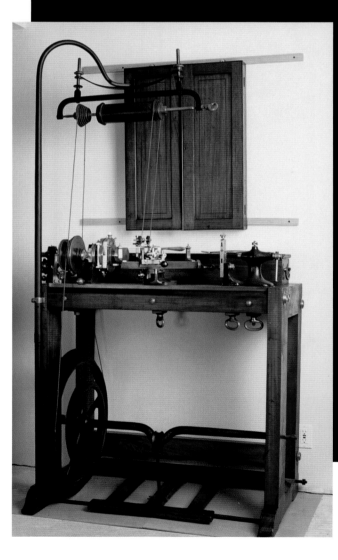

ful Holtzappfel ornamental-turning lathes (example shown at left), marvels of precisely machined and highly polished brass and iron.

Although most lathes are simple machines, they had an important role in the development of other machinery. Early precision lathes made it possible to turn perfectly round metal cylinders from which gears and pulleys were cut—components used in other early machines to transmit and regulate drive forces. So, if you think of a lathe as a wood tool for making bowls and chair spindles, think of where woodworking machinery would be if the lathe hadn't come along.

Spindle Shapers

POWERMATIC MODEL
270010 spindle shaper.

THE EFFICIENT SHAPING MACHINE

Do you feel the need to wear armor every time you run a big bit in your router table? (Those helicopter blade–diameter panel-raising bits are especially scary!) One way to steady your nerves is to up-grade to a spindle shaper, a sort of industrial-strength router table. Shapers use cutters that come in an endless variety of profile shapes and sizes. Better still, shapers have the power and strength to run even the largest cutters smoothly and safely.

A shaper has an motor-driven spindle that pro-jects vertically through a hole in a large, cast-iron table. A handwheel raises and lowers the spindle to change the height of cutters mounted on the spindle. Expensive production shapers even have tilting arbors for angled profile work.

SHAPER SIZES

Shapers are sized by the diameter of their spin-dles: $\frac{1}{2}$-in. and $\frac{3}{4}$-in. sizes are common on benchtop or open stand–mounted light-duty units, while 1-in. and $1\frac{1}{4}$-in. spindles are reserved for heavy-duty industrial models. A number of shapers, including the Powermatic model 270010, have interchangeable $\frac{1}{2}$-in. and $\frac{3}{4}$-in. spindles, enabling them to use a greater range of cutters. Some models also use collet chucks that accept regular $\frac{1}{2}$-in.- or $\frac{1}{4}$-in.-shank router bits.

THE FREUD PERFORMANCE SYSTEM RP2000
features interchangeable cutters.

POWER FEEDERS

CO-MATIC M/3 BABY POWER FEEDER

SHAPER CUTTERS

If you've got a shape in mind, there's probably a shaper cutter available that will form it. But because these cutters aren't exactly cheap, all but the busiest production shops do their small-scale shaping on a router table, using economical bits, and save the big jobs for the shaper. One way to economize on big shaper cutters is to buy a cutterhead system that uses knife inserts, such as the Freud Performance System RP2000, which is designed for cutting raised panels. The system's cutterhead uses a pair of removable carbide knives, and the set comes with enough pairs to produce five different raised-panel profiles, including straight-sloped, cove, and ogee shapes.

Besides a good fence with a cutterhead shroud, a power feeder (also known as a stock feeder) is such an important accessory that many veteran woodworkers wouldn't even use a shaper without it. Equipped with a small motor that drives multiple skateboard-size urethane wheels, a power feeder, such as the Co-matic M/3 Baby, propels stock past the cutter at a smooth, consistent rate; this rate is adjustable to suit the kind of stock and the size and type of cut (the M/3 can run stock at between $6\frac{1}{2}$ ft. and 40 ft. per min.). A power feeder not only assures clean, consistent results, but it keeps your hands away from the shaper cutter, a notorious source of catastrophic hand injuries. Mounted at the end of an adjustable arm, a power feeder can be set for stock of various thicknesses. Besides shapers, power feeders can mount to router tables, table saws, and jointers to provide smoother, safer operations.

Stationary Sanders

EDGE SANDERS

Sanding the edge of a door or face frame can be tricky business. A random-orbit sander may round the edge instead of leaving it crisp and square, and a belt sander is awkward to handle on such a narrow surface. Alternatively, a stationary edge sander can accomplish the task with aplomb. Edge sanders are extremely useful for cleaning up tearout on straight- or convex-edged parts, as well as flush sanding the ends of face frames or cabinet doors. You can also sand the sides of assemblies that aren't too tall, to flush up dovetail or finger joints on drawers or small boxes.

An edge sander has a long, wide sanding belt, which is set horizontally and driven between a drive roller mounted to the motor's shaft and an idler roller at the other end. The small shop–size Taiwan-made Enlon edge sander has a 6-in. by 80-in. belt, but production models have belts 6 in. by 132 in. or longer. The longer and wider the belt, the more length and area the sander's primary platen has (the platen is the flat plate behind the belt) and, therefore, the larger the sandable surface. A large table supports the work as it is pressed against the belt. Most tables tilt (for bevel sanding) and adjust up and down so that you can use different sections of the belt. A smaller table that wraps around the edge sander's rubber-covered idler roller lets you sand concave edges.

ENLON stationary edge sander.

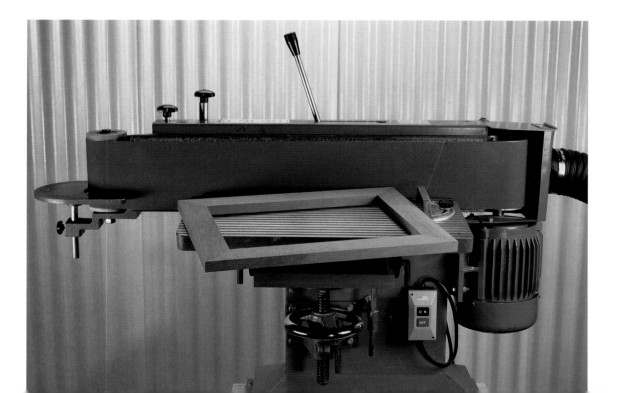

COMBO BELT/DISK SANDERS

THE DELTA SANDING CENTER extends its versatility through accessories, including a pneumatic drum.

DELTA 31-280 Sanding Center.

Some stationary sanders combine two (or more) sanding tools in one machine: narrow-belt/disk, belt/drum, etc. A combination belt/disk sander, such as the Delta 31-280 Sanding Center, teams up two of the most versatile sanding tools: a 6-in. by 48-in. belt and a 12-in. disk. Both are powered by a single 1½-hp motor. The Delta's belt sander pivots to run either vertically or horizontally. The horizontal position is better when sanding the bottom edges of boxes or drawers, while the vertical position is preferable when sanding the ends of long workpieces. The belt is backed up by a ground cast-iron platen, allowing extremely accurate work. The stationary disk sander (whether part of a combo sander or in a stand-alone unit) is very useful for smoothing straight or convex edges and shaping or trimming parts quickly. The sanding disk mounts directly to the metal disk's surface, so the abrasive cuts aggressively to produce surfaces that are surprisingly flat and accurate (patternmakers love to use stationary disk sanders for creating precisely sized parts). The disk sander has a tilting table for sanding beveled edges. A miter slot in the table accepts a standard miter gauge for truing up mitered frame ends or, with the table tilted, sanding compound angles.

An accessory arbor mount on the side of the Delta Sanding Center accepts numerous accessories, including abrasive wheels, flap wheels, a flexible shaft tool, or a pneumatic drum.

OSCILLATING AND RANDOM-ORBIT SANDERS

You can do a pretty good job of sanding concave edges with a sanding drum chucked into a drill press. But an oscillating spindle sander (OSS) uses a dual action that sands curves smoother and faster. An OSS's spindle (a tall sanding drum) moves up and down as it rotates, anywhere from $\frac{1}{2}$ in. to 1 in., depending on the unit. The oscillating action distributes wear over a greater portion of the spindle, and the oscillation prevents grooved scratches on the work.

Once available as only large industrial-duty machines, small-shop-sized oscillating spindle sanders, including benchtop models like the Ryobi OSS450, are now available and affordable. To suit the sanding of curves of different radii, interchangeable rubber drums, which range in diameter from $\frac{3}{4}$ in. to 3 in., fit over the machine's metal spindle. Sandpaper sleeves mount over the rubber drums (a $\frac{1}{2}$-in. sleeve fits directly over the spindle).

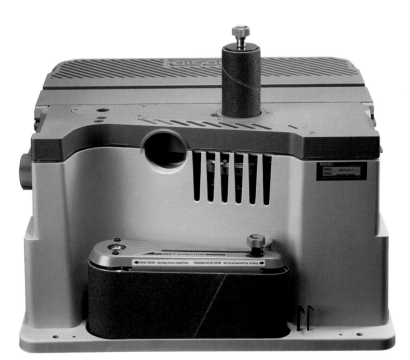

RIDGID EB4424 oscillating-belt and spindle sander.

THE RIDGID EB4424 doubles as an oscillating spindle sander.

DELTA 31-750 benchtop random-orbit sander.

OSCILLATING-BELT SANDERS

Taking the idea of an OSS a step further, an oscillating-belt sander moves its entire spinning belt assembly up and down. The gentle oscillation produces a cleaner sanded edge than you'd get from a regular belt sander, stationary or portable. The Ridgid EB4424's oscillating belt uses a standard 4x24 sanding belt, which lets you sand straight- or convex-edged parts on the flat section or convex shapes at either end of the belt. The table tilts for sanding chamfers or beveled edges. Remove the belt assembly and mount a rubber drum and sanding sleeve, and the machine transforms into a regular oscillating spindle sander.

BENCHTOP RANDOM-ORBIT SANDERS

A regular sanding disk cuts aggressively but tends to leave concentric scratches in the work surface. In contrast, the unique Delta 31-750 benchtop random-orbit sander spins and orbits its abrasive disk just like a portable random-orbit sander. Mounted in the center of a large, laminate-covered table, the 9-in. disk sands flat edges and surfaces quickly but leaves them with a swirl-free finish. The disk features an interchangeable sanding pad, which can use either PSA or hook-and-loop abrasive disks. For edge work and to steady small parts, a fence attaches to the table, overlapping part of the disk.

RYOBI OSS450 oscillating spindle sander.

WIDE-BELT SANDERS

It might be the most expensive machine you'll ever buy for your woodshop, but a wide-belt sander provides a lot of bang for the buck. Sometimes called "Timesavers" after the company that introduced them to American craftsmen, a wide-belt sander can quickly sand large panels, frames, and doors silky smooth and flat, regardless of grain direction. Fitted with a coarse-grit belt, the same machine also abrasively planes rough boards—just as a thickness planer would—yet without tearout in areas of irregular or figured grain.

The belt on a wide-belt sander runs vertically on rolls (rollers) above a conveyor-belt table, which adjusts up and down to set the depth of cut and to handle stock of various thicknesses. The lower roll is a rubber-covered drive roll, which presses the sanding belt against the work.

The Sheng-Shing SDM-15's 16-in. by 48-in. belt can sand panels up to 30 in. wide in two passes, thanks to its open-sided frame. The SDM-15 has many features that industrial machines have: massive, cast-iron parts; heavy, welded-steel cabinet construction; a motorized conveyor with a durable, rubberized belt; and efficient built-in dust collection.

To keep the belt tracking smoothly, the SDM-15 uses an air-powered automatic tracking mechanism that adjusts the angle of the top roller to keep the belt centered. This mechanism gives the belt a gentle back-and-forth oscillation, which distributes the sanding load evenly across the surface of the belt and prevents banding— the buildup of resin or other belt-clogging debris in one narrow stripe.

SHENG-SHING SDM-15 wide-belt sander.

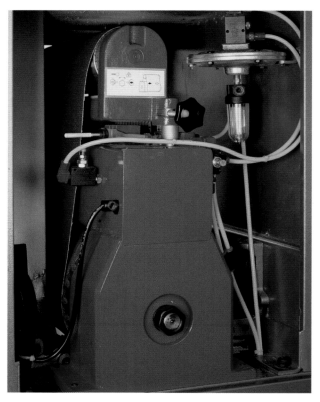

AN AIR-POWERED AUTOMATIC TRACKING MECHANISM on the SDM-15 keeps the belt centered and provides oscillation that prevents banding.

DRUM SANDERS

If you need to smooth and flatten glued-up panels or cabinet face frames and can't afford a wide-belt sander, consider a drum sander instead. Drum sanders can sand very thin stock (down to $\frac{1}{16}$ in.) safely, so luthiers use them to precisely sand the sides, tops, and backs of flat-top acoustic guitars. The biggest models can sand a 50-in.-wide panel in a single pass, but smaller models, such as the Performax 16-31 Plus and the Ryobi WDS1600 (shown in the photo above right), have an open-ended design that enables them to sand panels up to 32 in. wide in two passes.

Like a wide-belt sander, a drum sander uses a conveyor-belt table to feed the workpiece under a spinning abrasive head—a long cylindrical drum—to abrade it flat and smooth. The surface of the extruded aluminum drum is covered with a long, continuous strip of sandpaper wound on it spirally and held at the ends by special spring-loaded clips. The clips take up slack, which inevitably develops when the sanding strip heats up and lengthens by expansion.

The only significant disadvantage of small-shop drum sanders is that they are slow: The maximum feed rate for small-shop models rarely exceeds 10 ft. per min.—and that's during a very light cut. Heavier cuts can slow the feed rate down to a snail's pace of 2 ft. to 5 ft. per min.

RYOBI WDS1600 drum sander.

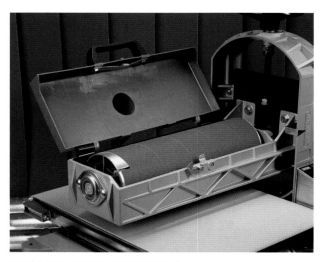

SANDPAPER IS HELD AT THE ENDS by spring-loaded clips that take up slack as the strip heats up under use.

RESOURCES

Advanced Machinery Imports, Ltd.
P.O. Box 312
New Castle, DE 19720
(800) 727-6553
Hegner

American Tool Companies, Inc.
701 Woodlands Parkway
Vernon Hills, IL 60061
(847) 478-1090
Irwin sawblades and drill bits

Beaver Tools
4031 Garvois Ave.
St. Louis, MO 63116
(800) 365-6677

Bridge City Tool Works, Inc.
5820 N.E. Hassalo
Portland, OR 97213
(800) 253-3332

Campbell Hausfeld
100 Production Dr.
Harrison, OH 45030
(800) 543-8622

Carter Products Co., Inc.
437 Spring St. N.E.
Grand Rapids, MI 49503
(616) 451-2928

CMT USA, Inc.
307-F Pomona Dr.
Greensboro, NC 27407
(888) 268-2487

Colonial Saw, Inc.
122 Pembroke St.
Kingston, MA 02364
(781) 585-4364
*Lamello biscuit joiners and
accessories*

Craft Supplies USA
1287 E. 1120 South
Provo, UT 84606
(800) 551-8876
Nova lathe chuck

Delta International Machinery
   Corp. (see Porter-Cable/Delta)

DeWalt Power Tools
701 East Joppa Rd.
Towson, MD 21286
(800) 433-9258

Dremel
4915 21st St.
Racine, WI 53406
(800) 437-3635

Emerson Tool Co.
8100 W. Florissant
St. Louis, MO 63136
(800) 474-3443
Ridgid power tools

Epic Machinery Group
5128 Westinghouse Blvd.
Charlotte, NC 28273
(704) 588-6627

Fein Tools
1030 Alcon St.
Pittsburgh, PA 15220
(412) 922-8886

Festool (formerly Festo)
Tooltechnic Systems LLC
1187 Coast Village Rd., Ste. 1215
Santa Barbara, CA 93108
(888) 463-3786

Forrest Mfg. Co.
P.O. Box 708
Hermiston, OR 97838
(541) 567-2105

Freud USA
P.O. Box 7187
High Point, NC 27264
(800) 334-4107

Garrett Wade
161 Avenue of the Americas
New York, NY 10013
(800) 221-2942
Inca machinery

General Mfg. Co., Ltd.
835 Cherrier St.
Drummondville, QB J2B 5A8
Canada
(819) 472-1161

Hitachi
3950 Steve Reynolds Blvd.
Norcross, GA 30093
(800) 829-4752

Holz-Her USA, Inc.
5120 Westinghouse Blvd.
Charlotte, NC 28273
(704) 587-3400

Injecta Machinery/Eagle Tools
2217 El Sol Ave.
Altadena, CA 91001
(800) 203-0023
Inca machinery

Jet Equipment & Tools
P.O. Box 1937
Auburn, WA 98071-1937
(800) 274-6848
Powermatic tools

Bonnie Klein
Klein Design, Inc.
17910 S.E. 110th St.
Renton, WA 98059
(425) 226-5937
Klein Lathe and mini tools

Lee Valley Tools, Ltd.
1090 Morrison Dr.
Ottawa, ON K2H 1C2
Canada
(613) 596-0350
Veritas tools

Leigh Industries, Ltd.
P.O. Box 357
Port Coquitlam, BC V3C 4K6
Canada
(800) 663-8932
Leigh Jig and accessories

Luthiers Merchantile International
P.O. Box 774
412 Moore Lane
Healdsburg, CA 95448
(800) 477-4437
Bishop Cochran rotary-tool router base

Makita USA, Inc.
14930 Northam St.
La Mirada, CA 90638
(714) 522-8088

McFeely's
1620 Wythe Rd.
P.O. Box 11169
Lynchburg, VA 24506-1169
(800) 443-7937
Quik Drive auto-feed screw gun

Metabo USA
1231 Wilson Dr.
West Chester, PA 19380
(800) 638-2264

Micro Fence
11100 Cumpston St., #35
North Hollywood, CA 91601
(800) 480-6427

Milwaukee Electric Tool Co.
13135 West Lisbon Rd.
Brookfield, WI 53005
(262) 781-3600

Panasonic Personal and
   Professional Products
One Panasonic Way 4A-3
Secaucus, NJ 07094
(201) 271-3476

Porter-Cable/Delta
4825 Highway 45 North
Jackson, TN 38302
(888) 848-5175

Professional Tool
   Manufacturing, LLC
P.O. Box 730
Ashland, OR 97520
(541) 201-7500
Drill Doctor

Rockler Woodworking
   and Hardware
4365 Willow Dr.
Medina, MN 55340
(800) 279-4441
Robosander

Ryobi America
1424 Pearman Dairy Rd.
Anderson, SC 29625
(800) 525-2579
Robosander

S-B Power Tool Co.
4300 W. Peterson Ave.
Chicago, IL 60646
(877) 754-5990 (Skil)
(877) 267-2499 (Bosch)
Skil power tools; Bosch power tools

Sears Power and Hand Tools
P.O. Box 14588
Des Moines, IA 50306-3588
(800) 290-1245
Craftsman power tools

Sioux Tools
2901 Floyd Blvd.
Sioux City, IA 51102
(800) 722-7290

Sommerville Design Mfg., Inc.
940 Brock Rd.
Pickering, ON L1W 2A1
Canada
(800) 357-4118
*Excalibur fences, sliding tables,
guards, accessories*

Sunhill Machinery
500 Andover Park East
Seattle, WA 98188
(800) 929-4321
*Co-matic power feeders; Sheng
Shing wide-belt sanders*

Tool Crib
P.O. Box 14930
Grand Forks, ND 58208
(800) 635-5140
Prazi chainsaw accessory

Virutex.Com
(formerly TNT Virutex Corp.)
601 West 26th St., 3rd Floor
New York, NY 10001
(800) 868-9663

Woodcraft
560 Airport Industrial Park
P.O. Box 1686
Parkersburg, WV 26102
(800) 225-1153
*Jacobs router collets; drill press
quick-action lever clamps;
Robosander*

Woodhaven
501 W. 1st Ave.
Durant, IA 52747
(800) 344-6657

Woodworker's Supply
1108 North Glenn Rd.
Casper, WY 82601
(800) 645-9292
*Arbortech carving wheels; M.A.C.
miter board*

Woodworking FasTTraK, Inc.
W5823 School Ave.
Merrill, WI 54452
(888) 327-7725
FasTTraK accessories; Cool Blocks